W9-CUK-792

1948

The Crossroads Year

James F. Nagle

ISBN: 1-4196-7142-1
ISBN-13: 978-1419671425
Library of Congress Control Number:

Visit www.booksurge.com to order additional copies.

Dedication

To my wife, Annie, my favorite member of the Class of 1948, for her proofreading, editing, and analysis of this book, but mostly for her companionship and love for a third of a century.

Acknowledgments

In researching this book, I used the facilities of the Library of Congress, the New York Public Library, and the Seattle Public Library, all of which are treasures for the documents they house and the personnel that grace their halls.

I owe special thanks to my secretary, Christine Jordan Smith, for her conscientious typing and her amazing ability to decipher my hen-scratching quickly and flawlessly; and to my son, Jimmy, for his incisive analysis and wordsmithing of what, for him, was ancient history; and finally to my wife, Annie, for all the work just hinted at in the dedication.

Table Of Contents

Dedication
Acknowledgements
Introduction 1
    A Year Of Movement 1

Chapter One 5
    The Year Begins 5
    The Baby Boom, Consumerism And Housing Shortage 5

Chapter Two 9
    The Political Year Begins 9
    Harry Truman - The Accidental Everyman President 9
    A Serious Attack From The Left 11
    Truman's Game Plan 12
    The 80th Congress And Truman's Strategy--Picking A Fight. . .14
    The State Of The Union - The Opening Salvo 14
    The Eisenhower Boom 16
    Civil Rights Touches Off A Southern Revolt 16
    Truman As Candidate 19
    The Strangest Man In Politics 20
    The Republican Contenders 22

Chapter Three 27
    The Death Of Isolationism 27
    Communism And Containment .27
    Technology Trumps Tradition 27
    The Torch Passes 28
    Greece 30
    The Marshall Plan 31
    The Plan's Guardian Angel 34
    Czechoslovakia 36
    Other Threats 37
    A Galvanized Congress Adopts The Marshall Plan 37
    Alliances 39
    War Talk 41
    America's Military 42
    The Atomic Bomb 43
    Personnel 44

Chapter Four 45
   The Berlin Blockade. 45
   The Dysfunctional Occupied Germany 45
   First Steps Towards Unification 47
   The Russians Respond 48
   The April Blockade 48
   Preparations For War. 49
   Currency 50
   The Blockade Begins 51
   The Airlift Starts 52
   The Chain Of Command 56

Chapter Five. 59
   Palestine - An International And Domestic Quagmire 59
   A Long Festering Imbroglio 59
   The Combatants Mobilize 60
   Indiscriminate Bloodshed 61
   The Elusive International Peace Force 61
   Political Maneuvers 63
   Recognition 65

Chapter Six. 71
   Politics 1948 Style. 71
   Truman's Nose-dive To Retirement .71
   Liberals And Conservatives Yearn For Eisenhower. 72
   The Spring Of The Democrats' Discontent 73
   Truman's Dry As Dust Speaking Style. 74
   The Supposedly Nonpartisan Train Trip 75

Chapter Seven. 81
   The Republican Catfight 81
   The New Hampshire Opener. 81
   Wisconsin 81
   Nebraska 83
   Ohio 84
   Oregon 85
   Handicapping The Field 87
   Television - The Cub Reporter 88
   The Republicans Converge For A Coronation 90
   The Vice Presidential Beauty Contest. 93

Chapter Eight...95
The Democrats Reluctantly Pick A Loser 95
The Pre Convention Maneuvering 95
The Democrats Gather For A Wake........................97
The Battle Over Civil Rights 99
Politicians And Television Adapt To Each Other 104

Chapter Nine..107
Dixiecrats, Progressives, Civil Rights And The Turnip Session 107
Dixiecrats..107
Wallace Self Destructs 108
The Progressive Convention 109
The Fight For Civil Rights.................................110
The Turnip Session 111

Chapter Ten..115
Domestic Communism And The Hiss Case 115
A Clammy Fear 115
The House Committee On UnAmerican Activities.........116
Prelude To The Hiss Case – The Communist Mata Hari.....118
Whittaker Chambers - The Charge 119
Alger Hiss Rebuts..120
Nixon Grabs The Opportunity............................122
The Public Confrontation 125
The Pumpkin Papers 127
The Grand Jury 128
Aftermath 128

Chapter Eleven..131
1948 – The Television Year 131
The Decline Of Radio -- The Advent Of Television.........131
Fears 132
TV And Sports..134
Milton Berle..136
Ed Sullivan 138
Other Legendary Beginnings 139
Cheap Shows...140
TV And Children..141
Commercials 142
Technology 143

Growth 144
The Result 145

Chapter Twelve 147
The Berlin Airlift - Confronting Stalin 147
The International Political Scene 147
The Airlift Gathers Steam. 148
The Berliners 149
An Assembly Line Approach 152
Assembling The Planes 153
Personnel. 154
Ground Crews. 155
Maintenance 156
Air Traffic Control 156
The Result. 157
The Berliners Adapt. 158
The Soviets Turn Up The Pressure 158
The Winter 160
The Third Airfield 160
Operation Little Vittles 162
The End 163

Chapter Thirteen. 167
The First Arab/israeli War 167
The Arabs Invade - But Will They Unite? 167
The Truce. 169
The War Resumes 170
Bernadotte - Man On A Tightrope 172
Diplomatic Maneuvers 173
The Effect On The Presidential Election 173
The War Bleeds To Its Inconclusive Conclusion 174

Chapter Fourteen 177
The Campaign Takes Shape. 177
Will The New Deal Continue Or Be Rolled Back 177
The Personalities - Who Are These Guys 178
The Underdog Had To Fight 179
Truman's Strategy - Fearmongering 181
Attacks On The 80th Congress 181

Dirty Harry 183
Why Give Money To A Loser .185
The Polls 186

Chapter Fifteen. 189
Union Men, Farmers And The Traveling Medicine Show 189
The Labor Vote 189
The Labor Day Trip 191
The September 17 Trip 192
The Farm Vote 193
Race Relations 195
The Courts Breach The Segregated Walls. 196
The Traveling Medicine Show 197
The Naysayers. 199

Chapter Sixteen 201
The Men Who Would Be King - Now Or Later 201
Dewey's Campaign. 201
Boring - Dewey's Reluctance To Fight. 201
Missed Chances. 203
Lazy. 204
The Pop Up Toaster 205
The Press Saw What They Wanted To See 206
Wallace 206
Thurmond. 209
Other Future Presidents On The Hustings. 209

Chapter Seventeen 211
The Final Stretch 211
Truman's Large Crowds 211
Signs Of Dewey's Weakness .212
Polls And Pundits Continue Their Unanimity 212
Foreign Affairs. 213
The Campaign's Last Two Weeks - Dewey Coasts,
    Harry Goes All Out. 214
Harry Courts Ohio - Dewey Ignores It 215
Truman's Final Whistlestop Tour 216
The Last Predictions 218
Election Eve. 219

Chapter Eighteen. 221
    The People - A Snapshot 221
    Family Life. 221
    Sex And The Kinsey Report 221
    A Woman's Changing Role. 224
    Lightning On The Ground. 225
    Cities. 226
    Common Life. 227
    Fashion 228
    Education - The Gi Bill Transforms America. 228
    Economy 229
    Business. 230
    Employment 231
    Labor 232
    Automobiles - The American Dream On Wheels 233
    Science And Technology 235
    Baseball - The Nation's Passion. 236
    Books. 239
    Music. 240
    Movies 240
    Westerns 241
    Conclusion. 242

Chapter Nineteen 243
    Election Day. 243
    The Day. 243
    Truman's Day. 244
    Radio And TV Prepare. 244
    The Evening 245
    Radio And TV's Performance 248
    The Reaction 249
    The Day After 250

Chapter Twenty 253
    What Happened And Why 253
    The Paper Thin Landslide 253
    A Bored Electorate Stayed Home .254
    The Party Victory And Reverse Coattails 255
    The Polls Made Truman A Legend 255
    Revolt Against The 80th Congress 257
    The States 257

Negro 258
Labor. 259
Farm 259
Wallace 260
Foreign Affairs. 261
It Was The Economy, Stupid 261
Dewey's Unscalable Obstacle 262
Winners And Losers 262

Chapter Twenty-one 265
A Return To Normalcy. 265
Harry Is Ejected From The White House 265
The Nation Gives Thanks 266
The Old Soldier Tries To Fade Away 266
China's Last Gasp For Help 267
Christmas And The Boom Subsides 268
Exorcising The Last Ghosts Of The War. 270
Epilogue 270

Bibliography 275

Endnotes. 289

Index 318

∾

INTRODUCTION

> "By a historical oddity, Western Civilization has twice during the last 300 years reached decisive turning points in the 49th year of the century. With the Treaty of Westphalia in 1648 ended the 30 Years War, the bloodiest human conflict before the two world wars. In 1848, the hopes raised by the American and French Revolutions exploded throughout Europe in an uprising that marked the end of the power formerly wielded by authoritarian monarchies. This week, all the historical signposts pointed to 1948 as the turning point in the struggle between western democracy, as exemplified by the United States and eastern absolutism as symbolized by the Soviet Union."

Newsweek January 5,1948.

A YEAR OF MOVEMENT

New Yorkers could not believe it. No one could remember it ever snowing that hard and fast. New York City lay under a record snowfall of 27 inches from the night of December 26, 1947. The city had averaged 1.8 inches an hour--dumping 99 million tons of snow--after the experts had forecast "mostly sunny" weather. While that blizzard still paralyzed the city, New Year's Day ravaged it further with a severe ice storm, cutting power lines and blacking out large portions of the city. For 24 hours, scarcely a bus or a taxi moved. Subways barely functioned.

The deep blanket of white made the familiar unrecognizable, transforming the landscape, changing how people lived, worked, played. The changes wrought by the blizzard were temporary and soon melted. The changes made by that year are still with us. The snow both greeted and symbolized the new year and era.

In 1948, America transformed itself and changed the world! Today, three day old newspapers go unread because this morning's events toppled them. Yet, sixty year old happenings dredged up from dusty library shelves resonate through our daily lives and define who we are and how we became that way. As one scholar wrote, "We may be finished with the past, but the past is not finished with us."[1]

Presidential biographers have focused on 1948 for Truman's world-shaping decisions and Nixon's career launching role in the Hiss case. Such studies, however important, are threads in a tapestry rich with diversity, vitality, and consequence. An historic blizzard caused a puppet to be a household name on the infant technology, television; a bill ignored in Congress' rush to adjourn for the conventions would cost the GOP the election; and a financial crisis in England shifted centuries old global responsibility to the New World.

World War II ended in 1945, after costing more lives and money than any conflict in history. The war still pulsed through the lives of all Americans as they struggled to restore lives that the war had put on hold.

The nation groped through the postwar environment, trying to understand its role in this new era. America stood pre-eminent, not only because of its wealth and might, but because so much of the world lay in smoldering or irradiated ruins.

As America tried to adjust to a world convulsing and reshaping, Americans asked: What was their role in this new society? How would they support their new families? They suffered a collective identity crisis.

The war had stripped soldiers of their individuality as surely, quickly, and completely as they had shed their civilian clothes. They were trained not as individuals but as part of a team with the same haircuts and clothes, all provided by the government. "GI" ("Government Issue") became the synonym for the soldier, not just what the soldier wore. "Uniform" described their life. Even those on the home front sacrificed their individuality for the war. Many enrolled in an army of mass producing cogs in an industrial effort never before imagined. Their names were secondary; only their function mattered, riveter, carpenter, etc. They became interchangeable parts.

The fighting had ended, but the regimentation continued. Veterans traded one uniform of olive drab or khaki for the company's work clothes or gray flannel suits. Nor was their anonymity confined to the workplace. Millions lived in homogenized houses mass produced in suburbia which architectural critic Lewis Mumford described as "a multitude of uniform, unidentifiable houses, lined up inflexibly, at uniform distances, on uniform roads, in a treeless communal wasteland, inhabited by people of the same class, the same income, the same age group."[2] Americans had to find themselves.

1948 was a journey, buffeting America and Americans with change, danger, fear, and opportunity - of endings but most importantly beginnings. In 1945, Readers Digest predicted that in this era, Americans had a precious "chance to make a second start."[3] Americans made the most of it. New life seemed everywhere – from the babies flooding hospitals to the new beginnings and opportunities for veterans, women, and minorities.

If 1948 had an image, it was movement. The whirlpool of war had moved tens of millions of Americans and made relocation no longer strange or forbidding. Men who had spent nights patrolling the North Atlantic or lying in foxholes in the South Pacific, dreaming of home, now left those homes in four major movements that swirled around the country.

The first movement saw Americans again going west as they had throughout their history. California reported a population of over 10 million, an increase of 45.2% since 1940, making it the nation's third largest state. The Los Angeles area was generating 1 out of 8 new jobs in the country and building 1 out of 11 of new houses. Unlike the migrations from the dustbowls of the 1930's, these people moved not from desperation - things were fine where they were - everything just looked even better where they were headed!

One hundred and sixty thousand Negroes[4] migrated from the South, continuing a trend begun early in the decade. War had taken many Negroes out of the South for the first time as they joined the military or worked in defense plants.[5] Once so exposed, many preferred to start anew up North rather than remain in Dixie.

About 24 million Americans farmed in the late 1940s, but that number was dwindling as people fled the farm in one of the most dramatic demographic shifts of American history.[6] Farmers left, not because farming was any harder than ever before - far from it; compared to the Great Depression, farming was riding high. They left because city folk had it so much better, primarily because of something we take for granted today - electricity. Only half the farmhouses had electricity. Many farm families could only read about such devices as radio, washing machines, and television.

A shorter, more subtle but no less profound migration measured from the city to a new land, suburbia. In all four migrations, the destination differed yet the goal was the same - a better life.

People moved not only geographically but economically and socially as class distinctions shattered. In the greatest land rush in history, they were moving into homes they owned![7] Citizens scampered up rungs of the American dream that their parents could only stare at in envy.

Motion always forces decisions - to move or stay, in what direction, how far. America and Americans had been on this journey of self discovery since 1945, but what makes 1948 so pivotal are the choices made that year which created the world we live in. America decided which bridges to cross and which to burn.

I have tried to paint a vivid picture of what happened in 1948; who made it happen and why. My goal has been to give two vantage points: the perspective of 60 years later and another from the view of 1948 – always a difficult mixture! As the historian C. Vann Wedgwood wrote: "History is lived forwards but it is written in retrospect. We know the end before we consider the beginning, and we can never wholly recapture what it was to know the beginning only."[8]

～

CHAPTER ONE

THE YEAR BEGINS

On the same New Year's Day in 1948 that stung New York, a freezing rainstorm with 60 m.p.h. winds hit Chicago, paralyzing traffic, wrecking radio towers and smashing store windows. In mid-January, the coldest front in eight years stormed from the Rockies into the South, freezing Florida's strawberries, celery, and vacationers who had fled the frigid North.

No matter what Mother Nature hurled, she could not dim the nation's exuberance. After suffering through two world wars and the searing Depression, the nation was prosperous, with high employment, and at peace. As TIME magazine noted: "It was a little saddening to the more daring spirits, but in 1948, it was difficult to want to be anything but an American."

THE BABY BOOM, CONSUMERISM AND HOUSING SHORTAGE

With World War II over, repressed desires erupted. Americans succumbed to the three basic urges: sex, shelter, and a new car.

Americans did for babies what they had done for B-29 bombers. They mass produced them! Bleary eyed maternity room nurses experienced the joys of overtime. The baby boom, officially begun on January 1, 1946, was two-years old and in full steam.

From pessimism born of the Great Depression and inability to feed the children it had, 1933 saw only 2,312,000 children born. In 1947, 3,910,000 arrived. In 1948, 3.6 million. The phenomenon had already pushed the population up 12 million over 1940. Now 144 million, the population was surging to reach 148 million by 1950, 20 years before the experts of the 1930s had estimated. They believed that 164,500,000 Americans would exist by 1990.[9] These births showed more than a galloping libido. They trumpeted confidence! - in the country's and the parents' future.

Sex was not the only thing that the war had repressed. For the first time in 20 years, the average American had money, a bright future, and a good reason to spend that money.

A boom greeted veterans back to civilian life. America confounded all the predictions, especially Marxist, of widespread post-war unemployment by remaining prosperous. Virtually every class had money to spend, as the war had flattened the economic pyramid somewhat for the only time that century. The piece of the national income held by the top 5 percent of its wage earners dropped from 22 percent to 17 percent and the share of the bottom 40 percent substantially rose. Full employment and wartime rationing had swelled savings accounts by 30 percent. Americans had $140 billion burning a hole in their pockets for consumer spending at war's end, compared with just $50 billion at the end of 1941.

"Plenty" is a relative term, but for average citizens, this was the most plentiful time in history. Americans had gone straight from the Great Depression into World War II. The home front had endured rationing, while servicemen had thought themselves blessed if they had a clean canteen cup. 1948's prosperity can only be appreciated - not by looking at the cold statistics of that year, but by considering what people that year had been used to!

The backlog of consumer demand and savings created a seller's market in which buyers seldom quibbled over price or quality. The Industrial Revolution entered a new phase. Previously, industrial power had been devoted to capital goods. Mass production of consumer goods had been limited, because most people did not have the funds to justify huge production runs - Henry Ford's Model T being a prime exception. Now, a massive, well-funded consumer demand arose exactly when industry, primed to mass production by the frenzy of World War II, wanted to convert to profitable civilian goods. The lure of dollars for industrialists and the enticement of consumer goods for the long deprived masses stimulated a mutually satisfying orgy of producing and buying.

To fund the buying since VJ Day, Americans had plunged into debt. Consumers owed a record $46 billion, much of it spent for goods that post-war Americans demanded: clothes, refrigerators, washing machines, televisions, dishwashers and electric stoves. "Between 1939 and 1948, clothing sales jumped three-fold, furniture and jewelry four-fold, liquor, household appliances, including TV, five-fold."[10] New car sales soared, although at twice the prices of 1941 models. The increased demand outpaced a supply economy converting from making munitions. Shortages and spiraling inflation resulted.

The cost of living soared to an all time high in April and kept rising. By mid-July, the Consumer Price Index reached 9.7% over 1947, up 76.2% over 1939. In October, officials paroled Walter Seward from the Indiana State Prison after 22 years. The high prices so shocked him that he persuaded the parole board to send him back to jail.

Seward was not the only one stunned. A house which cost $4,440 in 1939, now cost $9,060; clothing was up 93 percent; food, 129 percent; home furnishings, 93.6 percent; rent, 12.2 percent; only gas and electricity were down, 4.8 percent. A Spokane butcher shop advertised: "Choice Meats: The management will accept Cash, first Mortgages, Bonds, and Good Jewelry." In Kalamazoo, Michigan, butchers began passing out an aspirin with each meat purchase.

With high prices came a severe housing shortage. The baby boom overwhelmed the nation's stunted housing supply. Housing starts had slowed during the Depression and had stopped during the war. Men who had liberated Rome, stormed Iwo Jima, and closed pubs in England did not want to move back in with mom and dad and their confining rules. Returning veterans, especially those with families, wanted places of their own, a house if possible, an apartment if necessary.

Apartment dwellers had their rents hiked suddenly and drastically. To ease the problem, the government had enacted a Rent Control law, but not even its offices were immune. In Newark, the Office of Rent Control had to move when the landlord boosted the rent. Many husbands and wives stayed together only because they realized that if they separated, one of them would have no home.

The demand for housing caused a cultural, demographic and geographic shift. Families wanted new homes; builders wanted cheap developable land; thinly populated county governments wanted an expanding tax base. The convergence of those three desires created a new community - suburbia: communities not with individualized houses, built over decades, but row upon row of houses stamped out amazingly quickly and positioned with mind numbing similarity.

Critics carped that many venal builders flimflammed the over-eager veterans, but the criticism overshot the mark. The critics were established professionals, normally living in upscale houses nestled in good communities. Certainly veterans would have preferred to move into such surroundings, but such homes were rare and expensive. Most home buyers wanted them fast and inexpensive; so they sacrificed quality. Stripped to the essentials, tract houses lacked many amenities which would have added time and cost. In Houston, a 4700 unit development lacked porches or garages. A slight shade-giving roof eave supposedly offered such value that the builder touted it in advertisements.[11]

When new houses were started, applicants scrambled to buy. In the fall, people jammed the Long Island highways to look at a house that was not yet for sale. Five hundred offered cash immediately for houses that were not built. Levitt & Sons had decided to test public reaction to their concept of a $20,000 home. They built a sample near Manhasset, then put up a sign, 6 inches high and 3-1/2 ft. long, that read "The house of 1949 by Levitt." That was their only advertising. It brought swarms of visitors. So on September 28, buyers bought 53 houses to be erected by the following Spring. The next day, the remaining 47 homes planned for the development were snapped up.

"Levittown" was born. Its lot sizes nearly doubled the size of most turn of the century homes. The typical home had four and one-half rooms spread over a practical and well designed two-story Cape Cod style house, 25 feet by 30 feet. Each house included a twelve by sixteen foot living room with a fireplace, a kitchen, one bath, and two bedrooms (about 750 square feet) with expansion possibilities in the unfinished attic or outward into the yard. Later models had a carport.[12]

To produce such homes, Levitt simply transferred to home building the techniques he had used to build housing for war workers. As they had with aircraft and ship making, huge war contracts with tight schedules had transformed the home-building industry by introducing it to mass production.[13] Soon fleets of bulldozers were churning up dust storms as Levitt built 36 houses a day as opposed to the five a year the average contractor built before the war.[14] The 1,118,000 single houses began in 1948 were not enough. Two million couples had to live with relatives.

Inflation and the housing shortage emerged as central issues in the presidential election in November.

CHAPTER TWO

THE POLITICAL YEAR BEGINS

HARRY TRUMAN - THE ACCIDENTAL EVERYMAN PRESIDENT

As 1948 began, the country was led by its 33rd president, Harry S Truman. Nothing in his biography instilled great confidence in his leadership.

A financial gamble of his father, a farmer and mule trader, had lost the family savings. So Truman became the only President of the century not to attend college. Harry toiled at a series of dead-end jobs, farmed for a time, and joined the National Guard. He served in France during World War I as an artillery battery commander. After the war, he opened a men's clothing store in downtown Kansas City, participated in an Oklahoma zinc mine, and various oil drilling activities. All failed. In 1922, he entered local Democratic politics under the wing of political boss, Tom Pendergast.

Some people then and now misunderstood what that meant. They assumed that Truman was as crooked as the organization. Not so. In political fiefdoms like Jackson County, if you wanted to get into politics, you had to join the machine. But Truman remained so uncorrupted that as late as 1940, after being in politics for 18 years including six in the U.S. Senate, Truman was still too poor to save his mother's home from foreclosure.[15]

Elected to the U.S. Senate in 1934, and chided as the "Senator from Pendergast", he staunchly backed Franklin Roosevelt and voted consistently for New Deal legislation. During World War II, Capitol Hill correspondents had voted him the most effective senator, after he chaired a committee exposing waste in the war effort. Roosevelt and the party leaders chose him as FDR's running mate in 1944, because he would help relations with Congress and did not offend people the way the incumbent, Henry Wallace, did.

One incident during Truman's short vice presidency encapsulated the man. Tom Pendergast had been imprisoned for tax evasion. Virtually all politicians, especially national figures, shunned the now powerless pariah. Not Harry Truman. When Pendergast died shortly after leaving prison, Truman weathered the criticism, and went to Missouri for the funeral. To

Harry Truman, friends remained friends whatever their circumstances.

On April 12, 1945, less than twelve weeks after Truman became vice president, Roosevelt died. President Truman had muddled through, but always under FDR's shadow and never quite measuring up, in the minds of most Democrats. Truman had not yet announced his candidacy, but his close friends knew that he wanted to erase FDR's specter and win on his own.

Presidential elections force Americans to assess where they are, where they are going, and where they want to be. The election forms the spine of 1948, connecting many seemingly disparate events. 1948 would be the first presidential election since 1932 in which Franklin D. Roosevelt was not leading the Democratic ticket. Republicans smacked their lips at their golden opportunity to win after four losses.

America had held only one national election, on November 5, 1946, since Truman occupied the Oval Office. He was so unpopular that party leaders convinced him to stay out of the campaign. They replayed old FDR campaign speeches on the radio instead. The Democrats were still reeling from that drubbing. Under the slogan "Had enough? Vote Republican!", the GOP gained 11 seats in the Senate, 54 in the House and seized control of both Houses for the first time since the New Deal began.

The Democrats blamed Truman. Senator J. William Fulbright of Arkansas, a Democrat, urged Truman to resign. With no vice president, next in line of succession was the Secretary of State. Fulbright suggested that Truman appoint Republican Senator Arthur Vandenberg to that post. As President, Vandenberg could restore confidence and avoid the gridlock that a Republican Congress and a Democratic president would foster. The Chicago Sun and the Atlanta Constitution agreed and urged Truman to adopt the suggestion.

With that inauspicious record as the leader of the party, Truman faced the election year that would decide whether the New Deal should roll on or back. One thing remains the same in any election - everything the President does, fails to do, or can take credit or blame for - is magnified and used for political purposes.

The election marked a watershed in American politics - the last presidential election before television, computers, primaries, teleprompters, jet travel, political consultants, modern polling, and faxes transformed politics.[16] Yet, in many ways, it was the first modern campaign.

Since the 1946 reversals, Truman's popularity had rebounded. In late 1947, the Gallup poll showed him beating the top Republican contenders, Governor Dewey of New York and Senator Robert A. Taft of Ohio, decisively.[17] But, at year's end, he suffered a body blow when a festering dispute erupted.

A SERIOUS ATTACK FROM THE LEFT

On a national radio broadcast on December 29, Henry Agard Wallace announced his independent candidacy, declaring:

> There is no real fight between a Truman and a Republican. The bigger the peace vote in 1948, the more definitely the world will know that the United States is not behind the bipartisan reactionary war policy which is dividing the world into two armed camps and making inevitable the day when American soldiers will be lying in their arctic suits in the Russian snow. . . .
>
> We have assembled a Gideon's army, small in number, powerful in conviction, ready for action. . . .[18]

Not just another third party candidate, Wallace was a political icon with a resume of historic accomplishments. As the Vice President for FDR's third term, 1941-45, had FDR not replaced him on the ticket in 1944, he, not Truman, would be the incumbent in 1948.

Unlike Truman, Wallace's pre-political life had sparkled. Trained as an agriculturist and a plant geneticist, he served as editor of Wallace's Farmer from 1924 to 1933. He researched corn yields and developed several hybrid strains of corn including one with a high yield for feeding pigs. His Pioneer Hybrid Corn Company made so much money that, despite his appeal to the common man, he was 1948's wealthiest presidential candidate.

Originally a Republican, Wallace supported Roosevelt in 1932. He helped write FDR's Farm Platform; then served as an outstanding Secretary of

Agriculture from 1933 to 1940. Had Roosevelt not run for a third term in 1940, many would have supported Wallace as the candidate.[19]

But Roosevelt did run and chose Wallace as his running mate. By early 1944, however, Wallace's left wing views had offended too many party bigwigs. Roosevelt nudged him off the ticket by announcing that Truman would be an acceptable running mate. Wallace and Truman had gone head to head for the vice presidency at the Chicago Convention.

On the first ballot, Wallace received 429½ votes to Truman's 319½ votes. The remaining 428 votes split over 14 favorite sons and local choices. Since 589 votes were required, Wallace missed by 160 votes. But for those votes, Wallace would have been re-elected vice president and would have been the President seeking election in 1948. On the second ballot, the political bosses, Mayor Ed Kelly of Chicago, Ed Flynn of New York, and Mayor Frank Hague of Jersey City, pushed Truman over the top.

As a consolation, Roosevelt asked Wallace to be Secretary of Commerce where he remained until Truman fired him for publicly castigating American's hard-line policy toward the Soviet Union.

Far more pro Soviet than most Americans, Wallace went on a speaking tour sponsored by an umbrella group of leftist organizations. Enthusiastic supporters swarmed to hear him, often shouting: "We want Wallace!" "Wallace in '48." Buoyed and perhaps deluded by the fervor, he became the candidate of the new Progressive Party and began trying to lure disaffected liberals from the Democrats.[20]

No one believed he would win but everyone thought he would take enough votes (anywhere from 13 to 18 percent) from Truman to give the White House to the Republicans. Wallace's candidacy did not catch the President unprepared.

TRUMAN'S GAME PLAN

James Rowe eyed an election the way a street fighter sizes up a brawl. "Who will I be fighting? What are their weaknesses? How can I 'kneecap 'em'?" Rowe, a talented Washington attorney and former presidential assistant, had written a memorandum, "The Politics of 1948," in September 1947. The memorandum candidly looked at the country, the likely opposition, and Truman. It analyzed how to exploit Republican weaknesses and capitalize upon the powers of the Presidency. Clark Clifford, Truman's primary domestic advisor, revised and updated it, especially the civil rights section. The bulk, however, retained Rowe's language.[21] It became the game plan for the campaign, and Rowe was the spider who spun the web.[22]

Rowe predicted Dewey as the GOP nominee. This was by no means certain then or even on the eve of the Republican convention. But Dewey was the country's best-known Republican - its standard bearer in 1944 and the governor of the most populous state, New York. He seemed a logical choice. "He will be a resourceful, intelligent and highly dangerous candidate... with an extremely efficient group of men around him."[23]

Forecasting Wallace's candidacy, Rowe suggested the best way to undercut Wallace was "to identify him and isolate him in the public mind with the Communists." To avoid Truman's getting splattered in the mudslinging, liberals and progressives "and no one else" should point out that the core of Wallace's backing came from Communists and fellow travelers.[24]

Rowe assumed that "The South, as always, can be considered safely Democratic." Because of that firm base, "we could lose New York, Pennsylvania, Massachusetts, Ohio, and Illinois--all the big states--and still win." So Truman could ignore the South and concentrate on the other regions.[25]

Rowe believed that the northern Negro vote held the balance of power. "The Negroes not only vote in a block but are geographically concentrated in the pivotal, large and closely contested electoral states such as New York, Illinois, Pennsylvania, Ohio and Michigan." Rowe and Clifford worried that enough Negroes would return to the GOP, the party of Lincoln, to tilt those states to Dewey. Truman must emphasize civil rights.

On domestic issues, the memo suggested a liberal agenda targeted at traditional Democrats but attractive to the independents who would hold the balance of power. Rowe concluded that the major issues would be the high cost of living, intensified by the housing shortage. On these issues, Truman and the Republican Congress were diametrically opposed.

THE 80TH CONGRESS AND TRUMAN'S STRATEGY—PICKING A FIGHT

To understand the election, you must understand the 80th Congress. Truman labeled it the "Do-Nothing 80th Congress," but he lied. It did a lot, but not much to a New Dealer's liking. It rejected much of Truman's social legislation, not out of laziness or indecision, but philosophical opposition. The Republicans, especially Senator Taft of Ohio, viewed the 1946 election as a clear plea to revoke the New Deal. But by mid-summer 1947, polls showed that enough people disliked the Republican record in Congress to make the 1948 election look like a horse race.

Rowe's brilliant but cynical strategy was PICK A FIGHT! Rowe recommended that Truman tailor the State of the Union message and other pronouncements for the voter, not Congress, and propose liberal issues bound to antagonize the majority in Congress, the conservative Republicans. None of these bills would pass anyway, so Truman should pick a fight with Congress in order to win in November. Truman could take credit for whatever passed but could criticize Congress for whatever did not.

Starkly contrasting the liberal policies of the Democrats with the conservative rut of the Republicans could rally the New Deal coalition and win the election. After the State of the Union address, Truman would hit Congress every Monday with a popular proposal that Taft and his colleagues were sure to reject.

Like a battering ram repeatedly smashing against the wall of conservatism, Truman proposed broader civil rights legislation, federal housing, extension of wartime controls, and highway construction, all destined to become issues in November.[26] That memorandum set the stage and the tone for the election.

Truman loved it! He spoiled for the fight. On January 6, 1948, he wrote in his diary: "Congress meets--too bad, too. They'll do nothing but wrangle, pull phony investigations and generally upset the affairs of the nation." Congress reciprocated his loathing.[27] On February 26, the Senate set up a committee with unprecedented power to investigate the administration.

THE STATE OF THE UNION - THE OPENING SALVO

On a sunny but windy January 7, Harry Truman motored up Capitol Hill to announce the State of the Union. The Capitol was still laced with naked steel girders to protect it against Axis bombing. As in any election year, this supposedly non-political report was actually a carefully crafted opening salvo of the campaign, delivered to a national audience.

Truman played to all the voting blocs needed in November. Defiantly reaffirming the New Deal, he proposed a smorgasbord of socio-economic programs, national health insurance, continued support for farm cooperatives and rural electrification, boosting the minimum wage from forty to seventy-five cents an hour and a forty-dollar tax reduction for every American. TIME Magazine called it "The Bible for the Democratic Party."

Unfortunately, he botched his delivery. Reading his 5,500 words at about 120 words a minute, he often stumbled over terms, emphasized wrong ones, and bungled his punchlines. Even his wife and daughter looking down from the gallery appeared bored. No less than seven times, Truman obviously paused for applause, only to hear silence. The GOP audience glared acidly while even friendly Congressmen scowled, twiddled their thumbs, squirmed in their seats, suppressed yawns or fell asleep. The mood on both sides of the aisle ranged from frowning annoyance to sheer boredom.[28]

Only at 1:55 p.m., 22 minutes after he began his 43 minute address, did Congress make its first sound. The Republicans mockingly applauded after he promised to fulfill his Constitutional duty to administer the Taft-Hartley Act. He was interrupted only once more, when he urged a strong armed force. In fact, a Wallacite in the gallery began clapping out of pity, "I just decided," she explained, "it was time somebody got up enough nerve to applaud." James Reston reported in The New York Times the speech's "extraordinarily chilly reception." TIME related: "They had to cut a hole in the ice to get him out of the Chamber."

Truman had scarcely left the Capitol before the sniping began. Nearly everyone ridiculed Truman's proposed $40 tax cut as a pure election year ploy. Ways and Means Chairman Harold Knutson gasped: "My God, I didn't know inflation had gone that far. Tom Pendergast paid only $2 a vote and now Truman proposes to pay $40." The usually friendly Washington Post dismissed his address as "unmitigatedly demagogic . . . a transparently political move."

The next day, in the GOP response, Senator Taft, over ABC radio, sadly concluded that once again, Washington was masquerading as "a Santa Claus, with a rich present for every special group in the United States." Truman's program would add at least $5 billion to the annual budget. "Where is the money coming from?" Taft demanded to know. [29]

THE EISENHOWER BOOM

Besides the icy reception from Congress, the bad news on prices, and the Wallace rebellion, Truman also had to worry about running against the most popular man in the country: Dwight Eisenhower. A Gallup Poll asked: "Is General Eisenhower a Republican or a Democrat?" 22 percent thought he was a Republican; 20 percent a Democrat; and 58 percent did not know. It did not matter. Everybody wanted him!

But on January 23, 1948, Eisenhower announced that he was not running. "[M]y decision to remove myself completely from the political scene is definite and positive. . . . I would not accept nomination even under the remote circumstance that it were tendered me." So the Republicans wrote Eisenhower out for 1948.[30]

Unfortunately for Truman, this good news soon dissipated. In an attempt to court the Negro vote, Truman fractured the Democrats' grip on the South's 127 electoral votes.

CIVIL RIGHTS TOUCHES OFF A SOUTHERN REVOLT

Newsweek noted that in all his years in the White House, Roosevelt had never taken any stands on federal anti-lynching legislation, poll tax repeal, or similar civil rights bills. Truman now dared to go where FDR had never traveled.

Hailing from a state where owning slaves was legal until only twenty years before his birth, Truman apparently enjoyed racial jokes and often used racial epithets. Indeed, in 1944, one Negro newspaper called him a member of the Ku Klux Klan.[31] But he was a fair man who took his duty as Commander In Chief very seriously.

On February 12, 1946, a Negro named Isaac Woodard, only a few hours after receiving his honorable discharge, took a bus from Atlanta to his home in South Carolina. At one stop, Woodard still in uniform asked the driver if he could use a restroom. The driver refused and a violent quarrel ensued. At the next stop, the driver told a policeman that Woodard had made a disturbance. The policeman dragged him off the bus, beat him, carted him off to jail where he shoved the end of a club into Woodard's eyes and ground them like corn meal, blinding him. The FBI and Attorney General Clark pressured local officials into trying the officer, but the jury acquitted him in half an hour.

Horrified by this and other incidents, on Monday, February 2, 1948, Truman proposed an omnibus civil rights program, including an anti-lynching law and an anti-poll tax statute - the first 20th century President to submit a legislative package devoted to civil rights.

To close this "serious gap between our ideals and some of our practices," he pledged to issue executive orders ending discrimination in the federal government and segregation in the armed forces. The Nation, a liberal magazine, hailed the message as "a genuine and highly admirable document" and the Chicago Sun Times dubbed it "a noble deed."[32]

The South erupted. Dixie politicians tried to outdo each other in their metaphors. They accused Truman of "stabbing the South in the back;" practicing "outright political demagoguery;" trying to "out-Wallace Wallace"; "kissing the feet of the minorities," trying to "mongrelize the South."[33]

In early March, 400 Negroes had registered to vote in Johnson County, Georgia's Democratic primary. On election eve, a long line of cars pulled up to the ballpark in Wrightsville. Two hundred and forty nine men and women got out and solemnly donned their Ku Klux Klan sheets. At the courthouse lawn, they burned a large kerosene drenched cross while the Grand Dragon harangued Truman's civil rights policy. "The Klan will not permit the people of this country to become a mongrel race." The next day, no Negroes voted.

If you dismiss such actions as the deeds of a few extremists, consider this: Fifteen states did not permit whites to marry "Mongolians," i.e. Orientals; in 5, whites could not marry Indians. Thirty states prohibited marriage between Negroes and whites. These were not antiquated laws, on the books but never enforced. On December 17th, 1948, a jury took only 15 minutes to rule that Davis Knight was legally a Negro even though his Navy records never questioned his status as a white man. He had married 18 year old Junie Lee Spradley in 1946. But his great grandmother was part Negro and therefore the Navy veteran, being at least 1/8th Negro, was legally black. The jury sentenced him to 5 years in prison for violating Mississippi's miscegenation statute.

On February 12, 5,000 Confederate flag-waving Southern Democrats, in Jackson, Mississippi, called upon "all true white Jefferson Democrats to unite in opposing Truman's program." A week later, on February 19, at the annual Jefferson-Jackson Day dinner, Senator Olin B. Johnston of South Carolina humiliated Truman. He purchased a table right in front of the dais at the Mayflower Hotel in Washington, from which Truman would speak, and left it vacant. News photos showed Truman speaking past the empty seats, giving the impression that he was addressing a virtually empty hall.[34]

On Friday, 52 southern members of Congress, later backed by 30 more, adopted a resolution condemning Truman's civil rights program. As TIME reported, nothing good happened to the Democrats that week. The next week was no better.[35]

On February 23, several southern Democratic governors, led by Strom Thurmond of South Carolina, called on Senator J. Howard McGrath, chairman of the Democratic National Committee. They demanded that Truman withdraw his civil rights legislation. When McGrath refused, the southerners stormed out to Thurmond's suite and prepared a press release. Thurmond's 21-year-old wife, who had been his secretary until he dictated to her a formal marriage proposal the previous fall, typed copies while sitting on a bed with a portable typewriter on her lap. The statement ended, "The present leadership of the Democratic Party will soon realize that the South is no longer in the bag."

When someone pointed out to Thurmond that Truman's policy on civil rights did not differ markedly from Roosevelt's public utterances, the reply was blunt and accurate. "I agree, but Truman really means it." The bedrock assumption of the Rowe/Clifford memorandum was shattering. The Solid South was defecting.

18

TRUMAN AS CANDIDATE

Harry Truman suffered from one fundamental flaw -- he was not Franklin Roosevelt.

People, and especially presidents, are judged by three factors: First, what they do, the only thing over which they have some control; Second, what peoples' expectations are; and third, the yardstick against which they are measured. These last two are closely related but distinct. Truman's main disadvantage was that he was compared to FDR. Warren Harding would not have been a tough act to follow. Roosevelt was. In 1945, people expected so little of Truman that when he did reasonably well, he surprised them, but people always thought: "Roosevelt would have done it better."

A Chief Executive stuck in an assistant county clerk's body, the inconspicuous looking Truman seemed more like an owl with his slicked hair and thick glasses. One 16-year-old gasped, "Why, he looks like anybody else, only more so!" Everything about him cried out his mediocrity. Roosevelt had been dignified. Truman seemed coarse and impetuous. His flat, high pitched voice carried a farmer's twang rather than a cultivated gentility. Truman had a bourbon and poker ambiance and often introduced presidents and prime ministers to the White House butlers or doormen.[36]

His home state newspaper, the *St. Louis Post-Dispatch,* believed that Truman lacked "the stature, the vision, the social and economic grasp, or the sense of history required to lead this nation in a world crisis." Two jokes epitomized the feelings; "Don't shoot the piano player, he's trying hard"; "He reminds me of an uncle who played the piano in a whorehouse two years before he found out what was going on upstairs."[37]

Truman had contributed to that impression. When he arrived in Washington, he confessed: "I'm as ignorant as a fool about everything that's important." In his first days as the new and dazed President, he admitted in one national address: "I shall attempt to meet your expectations, but don't expect too much of me." As Mark Twain wrote: "Confession is good for the soul but bad for the reputation." The Wallace candidacy and the southern revolt assured that he would not be in that job much longer.

On February 17, a special election for the House demonstrated Wallace's feared potential. It became a battle ground as the Progressive and American Labor candidate Leo Isacson received Wallace's help against his Democratic opponent, Karl Propper, boss Ed Flynn's candidate.

The 24th Congressional District had always gone Democratic, but Isacson crushed the heavily favored Propper nearly 56 to 31 percent. The New York Times predicted the defeat would certainly "bring gloom to the Truman high command." Experts claimed the election proved that Wallace would throw New York, California, Michigan, Illinois, and Pennsylvania to the Republicans.[38]

On Wednesday, February 18, Wallace announced that his California supporters had obtained 464,000 signatures, more than enough to place his name on the ballot there. On February 23, Democratic Senator Glen H. Taylor of Idaho announced he would be Wallace's running mate.

An isolationist who opposed the Marshall Plan and voted to slash foreign aid funds, Taylor ended his formal education at age 15 when he dropped out of school to become a sheepherder, later a tent-show cowboy singer, then a Senator. He campaigned by crooning western songs off the back of a soundtruck, accompanying himself on a guitar. The flamboyant cowboy, who had once ridden his horse up the steps of the Senate office building for publicity, promised the perfect colorful counterbalance to the bland Wallace.[39]

THE STRANGEST MAN IN POLITICS

A gangling man, slightly stooped with a toothy grin, thick gray hair and an unmanageable forelock, who loped rather than walked, Henry Wallace had been the 34th Vice President of the United States. Looking at his resume, you would think that he would be a formidable candidate.

But the resume masked some fundamental problems. He was an awkward rambling speaker. While Truman's delivery was bad, his content made sense. With Wallace, an equally bad delivery transmitted a content of ethereal fog.

Truman called him a 100% pacifist who wanted to disband the armed forces, a "dreamer,"[40] and one of the most peculiar fellows he'd ever met. For once, Harry put it delicately.

Wallace was the strangest man in American politics. A person of vastly diverse interests, as the editor of Wallace's Farmer from 1924-1933, he would run an article on infant damnation beside one on hog cholera. He spoke Russian, French, German, Portuguese and Spanish, believing "When a person learns another language, he acquires another soul."[41]

The austere and parsimonious Wallace rarely drank and did not smoke, play cards, gamble, swear or tell off color stories.[42] A deeply religious man, his religion defied classification, however. Normally a High Episcopalian, Wallace dabbled in Buddhism, Judaism, Confucianism, Islam, Christian Science and remote Oriental cults, mysticism and astrology. Really a Pantheist, he believed that nature, science, and religion were one. He would often draw horoscopes for visitors while expounding on the healing properties of raw garlic. A health fanatic, he once flabbergasted the playwright, Lillian Hellman, by serving her a lunch of shredded wheat and eggs and no liquor.

The Rowe memorandum had predicted his candidacy but noted: "the most recent reports on Wallace's personality by men who know him well are that... his mysticism increases..." That mysticism had apparently begun in the 1930's.[43] While Secretary of Agriculture, Wallace had immersed himself in the teachings of a Russian mystic named Nicholas Konstantinovich Roerich, guru of a religious sect. For more than a decade, newspapermen and politicians had heard rumors that Wallace had written letters to Roerich.[44]

In March 1948, columnist Westbrook Pegler wrote four columns publishing some of the letters and demanding that Wallace admit or deny authorship. Pegler, a conservative who despised Wallace's pro-Soviet views, gleefully asked whether Wallace still regarded Roerich "as a god or supernatural master of mankind as many of your associates in the cult did."

Newsweek published snatches of the letters, filled with bizarre mystic allusions and political pontifications. They saluted Roerich as "Dear Guru," and used a jargon or mysterious code which named President Roosevelt "The Flaming One" or "The Wavering One;" Winston Churchill, "The Roaring Lion"; and Cordell Hull, "The Sour One." The writer boasted of ridding himself of headaches at formal Senate dinners by passing a Tibetan amulet over his forehead. The letters also sermonized on the mystic potency of such symbols as the Christian cross, the Mongolian lama's reliquary, and the Indian medicine man's charms.

> A typical sentence, reprinted by Newsweek, read:
>
> I have been thinking of you holding the casket--the sacred, most precious casket. And I have thought of the new country going forth, to meet the seven stars under the sign of the three stars. And I have thought of the admonition, "Await the stones."

Some of the letters were signed "Wallace," others "Galahad." Three newspaper chains had hired experts to review the handwritten letters, all of whom named Wallace as the author. [45] Pegler wrote that he had called and telephoned repeatedly seeking an appointment to confront Wallace with those letters. "All to no avail."

At a news conference later that year, the "guru" letters stared Wallace straight in the face. Several reporters including Pegler and H.L.Mencken posed the question, but a visibly agitated Wallace refused to answer. Eventually, the reporters got up and left, leaving Wallace alone with writers for Communist publications. Mencken wrote that Wallace handled the news conference like an "imbecile."

Wallace's campaign slid downhill, but Wallace still would likely deprive Truman of victory. Democrats worried that hundreds of thousands of Americans would agree with Wallace's attacks on Wall Street, internationalism, and the military. A popular cartoon that January showed the GOP on its knees thanking God for Wallace's candidacy.

THE REPUBLICAN CONTENDERS

Besides Wallace and the Southern revolt, Truman had to confront the traditional rivals - the Republicans. With Wallace in the race and the South on the warpath, the Republican nominee seemed sure to be the next president. So the battle for the nomination raged. The best proof of Truman's perceived vulnerability was the number of people itching to take him on - at least six serious candidates. As the party's 1944 nominee, Dewey remained its titular head and seemed the front runner, but the others were substantial: Robert Taft, Douglas MacArthur, Arthur Vandenberg, Earl Warren, and Harold Stassen.

Born in Owosso, Michigan in 1902, and educated at the University of Michigan, Thomas Edmund Dewey raced through the three-year course at Columbia Law School in two years. In 1935, he became special prosecutor for a grand jury investigating vice and racketeering in New York City. In this job, and as district attorney from 1937 to 1941, Dewey gained national fame as a crusading prosecutor in the war against Lucky Luciano, Dutch Schultz, and other gangsters.

In December 1939, Dewey had announced his presidential candidacy, at the age of 37. Secretary of the Interior Harold L. Ickes jibed, "Dewey throws his diaper into the ring." He was the front-runner at the 1940 convention and led on the first three ballots, only to be passed by Taft and Willkie on the fourth ballot and to lose to Willkie on the sixth. Elected New York governor in 1942, he used that as the steppingstone to become the Republican nominee in 1944, when at 42, he sought to be the youngest man ever elected President. He kept his presidential hopes alive in 1946 by being resoundingly reelected Governor, even carrying New York City.

Dewey was indestructibly honest, a genuine hero who had prosecuted Murder Inc. When he received a death threat announcing that he would be killed that evening on his way home, he made a point of leaving at his usual time through the usual exit and taking the same route, with one difference - he made sure that the lights were on inside the car. His wife, Frances, once received an anonymous call telling her to go to the morgue to identify his body. In restaurants, he continued to sit with his back to the wall, a legacy from the days when the underworld slapped a $25,000 price tag on his head.[46]

Politically, a forward-looking moderate, with extensive executive experience, the 5'8" Dewey was always neat and unruffled, with wavy dark hair, and nicely trimmed mustache. His voice, honed as an operatic baritone and part time choir soloist, resounded in well-modulated tones.

And yet, Dewey had a major handicap, his personality. Many agreed with the oft-quoted words of the wife of one New York GOP leader, "You have to know Dewey really well to dislike him."[47]

With his stiff manner, he came across as an aloof patrician far unlike Roosevelt, who loved mingling, and certainly unlike Harry Truman. His own minister said Dewey has never feared gangsters, only germs. When Dewey toured a state prison, he would not touch a door handle himself, but wait for someone else to open it. If no one got his message, he would discreetly cover his palm with a handkerchief to grasp the metal that prisoners held daily.[48]

The politics of the day called for a peculiar minuet. Rather than campaign publicly for the nomination, one worked furiously behind the scenes and through intermediaries to build a "spontaneous" grass roots movement to which the reluctant candidate was duty bound to accede. Dewey played his part to the hilt. On January 15, after supporters deposited a thousand names on petitions to qualify him for the Oregon primary, Dewey issued a 74-word statement. While his legislative responsibilities prevented him from actively campaigning for the nomination, he would accept it, if his party so honored him again. It seemed "an appropriate way," he told his mother, to get "an inevitable statement behind us."[49]

Dewey's chief opponent led the conservative wing of the party. Robert Taft lived an interesting childhood. His father was Solicitor General, Secretary of War, then President of the United States, and finally Chief Justice of the United States, the only man ever to head two branches of the government. Taft had gone to the Taft School (naturally!), Yale, and then Harvard Law School and graduated first in his class from all three. Since 1939, he had been a U.S. Senator.

In nine years, Taft had become the intellectual leader of the Congress even though he was not the majority leader. Dominating his colleagues by character and intellect,[50] by 1948, the New Republic wrote: "Congress now consists of the House, the Senate, and Bob Taft."[51]

Generally called a conservative and certainly reluctant to involve the United States in overseas entanglements, Taft was more accurately a nineteenth century liberal, hidebound in his anti-New Deal belief that the individual should be free from governmental regimentation. He did, however, support federal housing legislation and federal aid to education on the grounds that society must care for the education and environment of its children.[52] In 1947, he co-authored the Taft-Hartley Law that handcuffed Labor's most potent weapon - the strike.

An authentic aristocrat, Taft was brilliant, well-educated, hard working, and probably the only candidate who made Dewey seem like a cavalier. Taft's vested suits, galoshes, rimless glasses, thin-lipped smile, humorless demeanor, and half-bald head covered by long strips of side hair reminded people of an aloof, stuffy minister rather than the charismatic man that voters want in the Oval Office. [53] Taft's attempts to humanize himself seemed forced and futile.

Taft scarcely concealed his distaste for handshaking, baby kissing, and all the foolish photographs that are the obstacle course of politics. He courageously did not shy away from unpopular positions, once remarking that "it isn't honest to be tactful." Equally maddening to his advisers, he answered many questions on popular issues with "Haven't made up my mind." or "I'm not yet sure what to do myself."[54] Devoid of personal color and rhetorical flair, his speeches could put a stampede to sleep with their emphasis on statistics.

Nothing more typifies Taft's bluntness and his almost disinterest in what today is called "the sound bite" than his response in 1947 when asked what could be done about high food prices. "We should eat less." Nationally that comported with the law of supply and demand. If demand decreased, prices should fall. Aside from that, it did not come across as particularly caring, especially to individuals with families. Newspapers labeled him "eat less Taft."

Dewey faced another challenger, Harold Edward Stassen, the boy wonder of the Republican Party. Minnesota's governor from 1938 to 1942, Stassen had broken tradition and announced his quest for the nomination on December 17th, 1946 - by far the first aspirant to do so.

The 41-year old Stassen had no connection with the negative Eightieth Congress. Domestically, he held liberal ideas, but was vehemently against Communism. In foreign policy, he was an internationalist with a distinguished war record and a laudable performance on the U.S. delegation that helped establish the United Nations in 1945.

As an out-of-office candidate, he was not given much chance, but Stassen had extensively used charter airplanes to pursue delegates and had been running non-stop for over a year in a campaign run by Warren Burger, a 40-year-old St. Paul lawyer.[55] If vigor and enthusiasm counted, Stassen would be formidable.

Despite this array of challengers, Truman had not yet formally announced. He told a press conference that he had been "so darned busy with foreign affairs and other situations that have developed that I haven't had any time to think about any presidential campaign." Finally, on March 9, Howard McGrath, Democratic National Committee chairman, left a meeting in Truman's office and told reporters, "The President has authorized me to say that if nominated by the Democratic National Convention, he will accept and run."[56]

By that time, most people assumed that whether Truman ran or not would make little difference.

∾

CHAPTER THREE

THE DEATH OF ISOLATIONISM

COMMUNISM AND CONTAINMENT

After the war, Stalin spread his grasp throughout Europe like an overturned glass of burgundy, corralling the peoples of Eastern Europe behind the Iron Curtain that Churchill had named in 1946. Truman, the accidental President, stepped in to stop any further Soviet expansion because no one else could.

Stalin apparently made four assumptions: First, Britain posed no obstacle to his plans, considering its financial devastation. Second, the United States would soon relapse into isolationism as it had after World War I. Third, a post war economic collapse like that of 1921 would engulf the U.S. Fourth, Europeans would welcome or at least acquiesce in becoming Communists. He was right on only one. Britain was too weak to continue its prewar role. But Eastern and Central Europe disclosed no mass support for Russia or for Communist ideology. Most importantly, he totally misjudged Harry Truman, the American economy, and the American people.[57]

TECHNOLOGY TRUMPS TRADITION

"Avoid overseas problems!" warned George Washington and Thomas Jefferson. For almost 170 years, Americans had obeyed and shunned foreign troubles, especially European ones. Isolationism had not been a fad but a creed. Now, Americans reluctantly but unequivocally abandoned that religion wholesale to pursue the diametrically opposed grail of internationalism. They did so because the weapons of war demanded it. Before, the Atlantic and Pacific Oceans had insulated America from overseas perils. Now rockets, long range bombers, and aircraft carriers had reduced that vast moat to a puddle. Most frightening of all, however, were not the delivery systems, but the munitions. The atomic bomb weighed heavily on America's collective mind.

Britain had been the world's policeman until World War II bankrupted it. The Empire decided that its colonies, gathered over centuries, cost too much in coin and carnage. So it began peeling them off. India had gained independence in 1947 and split into India and Pakistan. On January 4,

Burma became an independent country, followed on February 10, by Ceylon. Most ominously, the British announced that their protectorate of Palestine would end in May.

Only the U.S. had the military, economic, and political power to fill the vacuum. This was not jingoistic boasting. It was globally recognized fact.

Not only did the United States have 50% of the world's wealth; but, as TIME noted: it "had not only reached a new maturity, but a position of pre-eminence in the world. It now seemed impelled to consolidate its social gains and learn more about the art of exerting leadership among nations."

Harold J. Laski, the British political scientist and historian, agreed: "World history is more likely to be shaped by American history for the next half century than by any other element in its making. . . . It is difficult to see how the world can beat its problems squarely without the moral and material leadership which only America is in a position to provide." For centuries, the world had been Euro-centric. Now center stage shifted. The world split into bipolar camps as a new balance of power emerged.

THE TORCH PASSES

The history of our time is largely composed of moments. One such moment occurred on February 21, 1947. The British Embassy in Washington called the State Department to say that the Ambassador had an important message to give Secretary George C. Marshall.

The Communists in Greece had ignited a guerrilla war, and Britain spent millions of pounds futilely trying to contain them and sustain the government. Concurrently, British money helped prop up Turkey against Soviet pressure for warm-water ports and military bases around the Dardanelles.

After six years of war, and with its money for food and raw materials dwindling after a freezing winter, Great Britain faced stark postwar reality. It could no longer bolster the governments of Greece and Turkey. Until that day, United States foreign policy had relied on the Pax Britannica, enforced by the Royal Navy. In that simple conversation, the baton of world leadership passed from the old world to the new. [58]

The British Ambassador met Marshall on February 24, but the State Department had already begun working out the details.

Marshall briefed Truman that afternoon, recommending that America continue the aid that the British had dispensed. The President agreed. Three days later, on February 27, Secretary Marshall and Undersecretary of State Dean Acheson briefed congressional leaders. The combination of Marshall's dry but sobering listing of the dangers ("The choice is between acting with energy or losing by default.")[59] and Acheson's impassioned advocacy stunned the select audience with the imminence and extent of the peril. Acheson stressed that not only Turkey and Greece could fall, but all of eastern and central Europe. Failing to act "might open three continents to Soviet penetration." Everyone recognized the sea change in responsibility this meant. Breaking the silence, Arthur Vandenberg turned to Truman and said, "Mr. President, if you will say that to the Congress and the country, I will support you, and I believe that most of its members will do the same."[60]

Two weeks later, on March 12, 1947, a grim faced Truman told a joint session of Congress that Greece was about to succumb to an armed minority and that not even the United Nations could save it. Its downfall, moreover, would have an "immediate and serious effect" on Turkey, spread "confusion and disorder" throughout the Middle East, and undercut those Europeans who were "struggling against great difficulties" to keep their independence. Then he uttered the core of his message that became the Truman Doctrine and matches the Monroe Doctrine in significance.

> I believe that it must be the policy of the United States to
> support free people who are resisting attempted subjugation
> by armed minorities or by outside pressures. The world is
> not static, and the status quo is not sacred. But we cannot
> allow changes in the status quo in violation of the Charter
> of the United Nations by such methods as coercion, or by
> such subterfuges as political infiltration.

Seeking $400 million to aid Greece and Turkey, he did not ask to use armed force, but to send civilian and military personnel to supervise reconstruction and training. Truman did not mention Russia. He did not have to. Truman committed the United States to world policing and unlimited economic aid to any nation opposing communism. It was the public declaration of the Cold War.

Although stunned by the sweep of the Truman Doctrine, Congress soon gave the Greek-Turkish aid bill bi-partisan support. On May 22, 1947, Truman signed the bill authorizing $100 million in military aid to Turkey and $300 million for Greece, equally divided between economic and military assistance.[61]

Thus began a chess game of escalating responses to match step by step Stalin's ever more ruthless aggression. That expansion plus the brutal Soviet repression of democratic ideals in Eastern and Central Europe (notably Hungary, Czechoslovakia and Germany) ended any lingering public optimism about the postwar world.

The Truman Doctrine evolved into blocking Communist expansion anywhere in the world. Truman had a visceral urge to confront the Communists. George Kennan gave him a philosophical and global vision - "containment."

In February 1947, Kennan was a little known State Department scholar of Russian history and psychology. Marshall ordered him to devise a plan for the United States to seize the initiative from the Russians. Kennan had one ready.

He had sent an 8,000 word cable to Washington while counselor in the Moscow embassy. This cable became Kennan's article, "The Sources of Soviet Conduct," published under the pseudonym "X" in the prestigious Foreign Affairs periodical. Kennan elegantly argued that Communism could be contained - within the nations already under its hex. He proposed that the West, especially the United States, devise political counters to Moscow's exploiting the weakness and instability of war ravaged countries. Greece was its first test.[62]

GREECE

Spread too thin, the U.S. Army could not send troops to aid the Greeks against the Communist guerrillas. Instead, it sent a substantial military advisory force, headed by Lieutenant General Jim Van Fleet. General Marshall told him: "Van Fleet, I want you to go to Greece and give them the will to win."[63]

When Van Fleet arrived in Athens on February 24, 1948, he reorganized and revitalized the Greek Army, modernized its tactics and logistics and thrust it on the offensive. He performed magnificently and became one of Truman's favorite generals. General Omar Bradley later opined that Van Fleet was worth two divisions. In 18 months, Greece was pacified, Turkey was secure. Containment had passed its first test.[64]

After the Truman Doctrine came two even bolder moves to check Soviet aggression--the Marshall Plan of economic aid to Europe and the North Atlantic Treaty Organization (NATO), a military alliance forging a united defense against the Russians. Truman's greatest triumph was changing the nation's foreign policy. After World War I, Wilson had failed in his attempt to involve America in Europe's affairs. Truman succeeded.[65]

THE MARSHALL PLAN

Britain's inability to continue propping up the Greeks and Turks dramatized Europe's plight. The continent's agricultural and coal production had nearly stopped, its people faced starvation, and tuberculosis reached epidemic proportions. Churchill called Europe "a rubble heap, a charnel house, a breeding ground of pestilence and hate." The Communist parties feasted on such chaos and discontent.

On May 27, 1947, William L. Clayton, Marshall's economic affairs advisor, reported that Europe's economy was hemorraging. He calculated that the United States would have to disburse at least $6 billion a year for 3 years to save Western Europe from economic and political collapse. Marshall agreed.

Lacking a flamboyant personality, Marshall did not wear pearl handled guns, flash a famous grin, nor sport a crushed hat with a corn cob pipe, but his government colleagues and subordinates, many of whom had egos that would allow them to look down on God, wrote of him with knee-bending awe. Presidents and prime ministers prized the apolitical general's calm, rocklike demeanor amid any crisis, unswerving loyalty, and what the public so recognized that pollster Elmo Roper could measure it - "his shear unwavering devotion to his duty as he saw it."[66]

For six years, he had steered America's war effort and become in Churchill's words - "The architect of victory." He had tried to retire to his Virginia farm, but duty kept calling him back.

Ironically, Americans trusted Marshall, the leader of the most lethal army in history, to safeguard and nurture the delicate peace.[67] He would win the Nobel Peace Price in 1953 - the only professional soldier ever to do so.

In Marshall's introduction at Harvard Commencement on June 5,[68] the honorary degree heralded him as "an American to whom Freedom owes an enduring debt of gratitude, a soldier and statesman whose ability and character brook only one comparison [George Washington] in the history of the nation."[69] Marshall spoke from eight pages, in a soft, almost inaudible voice, rarely looking up at his audience, for no more than fifteen minutes, and changed the planet.[70] The legacy of that speech is the world around us.

After portraying the torn "fabric of European economy," he offered virtually unlimited American aid. "Any government which maneuvers to block the recovery of other countries cannot expect help from us. Furthermore, governments, political parties, or groups which seek to perpetuate human misery in order to profit therefrom politically or otherwise, will encounter the opposition of the United States."

"Our policy is directed not against any country or doctrine but against hunger, poverty, desperation, and chaos. Its purpose should be the revival of a working economy of the world so as to permit the emergence of political and social conditions in which free institutions can exist."

TIME heralded The Plan "Hope for those that need it." Newsweek called it "the single greatest financial enterprise ever seriously considered by man."

As Acheson had suggested, the news of the speech had been dictated over a transatlantic phone to England, so no time would be lost. Early the next morning, a boy from the *Daily Telegraph* bicycled to the home of sleeping Foreign Minister Ernest Bevin with a copy of the news.[71] Bevin grasped this life preserver, as did France.

When the United States insisted on cooperation with capitalist Western Europe and an open accounting of how funds were used, the Soviets rejected the idea as American imperialism designed for the wholesale purchase of the whole European continent. Actually, if the Soviets had participated, it would have killed the Plan and the infant western union. The conservative

Republicans in Congress would never have approved it.

The lure of American dollars proved too tempting, however, and split the Soviet bloc. Yugoslavia's Tito grabbed the chance to better economic relations with the United States and caused an eventual break in the Greek civil war.

So "that free men can effectively join together to defend their free institutions against totalitarian pressures," Truman asked Congress to appropriate $17 billion from April 1, 1948, to June 30, 1952; with an immediate appropriation of $6.8 billion for the program's first 15 months. That was 18 percent of the 1949 budget and over 2.5 percent of the gross national product - a bold move before an election in which the Republicans planned to campaign for a balanced budget and reduced spending. Such numbers so shocked Congress that one congressman wanted the word "billion" stricken from the language, because it was flung about too carelessly.

Officially, named the European Recovery Program (ERP), Truman rejected Clifford's suggestion to name it the Truman plan. "We have a Republican majority in both Houses. Anything going up there bearing my name will quiver a couple of times, turn belly up, and die." He decided to name it the Marshall Plan because "The worst Republican on the Hill can vote for it if we name it after the General." [72] [73]

The wisdom of Truman's choice surfaced when Truman gave his frigidly received State of the Union address. While Truman waited in an antechamber, he heard loud sustained applause from the House Chamber, caused by the late arrival of Secretary Marshall. That very week, Marshall had appeared on the covers of both Newsweek and TIME, applauding him for his plan to save Europe. TIME had named him its Man of the Year, for the second time. When he arrived two minutes late, he tried to slip in unnoticed and take the nearest seat in the cabinet's front row, but the other secretaries would not let him. Blushing "a burnished copper" and protesting in embarrassment, he had to take his seat on the center aisle as the ranking cabinet member. By that time, the entire Congress had risen to its feet in a spontaneous ovation. The Washington Post reported the next day: "old timers on the Hill said that they had never seen anything like it."[74]

THE PLAN'S GUARDIAN ANGEL

Despite such bipartisan respect for Marshall, his plan would face an uphill battle. Besides the conservative critics, Wallace called it the "Martial" plan because it would antagonize the Soviets. Fortunately for Truman, Marshall and the nation, the bill had a guardian angel on Capitol Hill -- a rare but valued individual who, when his country and the world most needed it, changed his mind to pursue a diametrically opposed course - not for partisan advantage but because the welfare of the nation demanded it.[75]

Arthur Hendrick Vandenberg had grown up poor, a harness maker's son, but became a millionaire by his 30's. A Michigan Senator since 1928, he had been the leading spokesman for isolationism, howling against involvement in overseas problems.

But, in January 1945, Vandenberg converted, evolving from pretentious politician to statesman. After spending most of his first 16 years in the Senate preaching isolationalism, he spent his last few years denouncing it as foolhardy when a pummeled world needed America's leadership.

As chairman of the Senate Foreign Relations Committee and President Pro Tem of the Senate, Vandenberg dominated foreign affairs, as Taft ruled domestic policy. Although a potential Republican presidential candidate, he supported Truman's actions overseas and became the architect of the bipartisan postwar foreign policy.

Tall, rather heavy, barrel-chested, his black eyebrows contrasted with thinning gray hair atop a high forehead, Vandenberg's pompousness had helped to eliminate him as a serious presidential candidate in 1936 and 1940. James Reston recalled his first impression: "I thought he was a pompous windbag. He was a big, loud, vain, and self-important man, who could strut sitting down. He never seemed in doubt about anything." Although he was a former newspaperman, his pompousness kept him from writing well. He never used one word, if three or four would do.[76] He became a modern day Micawber spouting phrases like "sheer magicry," "Our mirific inheritances," and "Marcescent monarchy."[77]

What saved him from being obnoxious was his tireless friendliness and his charitable core. Richard Rovere, the New Yorker columnist, wrote: "He was one of the few men I have known whom one could describe as inoffensively pompous."

On December 19, 1947, Vandenberg presented the Marshall Plan Bill to the Senate, calling it "a calculated risk" to "help stop World War III before it starts."[78]

The January 12th issue of Newsweek called it accurately: "For the next three months, Vandenberg will be the most important person in Congress, in Washington, and probably in the world." Using his chairmanship and legislative skills honed since the Hoover administration, he expertly nudged the legislation ahead. Knowing the isolationist arguments, he neutralized them before the floor debate. Vandenberg kept repeating: "The only way to get Congress to face up to the Russians was to scare hell out of the American people."[79]

To pass the Plan, the Cabinet put on a full court press. Defense Secretary James Forrestal told the House Foreign Affairs Committee that if the program was rebuffed, he would need a 25 to 50 percent increase in defense appropriations. Secretary of Agriculture Clinton B. Anderson added the carrot to the stick. He noted that American farmers were producing one-third more food and fiber products than before the war and would need European markets. "[T]he prospects of a collapsing European economy, providing little outlet for U.S. farm products, would not be pleasant to contemplate."

The Plan received substantial support on January 20th when John Foster Dulles, the Republican foreign policy expert, testified before the Senate Foreign Relations Committee, "In certain respects I think the State Department proposal can be improved . . . but this is not the time to be a perfectionist."[80]

Despite the persuasion, as soon as the 80th Congress began debating ERP in January, Taft and his followers carped that it represented more "global New Dealism." It poured good American cash into a "European TVA," could bankrupt the United States, and foolishly ignored Asia, also threatened by the Communists.[81] Democratic Senator Richard Russell of Georgia sniped that the United States would save money by adopting England, Scotland, and Wales as states. Truman had to stall the civil rights legislation to avoid derailing the Marshall Plan. But then came the fall of Czechoslovakia. Stalin became the most effective floor manager for the bill.

CZECHOSLOVAKIA

In 1929, when the Communists first entered the Czech Parliament, the Communist leader, Klement Gottwald, had looked at the Czech leaders and announced, "You gentlemen are asking me what we are here for. My answer is simple. We are here to break your necks. I promise you most solemnly we will do it."

In 1946, the Communist party of Czechoslovakia and Gottwald had won 38 percent of the vote, the most of any party. In February 1948, as Soviet troops camped on the Czech borders, Premier Gottwald demanded a new government under his control.

On February 24, 1948, Communist Interior Ministry police surrounded most government offices and the Prague Radio station and sealed the border. Army police sacked the headquarters of the non-communist National Socialist Party. Gottwald had seized the government. The last relatively independent regime in Eastern Europe disappeared as the Iron Curtain goosestepped west.

The coup shocked the West. With Czech President Eduard Benes on its cover with the caption: "The curtain falls again," Newsweek reported: "12 years of Hitler and 3 post-war years of Stalin's diplomacy had almost convinced the world that it could not be shocked any more. Last week, the Russians proved that it could."

Americans shuddered because they had heard it all before. The Chicago Tribune observed: "The American people can very well reflect that this is where they came in. It was ten years ago this fall that the independence of Czechoslovakia was sacrificed at Munich." Immediately after the coup, the Washington Post ran a front page map of Europe with the area under Soviet domination shaded. The caption stated: "Russia moves westward - where next?" Arrows pointed to Italy, France, Finland, and Austria.[82]

Former Ambassador to Russia Averel Harriman warned that the Soviet Union was "just as destructive in their effect on the world and our own way of life as Hitler was, and I think are a greater menace than Hitler was." Columnists Stewart and Joe Alsop wrote that the country had changed from a postwar to a prewar attitude. The coup prompted such a war scare in February that World War II veterans joked that they would have to dust off their uniforms to prepare for the coming war. A Chicago reporter wrote, "a cold fear is gripping the people."[83]

OTHER THREATS

Nine months before the Czech overthrow, a Communist coup in Hungary had toppled that government. The New York Times had declared on February 26, 1948: "There is no reason to expect that Czechoslovakia will be the last target of Russo-Communist expansions." The very next day, its opinion proved correct.

On February 27, the Finnish government reported that its 77 year old President Juhok Paasikivif, a big tired man with the patient face of a St. Bernard, received a personal letter from Stalin. He proposed a Soviet-Finnish mutual assistance pact similar to the Hungarian-Soviet and Rumanian-Soviet pacts and the "mutual defense treaty" just proposed by the Communists in Czechoslovakia. The tone of the letter indicated that Stalin would not take "no" for an answer; so the Finnish Council accepted the Soviet proposal. On the open market, American dollars shot from 700 to 1000 Finnish marks as refugees fled the country.

The Italian elections were coming on April 18, and U.S. newspapers predicted a 50-50 chance of a Communist victory.

A GALVANIZED CONGRESS ADOPTS THE MARSHALL PLAN

On March 1, the 64 year old Vandenberg rose to his full 6'1" at William E. Borah's old second row desk. The irony was palpable. Borah, the leading isolationist of his day, had been succeeded as the isolationist champion by the man now formalizing its demise. Realizing they were witnessing history, senators packed their chamber while dozens of House members lined the walls. People filled the corridors leading to the chamber.[84]

Normally not a very good speaker, Vandenberg alternated between a sweeping side arm gesture like a baseball pitcher and fingering the heavy gold watch chain worn laterally across a great waist coat. He uttered his lofty phrases with organ-like solemnity. Sometimes the subject and timing match the pomp. His heart-felt convictions gave him a fundamental eloquence.

For 80 minutes, playing this climactic role of his distinguished career with just the right blend of humility and ham, Vandenberg read the 9,000 words which he had pecked out at home on his battered portable typewriter for 10 nights running. He presented "in the name of peace, stability, and freedom" the ERP - the final product of 8 months "of more intensive study by more devoted minds than I have ever known to concentrate upon any other objective in all my 20 years in Congress..."

The legislation, Vandenberg said, "seeks peace and stability for free men in a free world. It seeks them by economic rather than by military means. . . . It recognizes the grim truth--whether we like it or not--that American self-interest, national economy, and national security are inseparably linked with these objectives... If it fails, we have done our final best. If it succeeds, our children and our children's children will call us blessed."

He ended to the applause of galleries and floor alike. Acheson wrote that Vandenberg performed "a service for which this country should forever be grateful."[85] Vandenberg was vain, arrogant and would die within three years, but if all he had done in his career was make that speech, he would deserve a place in the pantheon of great senators.

His compromises and the mounting Communist threat had undercut any serious blockage to the Marshall Plan. Even Senator Taft now supported it. When the House vote came, the Washington Post portrayed: "As the roll call went on in a seething and excited House, shouts of "Aye" came from one Republican after another who had seldom, if ever, voted for any international legislation."[86]

Two weeks later, on March 14th, working against the deadline of the Italian elections, the Senate met in night sessions and passed, by a bipartisan 69 to 17, the European Recovery Program Bill.

ALLIANCES

Meanwhile, Stalin's actions scared the threatened countries into banding together. In mid-January 1948, British Foreign Minister Bevin warned Marshall that the Soviet bloc made it difficult to confront Russian actions individually. Bevin wanted to counter with a Western democratic coalition.

When Britain, France and the Benelux countries (Belgium, The Netherlands and Luxembourg) began meetings in Brussels, Secretary Marshall sent word that the US was prepared to join in establishing an Atlantic security system. With this encouragement, after an historic nine days, on March 17, the five nations announced "a treaty of economic, social, and cultural collaboration." The Treaty of Brussels, a 50 year pact, committed them to aid each other against any armed aggression. The pact would evolve into NATO in April 1949.

On the same day the Treaty was announced, Truman faced Congress. He had planned a St. Patrick's Day speech in New York, but the "grave events in Europe were moving so swiftly" that a delay was intolerable. Jauntily wearing a green carnation on his gray flannel suit and a green tie with his starched white shirt, Truman mounted the dais in the House chamber at 12:33 p.m.

The speech spotlighted the "increasing threat" to the very "survival of freedom." With his chin jutting, he did not mince words nor hesitate to name the villain. "The Soviet Union and its agents have destroyed the independence and democratic character of a whole series of nations in Eastern and Central Europe." He condemned "this ruthless course of action" and deplored "the tragic death of the Republic of Czechoslovakia." He blamed the world's turmoil chiefly on Russia's refusal to cooperate in establishing a just and honorable peace and actively seeking to prevent it.

To give Europe and the new treaty "some measure of protection against internal and external aggression," he warned that the Marshall Plan alone was "not enough." Because the armed forces lacked the strength to backup such commitments, he urged the adoption of Universal Military Training, and the revival of the draft that had lapsed a year earlier. Army Chief of Staff Bradley assumed that this courageous call for such measures in peacetime would cost him the election. Newsweek and the New York Times agreed.

Within 12 days, the House passed the Marshall Plan by 329 to 74. The Czechoslovakian coup and Vandenberg's and Truman's eloquence had not only galvanized passage of the Marshall Plan but shifted the direction of American foreign and defense policy. Congress approved the Selective Service Bill but rejected Universal Military Training. Instead, it funded a 70 group Air Force that was 25 percent larger than Forrestal or Truman had wanted. The Cold War had become the arms race.

Praising the Act as "perhaps the greatest venture in constructive statesmanship that any nation has undertaken," Truman signed the ERP on April 3, 1948. So, within three weeks, the Western alliance had been formed and financed. Congress voted exactly what Truman asked for - and more, the biggest peacetime aid program ever conceived.[87]

Churchill hailed ERP as "the most unsordid act in history." The London *Economist* called it "the most straight-forward, generous thing that any country has ever done for others."

Britain, France, Italy, Greece, Turkey, Belgium, Holland, Denmark, Norway, Austria, Ireland, Iceland, Portugal, Sweden, Switzerland, Luxembourg, and, later, West Germany applied to Washington for aid. By April 1948, an economic curtain divided Europe into Marshall Plan countries and Soviet bloc countries. The Cold War mirrored the trench warfare of World War I. Both sides became frozen in mutual unfriendliness with no changes for forty years.[88]

Much still had to be done but, by passing the Greek-Turkish Aid Bill and the ERP, America stopped Soviet expansion in Europe. As Walter Lafeber wrote: "During the Spring of 1948, a united administration, enjoying strong support on foreign policy from a Republican Congress, set off with exemplary single-mindedness to destroy the Communist threat which loomed over Western Europe. Within two years this threat had been scotched..."[89] Truman described the Truman Doctrine and the Marshall Plan as "two halves of the same walnut." They formed the philosophical twin pillars of American foreign policy for decades.

Eleven days after Truman signed ERP, the freighter John H. Quick left Galveston with nine thousand long tons of wheat.[90] When the ship arrived in Bordeaux, French children swarmed aboard and looked in the hold to glimpse the first food sent under the Marshall Plan.

The hope inspired by the Plan stiffened the Italian backbone. An anti-Communist poster in Milan read: "God can see you vote--Stalin can't." In April, anti-Communist forces decisively won the elections.

The Italian victory was merely the first. The program achieved both its immediate and long-term aims. When the aid ended in 1952, Communist control of Western Europe had been averted, the region's industrial production stood 35 percent above prewar levels. West Germany was independent, re-arming, and economically booming. Dirk Stikker, the Netherlands foreign minister, later stated: "Churchill's words won the war. Marshall's words won the peace."[91]

The Marshall Plan was to give Europe $12.5 billion, less than Marshall had thought necessary and far less than what the U.S. would spend on defense in one year. Yet it did far more for security.[92]

Thirty months later, when England was back on its feet, the *Manchester Guardian* said, "Ordinary thanks are inadequate. Here is one of the most brilliant successes in the history of international relations," and Hugh Gaitskell, then Chancellor of the Exchequer, added: "We are not a emotional people . . . and not very articulate, but these characteristics should not . . . hide the real and profound sense of gratitude towards the American people."

WAR TALK

Truman's March 17th speech to Congress launched the fear of war that had been ratcheting up with each land grab by the Soviets.

Newsweek reported that "talk of the next war was sweeping New England... The phrases 'wait until the Russians come' and 'when we fight Stalin' are clichés already." It continued: "It does seem to be a reluctant conviction that these three relentless forces, Communism abroad, Communism at home, and the atom bomb, are prowling the earth and that somehow they are bound to mean trouble for us."

The situation in Korea was especially ominous. On May 10th, under the aegis of the United Nations Temporary Commission, elections were held in United States occupied South Korea; but not in Soviet occupied North Korea. Communists tried to disrupt the voting and killed 35 people. 92% of Korea's 8 million registered voters cast ballots and elected Syngman Rhee president. On September 9th, communist North Korea announced the formation of the Democratic Peoples Republic of Korea in Pyongyang with Kim Il Sung as president. The summer of 1948 saw the birth of separate republics in the two Koreas - a war in the making.

AMERICA'S MILITARY

Despite all the saber rattling and war scares, the U.S. military was hollow. America's armed forces had won World War II decisively, but the flaws surfaced. Coordination between the services had often been spotty, especially in the Pacific where MacArthur in the south Pacific and Admiral Nimitz in the central Pacific essentially fought two separate wars. Interservice rivalries had impaired national defense.

To end such sibling jealousies and debilitating parallel efforts, Congress had established the Defense Department in July 1947. The new department unified the Army, Navy and Air Force, now an independent agency, to provide America with a coordinated multi-level military response. Only three and a half months old when 1948 began, the Defense Department was headed by a Secretary slowly spirally downward into paranoia.[93]

A slight, wiry man, with penetrating blue eyes and a brisk manner, James Forrestal had what Eisenhower described as a fighter's face – the result of a broken nose from a college boxing match. As Secretary of the Navy, Forrestal had vehemently opposed unifying the three services and stripped the office of Secretary of Defense of personnel to weaken it. Truman then chose him as the first Secretary of Defense to make it work.

Forrestal toiled in that task as hard as he had committed himself to the war effort. The effort killed him. Emotionally broken, he resigned and checked into the Bethesda Naval Hospital in the early spring of 1949. Two months later, on the night of May 22, he killed himself by jumping from the 12th floor of the hospital.

The U.S. and its new defense structure were groping, not only to understand America's new position in the world, but to deal with the terrible new weapons and ways to deliver them. Modern airplanes and the atomic bomb took some getting used to.

The Defense Department had been designed to unify the services; but a statute cannot erase almost two centuries of rivalries. Strategic air power divided the services. The Air Force claimed it as its domain and wanted 70 air groups. The Navy saw the carrier as its assertion of air power. To ensure its future, the Navy proposed supercarriers large enough to carry bombers able to drop A bombs. The administration concluded that with soaring prices, it could sate the demands of the services or it could have a sound economy. It could not do both. Truman decided that the nation needed a sound economy more than a strong military.

The Army reluctantly agreed but a war erupted between the Air Force and the Navy over who should get the largest slice of the appropriations.

THE ATOMIC BOMB

Surprisingly, the atomic bomb itself, which in many ways had ignited the warfare between the Air Force and the Navy, eased the strain between the two services.

In 1948, the military and the Atomic Energy Commission (AEC) tested three new bombs on Eniwetok Atoll in the Pacific. Rumors persisted that the new bombs had been far more devastating than anticipated.

At the end of July, the AEC vaguely reported that the test confirmed that the U.S. position in the field of atomic weapons "has been substantially improved." A few weeks later, Senator Edwin C. Johnson of Colorado blurted out that the new bombs had six times the power of the bomb that leveled Nagasaki. That meant a bomb with an explosive power of 120,000 tons of TNT. [94]

Air Force General Carl Spaatz then changed his mind and supported the Navy's supercarriers. The AEC could now produce bigger bombs but with less fissionable material per bomb. With the U.S. producing more fissionable material, the nation could have 400 bombs by the end of 1950. That was more than enough for the Air Force to share its monopoly. Besides, it made strategic sense to have extra launching pads for the Soviets to worry about, and mobile ones at that.

Meanwhile, the next generation of weaponry was being born. In January, the Air Force announced that Captain Chuck Yeager had broken the sound barrier in a rocket powered Bell X-1 at 35,000 feet in October 1947. This was the longest step in aviation since Kitty Hawk. Jet travel would soon dominate the skies and the aircraft industry would become the aerospace industry as missiles and space exploration began.

PERSONNEL

Even the most terrible weapons and delivery systems need personnel to operate them. After the war, the U.S. had returned to its tradition of a small standing army. The political and popular crush to "bring the boys home" produced not a demobilization but a riot. The military had shriveled from about 12 million in June 1945 to 1.5 million in June 1947, hardly equal to America's new role as world policeman. To meet Cold War demands, Truman had asked for the return of the draft which Congress did on June 24, 1948.

The Selective Service Act mandated the registration of all men between 18 and 25 and the draft of enough men to field an Army of 837,000, a Navy and Marine Corps of 666,882 and an Air Force of 502,000.

Major General Lewis B. Hershey once again became the Director of Selective Service. The man who had drafted 10,110,104 men for the Second World War geared up his old machinery. The U.S. began registering its young men for a new draft, 3 years and 16 days after World War II ended.

CHAPTER FOUR

THE BERLIN BLOCKADE

THE DYSFUNCTIONAL OCCUPIED GERMANY

As high as prices rose in the United States and as bad as the economy sank in the rest of Europe, Germany was far worse.

Germany and Japan suffered the centuries old ignominy of defeat. They were occupied by their conquerors and ruled by the victorious generals, installed like Roman proconsuls. Fortunately, for the vanquished and the victors, the two military governors, Douglas MacArthur in Japan and Lucius Clay in Germany, served outstandingly. MacArthur's imperial manner aside, he and Clay treated their defeated enemies with compassionate foresight and went a long way to seal the close bonds between the U.S. and its former foes that mark the postwar era.

Japan, at least, was whole and occupied by only one foreign force. Germany had been drawn and quartered, with each portion governed and occupied by one of the four allies: the U.S., England, France, and Russia. Berlin's situation was bizarre. The traditional capitol sat 100 miles inside the Soviet quadrant. Yet because of its historic and political significance, it too was divided into four sectors ruled by the allies in a Kommandatura. The Western powers had not even negotiated a pact guaranteeing surface traffic between Berlin and the western zones. That absurdly optimistic system, negotiated in the euphoria of wartime comradeship, depended on the continued good will of Joseph Stalin. Without it, the Allied troops and the people in Berlin were prisoners of war.

Germany was starving. In 1936, Germans had produced 85% of their food. In 1948, the figure sat at 25%. The official ration of 1550 calories a day, little more than one-third the normal American diet, dropped to 1400. Some regions ate far less. Each town had at least one brotbaum, "bread tree," where people would pin little notes "Want bread, will trade for German cigarettes," "Will sell linen tablecloth and curtains for money or food". A stifling inflation had crippled the food supply. Prices rose so fast that farmers had no incentive to produce. Any money earned rapidly lost its value.

Because Germany lies at the heart of Europe and historically spun the continent's industrial hub, its economic spiral was sucking all of Europe down with it. The Marshall Plan would pour money down a rathole unless Germany's economy became self sufficient – and fast! Inflation was the specific curse: its cause was the worthless currency. Its solution depended on the four military governors.

The military governors were Marshal Vassily Danilovich Sokolovsky for Russia, Lieutenant General Sir Brian Robertson for the United Kingdom, Lt. General Joseph Pierre Koenig for France, and, representing the United States, General Lucius DuBignon Clay. [95]

The son of a United States Senator from Georgia and great-grandnephew of Henry Clay, Clay had not wanted to be a soldier but strained family finances made West Point the only affordable path to college. In the interwar years, the young officer progressed through a succession of increasingly important engineering posts.[96]

Anointed as one of the Army's premier administrators, Clay spent most of WWII in Washington as deputy director of the Office of War Mobilization and Reconversion. Finally, transferred to Europe to command the Normandy base and the port of Cherbourg, he unplugged a serious bottleneck there in November 1944. After the Allied victory in 1945, a surprised Clay became military governor of the U.S. zone of occupied Germany. Secretary of State James F. Byrnes, for whom Clay had worked in the Office of War Mobilization, had endorsed him as "the most civilian-minded man in the Army...He could run anything from General Motors to General Eisenhower's army."[97]

A slightly built, dark-eyed man, Clay had performed magnificently, without MacArthur's egocentricity. In his three years in Germany, he had acquired a good deal of gray hair at his temples, along with an order of Kutuzov (1st class) from the Soviets, but without missing a single day's work. He did not eat lunch, considering it a waste of time. He smoked two packs of cigarettes a day while slurping twenty cups of coffee. To relieve stress, Clay walked in his flower garden with his Scottie, George, and played cards. With Ambassador Robert Murphy, Clay's State Department political advisor, he formed an effective and friendly partnership. They conducted much of their business each afternoon at their brief gin rummy session.

The best measure of Clay's ability can be simply stated. In a hierarchy of warriors, he had become a four star general without ever leading men in combat. Men who had brilliantly led divisions, corps, and even armies had not reached that rarefied plateau. Clay had become the Army's greatest administrator by merging the attributes of engineering and management. Unlike many engineers, he did not mire himself in minutia and ignore the big picture. Unlike many managers, he did not flinch from the details that make the process work.

Probably most important for his present position, he was not anti-Soviet. In 1946, Wallace had noted that of all the military people polled by the Pentagon, only Clay thought the U.S. could learn to get along with the Russians. All the others had preached a hard-line approach and expected war.[98]

FIRST STEPS TOWARDS UNIFICATION

The Allies had already begun to strengthen Germany, economically and politically. Byrnes and Bevin had agreed to join the American and British zones, forming Bizonia, effective January 1, 1947. The U.S. and England soon announced a merger of the eight states in Bizonia to create a West German economic government. Branding this an anti-Communist measure, the Soviets demanded that it be disbanded. To tighten the pressure, the Soviets began boarding all trains entering the Soviet zone to check the identity of passengers and to examine cargo for contraband. They also halted road traffic on the autobahn, claiming road repairs. The Americans put armed guards on one train to test whether the Russians would use force. The Russians simply switched it electrically onto a siding and stranded it there for several hours until it slinked back the way it had come.

The Soviets had two purposes: to show that they could prevent others from reaching Berlin; and to test how effectively the Allies could respond.[99]

Truman realized that, as the West continued to strengthen Germany, Stalin would likely sqeeze Berlin. Believing that the Continent needed a healthy Western Germany to fully contribute to European recovery, the Western powers met in London to discuss Germany. The Allies invited Belgium, Holland and Luxembourg, the Benelux countries. As Germany's neighbors and traditional trading partners, the inflation and hunger in Germany directly afflicted them.

The Soviet aggression throughout Europe caused the London conferees to agree to items unimaginable. For over 100 years, Germany had been the bogey man to these men, their fathers and all their countrymen. Now they were discussing ways to strengthen the dessicated Germany because they realized that the real danger was the Soviet Union.[100]

To bring West Germany within the "economic reconstruction of Western Europe,"[101] on March 6, 1948, the U.S., England, France, Belgium, Holland and Luxembourg announced the Allies would fuse a "federal form of government" by merging the three western zones.

THE RUSSIANS RESPOND

The Russians erupted. As the March 20 Allied Control Council meeting began, under the Image of Justice surrounded by cherubs, Sokolovsky launched into a tirade and read a long condemnation. As Robertson began to reply, the beaknosed barrel-chested Sokolovsky swept his papers together and announced: "I see no sense in continuing this meeting. I declare it adjourned." Sokolovsky pulled out a typewritten statement that read: "The Allied Control Council no longer exists as an organ of government." The whole Russian delegation then stormed out.[102]

The Council never met again. General Clay instinctively knew a sea change had occurred and that something was going to happen. On March 23, the British, French, and American commandants in Berlin began to plan how to counter Soviet aggression. That same day, March 23, the White House canceled the planned turnover to the State Department of the administration of the U.S. zone, scheduled for July. The Russian walk-out extended Clay's proconsulship. Keeping Army control in Berlin strongly reassured the German people and heightened war fears in the U.S.

THE APRIL BLOCKADE

The day after that announcement, on March 24, the Russian newspapers in Germany announced a sudden increase in murders, robberies, banditry and black marketeering on the borders of the East Zone. As Murphy fatefully reminded Washington, "the Soviet government (like the Nazi government) charges the other person with those things it itself intends to do." The newspapers warned that an influx of "starving thousands" from the West was depleting food supplies. To safeguard the food supply and the peace of the community, they called for stricter guarding of the borders.[103]

Cooperation evaporated. On March 26, Lt. General G. Lukyanchenko, the Soviet Chief of Staff, accused the Western powers of aiding illegal traffic into Berlin. Four days later, he warned that the Russians had to protect Berlin against "subversive and terrorist elements." Very late on the evening of March 30, the Soviets gave the Western military governors 24 hours notice of "certain supplementary regulations" for traffic between Berlin and the West.

Starting April 1, all persons traveling to Berlin on the autobahn or railway would have to show their identity documents at Soviet control points and have their luggage searched. No rail freight could leave the capital without Soviet permission. Later, the Russians extended these restrictions to barges, secondary rail routes, and other waterway traffic. The "baby blockade" had begun.

On the night of 31 March, military trains were stopped and forced back, including two American trains. Clay had put armed guards on the trains to keep the Soviets off. He cabled Washington asking permission for the guards to fire if Soviet troops tried to enter the trains but was refused. Instead, Clay ordered the 61st Troop Carrier Group at Rhein-Main Air Base near Frankfurt to fly in supplies, starting April 2, to supply the 6500 troops in the Berlin area plus families and support personnel.[104]

During the 3 days of the April blockade, 125 flights, mainly C-47s, landed at Templehof, the Berlin airport. The C-47s, which had dropped paratroopers into Normandy, could carry three tons of cargo. So 12 C-47s daily could deliver the 35 tons of food the 23,000 allied population in Berlin needed.

PREPARATIONS FOR WAR

Such chest thumping hostility forced the Allies to plan for a shooting war – a dismal prognosis. The surrounding Soviets outnumbered the 6500 troops in Berlin 3 to 1. Unable to mount a quick land offensive to save the city, the Allies' only hope, albeit slim, was the air.

In Europe, the United States could marshall only approximately 275 aircraft, plus approximately three squadrons of the Royal Air Force. Arrayed against this, the Soviets boasted a tactical force of some 4,000 aircraft in Eastern Europe.

Major General Curtis LeMay, who had commanded the B-29s that bombed Japan, led the Air Force in Europe. Clay tasked him to plan for war. General LeMay organized a web of air bases well to the west of the Rhine in France and Belgium. Quietly, he stockpiled these new bases with bombs, fuel, spare parts and 2,000 USAF ground crew personnel in civilian clothing. By the end of April 1948, LeMay had a network of air fields ready to bomb all the Soviet air bases in Germany.[105]

CURRENCY

Amidst all this posturing, the continued circulation of the Reichsmark bound together the four occupation zones. That was about to be snapped.[106]

To thwart German recovery and to buy western goods at bargain prices, the Russians had been flooding the western zone with paper money printed with plates in use since the occupation began. That currency had caused the inflation that blocked any real recovery. The Allies decided to change the currency to halt the inflation and widespread black marketing caused by the weak Reichsmark. The planning began immediately and in the utmost secrecy, even from the Germans.

On Friday, June 18, the Allies announced that a new currency, the Deutschemark, would replace the Reichsmark in the Western Zone on Sunday, June 20. The rate of exchange was to be 1 new mark for 10 old ones, a 90% devaluation of a fantastic volume of currency in circulation. The officials hoped that the change would return the American cigarette, for three years Germany's generally accepted exchange medium, into something smoked.[107]

The Soviets turned apoplectic. On June 19, Sokolovsky declared, "Bank notes issued in the Western Occupation Zones of Germany are not being admitted for circulation in the Soviet Occupation Zone of Germany and in Berlin, which is part of the Soviet Occupation Zone." With this first "official" announcement that all of Berlin was part of the Russian zone, Sokolovsky professed that the currency reform "completes the division of Germany."[108] The split between East and West was final.

The Soviets then announced their own currency reform, effective June 24, not only for the Soviet part of Berlin but their entire zone. The new Soviet marks were merely the same money with a new thumbnail size stamp. The Germans called it Tabetenmark--wallpaper money. The Western powers refused to go along and so, on the same day, they introduced the Deutschemark into Berlin, effectively splitting the city. The Berlin City Assembly courageously voted to apply the Soviet currency only to the Russian sector. The Berliners had sided with the West.

THE BLOCKADE BEGINS

TIME's bureau chief, Emmett Hughes, announced with prescience "the grimmest Russian pressure is not directly on the Allies, but on Berlin's people." The Soviets soon tightened the noose.

On June 23, the teletypes of the Soviet sponsored news agency in the western newspaper offices burped: "Berlin, June 23...Transport Division of the Soviet Military Administration is compelled to halt all passenger and freight traffic to and from Berlin tomorrow at 0600 hours because of technical difficulties... It is impossible to reroute traffic in the interests of maintaining rail service, since such measures would unfavorably affect the entire railroad traffic in the Soviet Occupational Zone."

Later another message announced: "Water traffic will be suspended. Coal shipments from the Soviet Zone are halted. The Soviet authorities have also ordered the central switching stations to stop the supply of electric power from the Soviet Zone and the Soviet Sector to the Western Sector. Shortage of coal to operate the plants is the reason." They also closed the autobahn because of "technical difficulties" and stopped traffic over various highway bridges for "repairs."

At 6:00 the next morning, as promised, they severed all road and barge traffic to and from the city and halted all supplies including coal, food and fresh milk, from the Soviet sector. Railroad passenger and freight service, electricity, mail and parcel post were completely cut off.

The Berlin blockade had begun - a total land blockade in a ruthless attempt to use mass starvation for political coercion.

Adam Ulam called the Berlin Blockade a masterful stroke of strategic-political pressure in location and timing. America was focusing on its election campaign; Britain was suffering a serious economic crisis. Moreover, if the United States took drastic countersteps, the Soviets could retreat simply by alleging "the repairs were completed." It seemed like a no-lose proposition for the Soviets.[109]

The Blockade marked the first feint of Brinkmanship. Clay sensed the new attitude - "from Sokolovsky on down,... faintly contemptuous, slightly arrogant , and certainly assured." Rather than cave in, Clay drew a line in the sand. "When Berlin falls, western Germany will be next...If we withdraw, our position in Europe is threatened. If America does not understand this now, does not know that the issue is cast, then it never will and Communism will run rampant... I believe that the future of democracy requires us to stay."[110]

Brave talk, but since 1945, one-half to two-thirds of Berlin's food had come from western Germany. Much of the rest and large portions of its fuel and electricity had come from the east. Clay calculated that there was food for 36 days and coal for 45. So, in about one month, people in the western sectors would begin to starve. In response to a reporter's question, Clay snapped his fingers, "I wouldn't give you that for our chances."[111]

THE AIRLIFT STARTS

Clay acted swiftly. On June 23, he had amassed a convoy of a 6000 man regimental combat team with armor and artillery and an engineer battalion with bridging equipment to ram its way into Berlin. He hoped that the French and British would each attach a battalion. Clay did not see any other solution. Truman was ready to authorize the convoy, but the rest of the military and General Marshall dissuaded him.[112]

Rather than risk starting a world war, Washington would allow the troops to go, but without ammunition, and they would have to retreat at any sign of Soviet resistance. Ambassador Murphy, the career diplomat, later reflected that he should have resigned over that refusal because it portrayed the Allied response as weak.

Washington feared that if a war developed it would quickly mushroom, literally and figuratively. The Allies could muster three divisions while the Soviets had 25. Furthermore, the Allies would need supplies from the U.S., since the ravaged French and British had little to give. Believing that the atomic bomb would be quickly used, the Pentagon sought control of the bomb. Truman refused, saying he did not intend "to have some dashing lieutenant colonel deciding when would be the proper time to drop one." Truman confirmed to Marshall and Forrestal: "I pray that these bombs will never be used but "if it becomes necessary, no one need have a misgiving but what I would do so." The next evening, a meeting of leading newspaper publishers agreed that, if war occurred over Berlin, Americans would expect the bomb to be dropped.[113]

On the morning of June 24, General Clay telephoned LeMay and asked if LeMay's forces could airlift 500 to 700 tons a day from Rhein-Main or Wiesbaden to Templehof for maybe four weeks. Clay cited only a month because he could not believe that the Soviets would really starve the entire city. He planned to supply the U.S. garrison in Berlin, not the entire population.

At dinner in late June, Clay had a fortunate guest. Lieutenant General Albert Wedemeyer had commanded U.S. forces in China during the war when his men and the Chinese had been supplied principally by plane. In July 1945, alone, the U.S. flew 71,000 tons of cargo over the Hump of the Himalayas from India into China. He suggested supplying the city by air. Independently, the British had arrived at the same idea.

The Hump had been the only large scale prolonged air supply operation; but two and a half million people lived in West Berlin, more than Los Angeles, Philadelphia, Detroit, or Cleveland. No one had ever tried to supply a community anywhere close to that size, by air.[114]

Just keeping Berliners alive would require 4,000 tons a day of food and supplies - the takeoff or landing of one C-47 every three minutes and 36 seconds around the clock; an impossible task without even considering loading, unloading, maintenance and refueling. To function normally, the city needed 8,000 tons a day, a takeoff or landing every minute and 48 seconds.[115]

Clay then called LeMay and asked: "Curt, can you transport coal by air?" There was silence on LeMay's end of the line until he uttered, "Excuse me, General, would you mind repeating that question?"[116]

The Americans called their version of the Airlift – "Operation Vittles," while the British called theirs "Operation Planefare." At first, the workhorse was the C-47, a twin engine passenger plane known commercially as the DC-3 but affectionately called "the gooney bird". The British also used converted DC-3's that they called Dakotas. Unfortunately, not a freighter, it could only haul about three tons.

LeMay scraped together approximately 100 to 110 C-47s. With that armada, the Airlift began on June 26 and made 32 flights landing 80 tons in Berlin, mostly fresh milk for children, flour and medicine. The skies over Berlin began to roar like an idling Mack truck. At both Berlin fields, soldiers hurriedly transferred sacks and boxes to waiting trucks.

While the Allies were pressing trucks, C-47s and every other type of aircraft into service, the Soviets barred Western newspapers from their sector so 1 million Berliners could only get Communist papers. A British correspondent asked a Soviet sector Berliner how much he believed in the Communist press. The reply: "The date."

TIME pointed out, "Never before had such a major city, in time of 'peace' been summoned to surrender or face the threat of starvation, civil war within, or a bigger war without." If the Airlift failed, General LeMay's battle plan might be triggered. Twenty more B-29 bombers landed in Germany raising the total to 30. A woman correspondent in the American Press Club in Berlin cried, "My God, why does everyone pretend to be so calm?"[117]

LeMay and Clay had cabled Washington for more and bigger planes. Within two hours came an amazingly quick and global response. On June 27th, the Air Force ordered 39 C-54 Skymasters to Germany. The military equivalent of the DC-4, the C-54 had four engines and could carry up to ten tons. Still, it was not a freighter. So ground crews ripped out seats and any other extraneous items, such as long range navigational equipment, not needed for the short and monotonous trips to and from Berlin. Bombardiers practiced dumping coal from their bomb bays while duffel bags, each containing 100 lbs. of coal, dropped from the gaping noses and fuselages of the C-54s into 10 ton trucks backed up to the aircraft.

The afternoon of June 29, the first four Skymasters landed at Templehof. On June 30, squadrons of C-54s began arriving from Panama, Hawaii, and Alaska. One correspondent, who later flew to Berlin in a C-54, noticed that the tail and wing tips were painted bright red. The pilot explained, "our squadron came here from Alaska. That was so that they could find us if we cracked up in the snow." The squadron had left Anchorage 12 hours after getting its orders.

Planes flew three air corridors: each 20 statute miles wide (32 kilometers), extending from ground level up to 10,000 feet. Two ran from the British zone to Hamburg and Hanover, and one from the American zone to Frankfurt. The terminus for British aircraft in Berlin was Gatow, an old Luftwaffe training center. The American airfield in downtown Berlin, Templehof, had been Berlin's principal civil airport, once the world's largest. The main American airbase in Germany was Rhein-Mein, a former Luftwaffe fighter base and, before that, a dirigible base from which the Hindenberg had begun its fatal journey. Rhein-Mein quickly became known as Rhein-Mud.

Brigadier General Joseph Smith, the initial Task Force Commander, promised 450 flights a day with a fleet of 52 C-54s and 100 C-47s. At a meeting, Major Edward Willerford, an operation planner, stood to answer General Smith's question on potential performance. "I estimate by July 20th, we will be flying in 1500 tons every 24 hours." Everyone scoffed at his gross optimism.[118]

TIME reported, "West Berlin depends on the most part on 2,000 tons of food a day brought in by rail from Bizonia, 100 miles away--more than could be supplied by the cargo planes which the U.S. and Britain were able to press into immediate service last week." But TIME in a footnote stated, "With added planes, however, and ideal weather conditions, it would not be impossible to lay down 2,000 tons of food a day onto Templehof and Gatow airfields." Initially, the Berliners could not believe that the Allies would fly supplies in and secondly, that they could do it. A woman described how her father began believing but still remained a pessimist.

> Then came the day [when the Airlift starts]. Father naturally didn't believe, therefore he rode to Templehof on

his bicycle. He was away a long time. When he came home he said: 'They're actually doing it! They're flying food to Berlin. But they won't be able to bring in enough. Think of this huge city with its millions of people![119]

The pessimism was understandable. In the beginning "Operation Vittles" toddled. During June and July 1948, the airlift averaged just 1,147 tons a day, and it looked as though the siege would succeed. But greater resources were being assembled and problems were being identified and corrected.

THE CHAIN OF COMMAND

The beginning of this struggle saw firmness by the Berliners and by Clay.

Clay's sad brown eyes and courtly manners belied a steel backbone. "I have firmly made up my mind that I will not be bluffed . . . Anxiety or nervousness among Americans here is unbecoming." TIME recognized that Clay very often seemed to have to make his own U.S. policy. A Frankfurt barber noted: "I feel sorry for General Clay. Every Russian from Marshal Sokolovsky down to the last sentinel seems to know what his government's policy is and what he's supposed to do about it. With the American government, I sometimes wonder whether it knows itself what it's doing." Actually, focused on the Republican convention in Philadelphia, official Washington deferred many matters to Clay's judgment. Another reporter wrote, "How had the U.S. got itself into a fix where one general and 6,000 GIs were supposed to hold an outpost deep inside a red sea of Russian power."

On the afternoon of June 28, the nation's top military and diplomatic leaders met with Truman but split on whether to try to hold Berlin. No clear consensus had evolved, but when Undersecretary of State Robert Lovett mentioned the possibility of withdrawal, Truman interrupted him. "I think we have to stay in Berlin. There is no need for further discussion on that issue".

When a worried Secretary of the Army Kenneth Royall wondered if the President had thought the consequences through, Truman responded: "We will have to deal with the situation as it develops. We are in Berlin by the terms of an agreement, and the Russians have no right to get us out by either direct or indirect pressure."

These are times in the life of a man and a nation when decisions are made quickly and quietly. When issues of transcending importance are stripped of their complexities and decided not on future geo-political advantage or the applause of an audience, but on what's right. This was one.

The reply was vintage Truman. He ignored the nuances of world strategy and the consequences of complicated logistics and diplomacy. He saw it and decided it on the simple basis of what was right and wrong. Truman was decisive, sometimes impulsive, often without the full facts and often without thinking all the consequences through. His private opinions could be surprisingly naïve and ill informed, but he made decisions. He did not wait for public opinion and did not hesitate to reject the advice of the State or Defense Departments. Fortunately, he had good instincts and a fundamental belief that the morality of right and wrong should govern policy issues - not political advantages that are often only temporary. For that reason, as Sam Rayburn, a staunch supporter noted, Truman was "right on all the big things, wrong on most of the little ones."[120] Historian Samuel Elliot Morrison added: "with more fateful decisions than almost any President in our time, he made the fewest mistakes."[121]

On the evening after the White House meeting, Lovett cabled the American ambassador in London, "We stay in Berlin."

CHAPTER FIVE

PALESTINE - AN INTERNATIONAL AND DOMESTIC QUAGMIRE

A LONG FESTERING IMBROGLIO

In a year of crises, no international dilemma was more braided into domestic politics than Palestine.

Since 1897, the Zionist movement had clamored to create a Jewish homeland in Palestine, which three of the world's great religions - Christianity, Judaism and Islam - held sacred.

In 1922, the League of Nations mandate entrusted Great Britain with administering Palestine and with aiding the Jewish people in "reconstituting their national home in that country." The British High Commissioner for Palestine governed the country, controlling defense and police, immigration, postal service, transportation, and port facilities.

In 1947, exhausted by six years of war and eager to withdraw from colonial commitments, Great Britain decided to leave. It tossed Palestine to the U.N. to resolve. At the U.N.'s first special session on November 29, 1947, the General Assembly passed a resolution calling for partition of Palestine into Jewish and Arab states, with Jerusalem as an international zone under U.N. jurisdiction. The Jewish and Arab states would form an economic union with an international police force to ensure peace.

Palestine thus became a bone of contention with Truman caught in the middle. Palestine more irritated Anglo-American relations and more strained Truman's relationship with his beloved General Marshall than every other issue combined.

The United Jewish Appeal began its 1948 Destiny Campaign to raise $250 million to fulfill the dream of a homeland. Jews throughout the world, staggered by the enormity of the Holocaust, contributed mightily of their time, talent, and treasure. Through the second half of 1947, Truman received about 135,000 letters, telegrams, and petitions, almost all of them backing the Jewish cause.[122] In one three month period in 1948, he received another 300,000 postcards, nearly all of them from Jewish interest groups and their supporters. Thirty three state legislatures had passed resolutions favoring a Jewish state, while 40 governors, 54 senators and 250 congressmen signed petitions to the President.[123]

The political pressure was so enormous that Truman later recalled: "Well, there'd never been anything like it before, and there wasn't after. Not even when I fired MacArthur, there wasn't."[124] It put Truman, the realistic politician facing an uphill battle for election, in a pickle.

 Rowe's memo had warned that unless the Palestine issue was "boldly and favorably handled," Jewish voters would defect to the "alert" Dewey or to Henry Wallace.[125] With them would go Ohio, California, Illinois and New York, because of the 2.5 million Jews concentrated in New York City. Since 1876, only Woodrow Wilson in 1916, had won the presidency without carrying New York.

THE COMBATANTS MOBILIZE

To secure the best tactical advantage once the mandate ended, the Jews frantically smuggled men and material into Palestine. Many of these immigrants enrolled in the Haganah, the Jewish defense force, mobilized to protect the settlements. Others joined two extremists groups: the Irgun Zvai Leumi (IZL) led by Menachem Begin, later prime minister of Israel; and the Stern Gang.

To arm those new recruits, Haganah agents bought arms whenever and wherever they could. Truman had imposed an arms embargo after the U.N. vote for partition, but the U.S., still teeming with excess munitions, was too tempting a source, and it leaked like a sieve.

On January 3rd, at pier F in Jersey City, dock workers were loading 26 big crates marked "Used Industrial Machinery" onto the Palestine-bound freighter, Executor. The twelfth case slipped from the loading fork and crashed six feet onto the concrete. The cooper found 50 one lb tins labeled "US Corps of Engineers - TNT - for Front Line Demolition Only." A shipment of 65,000 lbs. of TNT was seized.

The worried Arabs sought reinforcements. By January, the so-called Arab Liberation Army began to infiltrate into Palestine. Seven detachments with an estimated strength of 5,000 had arrived by the beginning of March.

INDISCRIMINATE BLOODSHED

With so many weapons and fighters crammed into a confined area, a total guerrilla war soon raged. The first armed Arab invasion of Palestine struck on January 9th when about 600 uniformed irregulars from Lebanon attacked two Jewish settlements in the northeast. The villagers held them off until British armored units and Jewish volunteers repelled the invaders. The next day, in a three-sided battle among British, Jews and Arabs in Southern Palestine near Gaza, 20 persons were killed before British troops restored order. More deadly, however, than the actual battles were the ongoing terrorist bombings. On January 4th, Jews dressed as Arabs parked a lorry loaded with high explosives in a narrow lane in Jaffa, next to the headquarters of the Arab Higher Command. The detonation killed 14 and wounded 90. The next day in Jerusalem, Jewish terrorists bombed the Arab owned Semiramis Hotel, a meeting place of Arab leaders. Twenty people died, including the Spanish consul.

On February 1st, the Arabs reciprocated by blowing up the office of the Jewish-owned Palestine Post. Mutual bombings continued. By the middle of January, approximately 828 British, Jews and Arabs had died in 6 weeks of relentless Holy Land fighting.

THE ELUSIVE INTERNATIONAL PEACE FORCE

On January 15th, the Jewish Agency for Palestine warned the U.N.'s Palestine Commission that an international force had to enforce partition. That call brought matters to a head. The U.N. had no army, and the demobilized American armed forces were spread too thin.

The Joint Chiefs of Staff estimated that approximately 100,000 U.N. peacekeepers would be needed and that the United States probably would have to provide nearly 47,000 of them, virtually the nation's entire ground reserve.[126] On February 19, the Pentagon hiked the U.S.'s probable participation to the 89,000 to 120,000 range.[127] With Europe a tinderbox, the U.S. could not bear such a burden.

Furthermore, the fear of war with the Soviets over Europe made access to Arab oil and air bases essential. The Arabs announced that if the U.S. continued to support partition, the U.S. would get no more Middle Eastern oil - particularly scary because Newsweek estimated that by 1952 the United States might have to import 2 million barrels of oil a day. Defense Secretary Forrestal voiced his "grave concern" to the House Armed Services Committee over a "strategic oil shortage vital to the European Recovery Program." Forrestal complained that he was tired of hearing about how the Democrats might lose three states and that someone should consider "whether we might not lose the United States."[128] He told Clifford: "oil--that is the side we ought to be on."[129] Columnist I.F. Stone described it as "a cynical policy of swapping Jewish blood for Arab oil."[130]

Palestine thus cleaved the American government, as officials differed over whether the strategic and economic concerns of the United States and its Allies should prevail over humanitarian concern for European Jews.
The State Department vehemently opposed partition and recognition of the Jewish state. It favored the formation of a federal state equally shared by Jews and Arabs.[131]

The decision stemmed not from the right or the wrong, but pure political and military reality. As Forrestal stated, "There are 30 million Arabs on one side and about 600,000 Jews on the other. It is clear that in any contest, the Arabs are going to overwhelm the Jews." Marshall told the Jewish Agency, "Believe me, I am talking about things which I know. You are sitting there in the coastal plains of Palestine while the Arabs hold the mountain ridges. . . . The Arabs have regular armies. They are well trained and they have heavy arms. How can you hope to hold out."[132] Powerless to stop the inevitable Jewish annihilation, the U.S. did not want to back the loser and thus cutoff its oil.

Marshall and the others totally misjudged the situation. As his former subordinate, Eisenhower, realized, "It's not the size of the dog in the fight, but the size of the fight in the dog!" They failed to fathom the effect the Holocaust had on Jewish desire for a homeland; and they overestimated the fighting abilities and cohesion of the Arabs.[133]

On the other side of the debate sat Truman whose humanitarian instincts and sense of history impelled him to help the Jewish people.[134]

Moreover, keeping liberal and Jewish voters happy in an election year was smart politics. As he pointed out to the State Department: "I do not have hundreds of thousands of Arabs among my constituents."[135] Besides their votes, Jewish contributions funded much of the party's campaign chest. Any misstep on Palestine would jeopardize that vote and money. Ed Flynn warned Truman that he must either "give in" on Palestine or expect New York's opposition to his nomination in July.[136] Trapped in a quandary, the Truman Administration juggled and expounded – with no clear goal. As one U.N. delegate explained: "We must do nothing - and do it quickly."

On February 27, the Jewish Agency for Palestine called everyone's bluff. It notified the Security Council that it would set up an independent Jewish state with or without the backing of an international police force.

On February 6th, the Arab Higher Command warned U.N. Secretary General, Trygve Lie, that the Arabs would fight "to the last man" against any forces sent to enforce partition. King Ibn Saud of Saudi Arabia threatened that the United States would have to choose "between an Arab land of peace and quiet or a Jewish land drenched in blood."[137]

POLITICAL MANEUVERS

On Thursday, March 18th, the infirm, almost blind Chaim Weizmann visited the White House. Truman assured him that American support for a Jewish state would not slacken. But Truman had seen and approved a plan proposing trusteeship.

On February 21st, while Truman was cruising on the Presidential yacht, the State Department sent him a message that, if a satisfactory solution in Palestine was not worked out, "some form of United Nations trusteeship for an additional period of time will be necessary." The next day, Truman cabled to Marshall, "I approve in principle this basic position."[138]

At a March 8th meeting, Marshall and Lovett again proposed a trusteeship as a fallback position and presented Truman with a draft of remarks for U. N. Ambassador Austin to deliver. Truman acquiesced but apparently did not grasp the diplomatic and political distinction between one solution and another.[139] He apparently understood the trusteeship would be offered after the Security Council announced that partition had proved impossible to carry out without a bloodbath. That way the record could be clear.

Warren Austin did make an important speech in the U.N. the day after Weizmann's visit, March 19, 1948. But it was not what Truman expected. Carrying out Marshall's instructions, approved by Truman, Austin declared that with the mandate's end on May 15th, chaos and more bloodshed would erupt. To avoid that, he proposed suspending the plan to partition Palestine and urged a special session of the General Assembly to reopen the issue. Pending a decision on its permanent status, the Holy Land should be placed under U.N. trusteeship without prejudice to the rights of the parties involved. Thus American policy suddenly flip-flopped.

Austin spoke when the Security Council had obviously given up on partition, but without voting. That made little difference to the State Department but Truman's standing with the Jews plummeted.[140] Vying for Jewish votes, Wallace charged that "Truman talks Jewish but acts Arab."

TIME reported: "Now no one in the world could be expected to know where the U.S. stood on Palestine. Harry Truman's comic-opera performance had done little credit to the greatest power in the world." The New York Times accused the Truman administration of unprecedented ineptness. Newsweek assumed that the turnabout and Truman's call the same week for the draft had "all but erased whatever small chance of reelection he had."

Passing the buck, Truman later wrote in his *Memoirs* that the State Department should have known that both Jews and Arabs would see trusteeship as an abandonment of partition. He lamely contended: "the trusteeship idea was at odds with my attitude and the policy I had laid down."

Marshall took full responsibility for the confusion. Over the next few days, he and Truman emphasized that trusteeship was not a substitute for partition, but only a temporary expedient to maintain peace pending a political settlement.

The domestic turmoil meant nothing in the long run. On March 20, David Ben Gurion, the head of the Jewish Agency, declared that establishing the Jewish state did not depend on the U.N. partition resolution but on the Jews' ability to fight. "It is we who will decide the fate of Palestine."[141]

Meanwhile, the war had continued and become more organized. Before, battles had raged for hamlets or neighborhoods. Now the Haganah began to battle with battalion size units, while Irgun and the Stern gang fought together as a tactical force, but independently of the Haganah. As TIME Magazine noted in its April 19th, issue: "For the first time since the Romans leveled Jerusalem, a Jewish army ate Passover matzoth and put their herbs around campfires in the field." However new, that army was inflicting substantial damage on the Arabs. For the first time, the Arabs were "glimpsing the sickening possibility of defeat."

RECOGNITION

On the diplomatic front, a race had begun. Torn between what he personally wanted to do and what he felt was political and military reality, Truman asked Clark Clifford to debate recognition with Marshall and other State Department officials, at a legendary confrontation in the Oval Office.[142]

At 4 p.m. on May 12, 50 hours before the new nation would be born, they gathered. To Truman's left sat Marshall, Robert Lovett and two other State Department officials. On the other side, sat Clifford and two White House aides. Lovett and Marshall laid out their plans and their arguments. Clifford rebutted with persuasive, quiet eloquence. He concluded with: "I fully understand and agree that vital national interests are involved. In an area as unstable as the Middle East, where there is not now and never has been any tradition of democratic government, it is important for the long-range security of our country, and indeed the world, that a nation committed to the democratic system be established there, one on which we can rely. The new Jewish state can be such a place. We should strengthen it in its infancy by prompt recognition."

TIME described Marshall as a man who was curiously unimpassioned and unimpressive when heard on the radio."[143] But when Clifford finished, Marshall was furious. "Mr. President, I thought this meeting was called to consider an important and complicated problem in foreign policy. I don't even know why Clifford is here. He is a domestic adviser and this is a foreign policy matter." Truman replied simply and directly, "Well, General, he's here because I asked him to be here."

Thinking Truman and Clifford were engaged in a "transparent dodge" to win votes in the election. Marshall stunned those present. "If you follow Clifford's advice and if I were to vote in the election, I would vote against you."[144] With the meeting spiraling downward, Truman adjourned the meeting.

Calling the meeting as "rough as a cob," Truman told Clifford to let the dust settle for a while, but to be careful because he feared that Marshall would resign. Truman could not afford to lose General Marshall - the political ramifications would be fatal. Truman needed the aura of respect that Marshall gave his otherwise tarnished administration.

Fortunately, Clifford and Lovett began meeting privately to overcome the stark and bitter confrontation. Eventually they came up with a plan that Marshall said he would not oppose - de facto recognition, not de jure.

Time was running out. On May 13th, the Arab League Secretary General in Damascus proclaimed a state of war between the seven Arab states and Palestine Jewry. Syria, Egypt, Lebanon and TransJordan announced their regular forces would invade the Holy Land within 48 hours of the mandate's end. Unimpressed, Jewish representatives met with Marshall on May 13 and told him that the Jewish state would be declared on May 14, 24 hours before the British mandate expired, because May 15th fell on a Sabbath. Marshall advised them not to, but basically said the U.S. would back the winner.[145]

Truman decided to recognize the new state immediately to be the first nation to do so, ahead of Russia. Such a move would help immeasurably in healing problems with American Jews over his previous fumbling.

Clifford had asked Eliahu Epstein, the Jewish Agency representative in Washington, to formally ask President Truman to recognize the new state. He was overjoyed to do so, but no one knew what the name of the new country would be. They assumed it would be called "Judea", but on the safe side, they typed in "the Jewish state." While the aide was carrying the letter to the White House, Epstein received word via short wave radio that the name would be Israel. A second aide intercepted the first, and, two blocks from the White House, they took a pen and crossed out the words "the Jewish state," and inserted "Israel."[146]

At midnight on May 14, 6 p.m. in Washington, the British would relinquish control of Palestine. Simultaneously, the Jewish agency under David Ben Gurion would proclaim the new state. At 5:40 p.m., Clifford told Lovett that at 6:00 Truman would recognize the new State of Israel. At 5:45 p.m., Dean Rusk received a similar call from Clifford. Rusk was stunned. He had kept negotiating for a trusteeship and thought he had the votes to accomplish it. Rusk then called Ambassador Austin. A messenger pulled Austin from the Assembly and into the anteroom to take the call. When Rusk told him what was going to happen, a stunned and furious Austin just put on his hat and went home without telling the rest of the American delegation.

At the White House, at 6:11 p.m., lanky, sad looking Press Secretary Charlie Ross announced to the press, "Statement by the President. This government has been informed that a Jewish state has been proclaimed in Palestine. ... The United States recognizes the provisional government as the de facto authority of the new State of Israel."[147]

At 6:01 p.m., newsreel photographers had focused on the clock in the half-filled U.N. General Assembly Hall. Awni Khalidy of Iraq went to the rostrum and announced, "The time is one minute past six o'clock." The U.N. had not repealed partition and had not voted a trusteeship. Khalidy declared that since the British mandate ended, "the whole game is up." As the Zionists celebrated, the delegates listlessly continued to debate trusteeship status. Then rumors hit the Assembly of the recognition. At first, the delegates scoffed that it was obviously untrue, if not a downright joke. But by 6:35, a flurry of excitement in the press section brought Dr. A. Gonzalez Fernandez to his feet. The Columbian representative wanted to know whether the American delegation could confirm news dispatches the United States had recognized the newly proclaimed Jewish state.

Truman had moved with such secrecy that not only were friendly U.N. delegations unprepared, but his own representatives as well. One member of the delegation, compelled to say something, went to the podium, scratched his head and solemnly announced that he had not the "faintest idea what was going on."

Not until 7:30 could another American delegate confirm the news and feebly explain it as a "practical step taken in the development of the difficult question of Palestine." The shock produced a violent reaction. A member of the U.S. delegation had to physically restrain the Cuban ambassador to keep him from going to the podium. Furious because three hours earlier he had helped the United States get the Trusteeship Resolution through Committee, he wanted to withdraw from the United Nations rather than sit in an organization in which a leading member was so duplicitous. Instead, he yelled: "The representatives of the Soviet Union and Poland are better informed on Washington plans than the United States delegation." The New Zealand delegate expressed the views of most of the delegates, "I am just dizzy, that's all, just dizzy."[148]

The most frequently heard explanation of the move was that Truman was more interested in winning the election than in maintaining his own and the U.N.'s prestige. The move certainly helped him in New York. Dancing erupted in the streets in Brooklyn and the Bronx and a huge "salute to Israel" rally began at the Polo Grounds.[149]

Truman's swift action allowed him to steal a march on the Soviet Union which recognized Israel on May 17, but speed came at the expense of smoothness. Newsweek noted the amateurish handling of the process. "As an unprecedented example of diplomatic confusion, President Truman's handling of the Palestine issue had long ago taken on most of the properties of a pretzel-bender's nightmare."

In Tel Aviv on the Sabbath Eve of May 14, 1948, the Provisional State Council, "representing the Jewish people in Palestine and the World Zionist Movement," hastily convened in the main gallery of the modern two-story Tel Aviv Museum of Art under the protection of Haganah gunners.

The thirteen men who would rule the new state sat at a long table on a raised dais. Over their heads hung white Zionist flags bearing two pale blue stripes and a blue Star of David. At exactly 4 p.m., David Ben Gurion, a stocky man with a wreath of electric white hair banged his fists on the table. Standing under a huge portrait of Theodor Herzl, the founder of Zionism, Ben Gurion declared, "We hereby proclaim the establishment of the Jewish State in Palestine, to be called Israel,... open to the immigration of Jews from all the countries of their dispersion." The audience cheered and wept.

Shortly after sunrise, the Union Jack was hauled down from Government House on Jerusalem's Hill of Evil Counsel. Simultaneously, the Union Jack fluttered down from British headquarters in the King David Hotel and a Red Cross emblem rose in its place. To the soft lament of a single bagpipe mingled with the occasional pop of a distant rifle, Lt. General Sir Alan Gordon Cunningham left his official residence as British High Commissioner for Palestine for the last time. At Haifa, after walking between lines of grenadier guards and royal marine commandos, he stepped onto a Naval launch for transport to the Royal cruiser, Euryalus, in the anchorage.

A band began playing, "The Minstrel Boy," as rockets lit up the night sky over the harbor and searchlights illuminated the Euryalus. Soon, the warship hoisted its anchor and headed to sea. The British mandate had ended and the first Arab/Israeli War was about to begin.

∾

CHAPTER SIX

POLITICS 1948 STYLE

TRUMAN'S NOSE-DIVE TO RETIREMENT

The bottom had fallen out! By the time McGrath announced that Truman was running, his chances of winning, so respectable in the fall of '47, looked miserable. In a few months, he had offended the South and the Jewish community - two stalwarts of the Democratic party. That plus Wallace's campaign had torpedoed his popularity. Between October 1947 and March 1948, the percentage of Americans who felt he was doing a good job sank - from 52 to 36 percent. In January, a poll had shown him beating Dewey 46 to 41. In mid-April, George Gallup revealed him losing 39 to 47 and also losing to Stassen, MacArthur, or Vandenberg. Both polls showed Henry Wallace reaping 7%.[150]

Truman's waffling on Palestine hurt him, but the Civil Rights package swamped him. The Gallup Poll released on April 5th showed only 6% support nationally for the program. Truman had a 57% disapproval rating in the South.[151]

Roosevelt could afford to lose the South. Not Truman.

On Saturday, February 21st, the Americans for Democratic Action (ADA) refusal to endorse him showed the dichotomy among liberals. They liked the message but scorned the messenger. The overwhelming sentiment on Truman was, "He means well, but he just doesn't do well."

Commentators became a Greek chorus of gloom. Edward R. Murrow proclaimed him a "dead duck." Ernest K. Lindley, Washington correspondent for Newsweek, doubted whether Truman "realizes that almost nobody in his party really wants him to run again...The most popular, and probably the best, service that Truman could render to his party now is to step aside and, assuming Eisenhower is completely unavailable, to assist in vesting the Party leadership in younger hands." On March 29th, Newsweek related, based on inside sources, that "Truman had resigned himself to defeat next fall and henceforth will conduct himself accordingly." To avoid the disgrace of an official rebuff, Truman's supporters simply wanted to get him nominated, even though they felt victory was impossible. "If Truman is nominated," Joseph and Stewart Alsop told their readers, "he will be forced to wage the loneliest campaign in recent history."[152]

If Truman were trying to doom his chances, he was doing a great job. Not since 1929 had the taxpayer received a substantial tax cut. Taxes had risen eight different times to boost sagging revenues during the Depression, to pay for the New Deal, to get ready for war, and finally to finance the costliest conflict in history. Congress finally reduced taxes to the lowest point since Pearl Harbor. What did candidate Truman do? He vetoed it, becoming the first President ever to veto a tax cut. On Friday, April 2nd, only three hours after his veto, both Houses, including most Democrats, voted overwhelmingly to override it. Only 10 Democratic senators backed the leader of their party.

Republicans giggled with anticipation. Taft captured the mood at the annual Gridiron Dinner in April. "We alone today earnestly and unanimously desire to see you renominated, Mr. President," he quipped to Truman.[153]

Democratic kingpins began talking privately about persuading Truman not to run and searched desperately for an alternative. Southern extremists, ADA liberals, and big city bosses could agree on only one thing - campaigning with Truman would spell disaster.

LIBERALS AND CONSERVATIVES YEARN FOR EISENHOWER

The desperate Democrats took up where the Republicans had left off and sought the most popular man in America!

Senator Johnston of South Carolina boomed Eisenhower as "the best available candidate" and announced that he would nominate Eisenhower at the Democratic Convention. FDR's sons, Franklin Jr., Elliott, and James announced they favored Eisenhower. Hugh Mitchell, Democratic leader in Washington State, even telegraphed the White House asking Truman to serve as chairman of the Draft Eisenhower Committee.[154]

Some liberals marveled about the enthusiasm for Ike when no one knew anything about his politics.[155] The New Republic answered, "Democratic politicians are not concerned about Eisenhower's views. What they want is a winning candidate who will carry local candidates to victory."[156]

Ticket-splitting was rare. "Vote Row A All the Way!" was not only a common slogan but a reliable outcome. If voters liked the top of the ticket, they would likely vote for all the other members of that team. A loser at the top sank numerous straphangers with him. So the bosses needed someone to head the ticket who would carry all state, county, and city office seekers to victory.

Ike, however, was still not interested. On March 29th, Ike announced that "under no conceivable circumstances" would he accept a Democratic draft. Eisenhower's denials did no good. Democrats still planned to put his name in nomination on the first ballot.

THE SPRING OF THE DEMOCRATS' DISCONTENT

So a badly fractured party, held together with Band-Aids and hoping for a new leader, began the nomination process. To understand the nomination process and political conventions in 1948, you have to understand two connected concepts: "favorite sons" and "political bosses."

A favorite son was the most prominent elected politician in a state - maybe the governor or a Senator - to whom the state's delegates would be pledged. This let the state keep its options open as long as possible. Until the 1950's, multi ballot conventions were common. In 1924, John Davis won nominatation on the 103rd ballot. So a shrewd state could trade its favorite son delegates to a needy but winnable candidate for a cabinet position, a dam etc.

Primaries and caucuses were uncommon in 1948, and most contests were shams in which the favorite son ran unopposed. For example, on March 27th, MacArthur and Stassen dropped out of the California Republican primary, leaving the field clear for Governor Earl Warren. Open primaries and political bosses were mutually antagonistic, like cobras and mongooses. Open primaries would destroy the power of the bosses, so they would happen only over the bosses' dead bodies.

But some open primaries did happen such as Wisconsin and Oregon, with glaring importance. An individual primary had more impact than today when, from February to June, primaries are a weekly event. In 1948, the rare open primaries, however small, gauged a candidate's vote-getting ability.

The committed votes were thus split over numerous favorite sons, plus a handful of real candidates fighting for the nomination. So rarely, prior to the 1980's, did any candidate arrive at the convention with the nomination really sewn up. The nomination was decided in the smoke-filled back rooms where political bosses traded for favors.

Political bosses meant just that: potentates elected or not who dominated the politics of an area. They were a dying breed, once prevalent but now prominent only in such cities as Chicago, Jersey City, New York. The political bosses were primarily Democratic, because they flourished in cities teeming with immigrants and minorities. Time and demography had eliminated the political bosses of the Republican Party. Its main strongholds had become the agricultural states, and political bosses did not grow well in farm country.

TRUMAN'S DRY AS DUST SPEAKING STYLE

Truman's miserable delivery of the State of the Union address typified his speaking. He lacked any oratorical ability. His problems started with his eyes and went down. Bright lights bothered him. Moreover, myopia made it difficult for him to return to a line once he had raised his eyes to look at the listeners. To get the words right, he sacrificed eye contact with his audience; usually stomped on his applause lines; and his nasal voice became a monotonous twang-filled drone, with no sense of pace or emphasis.

Incapable of the deft gesture, exquisitely timed for emphasis, he kept pumping his hands up and down as if delivering a two-handed karate chop, out of sync with his words. In Truman's 1940 Senate re-election campaign, a fellow senator effusively praised Truman's work. He then concluded his introduction with "I need not tell you that Harry Truman is not an orator. He can demonstrate that for himself."[157]

In ad-libbed remarks, he became lively and built a real rapport with his listeners. So, his staff convinced him to speak more extemporaneously. On

April 17, 1948, with his popularity at an all-time low, Truman addressed the American Society of Newspaper Editors in Washington. His prepared speech drew only tepid applause. But instead of sitting down, he launched into an off-the-record half-hour improvised discourse on American-Soviet relations, saying what he thought bluntly and vigorously. The editors cheered. About 40 guests told Charlie Ross that if Truman campaigned with that same fervor, "He'll be a hard guy to beat."[158]

TIME gasped: "Washington took startled note last week: a speech by Harry Truman had been well received." Roscoe Drummond of the Christian Science Monitor echoed: "I have never heard any political personage receive any longer, more sustained or more spontaneous applause than came from that group of overwhelmingly Republican newspaper editors. They liked what Mr. Truman had to say and they liked the way he said it. They felt an integrity, a morality of purpose... which stirred their esteem, their regard and their goodwill." Newsweek reported the roaring success of his remarks and spoke of two Harry Trumans--"the dry as dust reader of prepared speeches and the forceful, applause-winning impromptu speaker."[159]

THE SUPPOSEDLY NONPARTISAN TRAIN TRIP

In mid-1947, Gael Sullivan, staff director of the Democratic National Committee, advised the White House that:

> Sometime before the National Convention in 1948 the President should show himself to the nation via the back platform of a cross-country train.

Rowe's memorandum had spotlighted the West's priority. So, Truman's staff wanted him to go West.

A terrific idea! But expensive and the Democrats were flat broke, partly because the South had barely kicked in a nickel since Truman's civil rights message. Truman's dim prospects discouraged any bandwagon contributors who ordinarily filled the Democratic presidential campaign chest. McGrath had to cancel a Manhattan dinner for a score of wealthy long time contributors because only three accepted the invitation.

The $30,000-a-year presidential travel allowance could fund a cross-country train trip but Truman needed an excuse to make a "nonpolitical" tour. Rowe had suggested that since the President cannot be politically active until after the July convention, he must resort to "subterfuges." By happenstance, the president of the University of California in Berkeley asked Truman to give the commencement speech. The President pounced on the offer.[160]

Presidents could legitimately use taxpayers' money on nonpartisan trips, but this junket was embezzlement. The itinerary let Truman steam through eighteen strategic states, giving major speeches in Chicago, Omaha, Seattle, Berkeley, and Los Angeles, plus scores of impromptu back-platform talks where people could see and hear him and his new style rather than as interpreted through the predominantly Republican press. He planned to rally the majority party – the Democrats, two-thirds of whom had stayed home in 1946. Democrats needed to vote in '48 if they wanted to avoid another Republican Congress.[161]

The trip began at the nadir of Truman's chances but, on June 2nd, Truman replied to a letter urging him to drop out of the race, I "was not brought up to run from a fight." This trip proved it.

On June 3 at 11:05 P.M., the *Presidential Special* rolled out of Washington's Union Station in a pathetically disguised "non partisan" trip that fooled no one. TIME branded it Truman's first all-out political trip of the campaign. The Republicans accurately stamped it as "nonpolitical as the Pendergast machine." The Washington Post editorialized, "to have the President himself extending the period of interparty strife by making a campaign tour in early June seems particularly out of keeping with his responsibilities."

The 16-18 car long train, typically carried approximately 125 persons, including train crew, 59 reporters, and Presidential support staff who worked in cars set aside for their use. In the communications coach, a converted baggage car, Army Signal Corpsmen manned radio teletype to provide continuous contact with Washington, a necessity because of the Berlin crisis. One car served as a reception area in which the President met local politicians who greeted him at every stop and rode along awhile for the publicity.[162] No one could mistake the last piece of rolling stock. The Ferdinand Magellan was painted the standard dark green of the Pullman Company but that's where the similarity ended.

The Association of American Railroads had built the Ferdinand Magellan for FDR during the war according to specifications of the Secret Service. At 142 tons, it was the heaviest railroad car ever, weighing as much as a locomotive. Armor-plated, with windows 3 inches thick of green tinted bulletproof glass, it had a shielded undercarriage to protect the President from any bomb on the tracks plus a couple of escape hatches.

Its most conspicuous feature was a rear platform protected by a striped canopy. It could hold six or more people, carried the Presidential seal below its railing and had a built-in lectern wired to loudspeakers mounted overhead for public addresses.

At most stops, Truman joked that he was on his way "fur to get me a degree" - what LIFE Magazine called his "Li'l Abner Ozark style" in keeping with the popular comic strip.[163] He started out trying to appear bipartisan, but in Crestline, Ohio, a housewife in the crowd of 2,000 interrupted, "Aw, we don't want to hear that; we're all Democrats here." Laughing, Truman declared: "On this nonpartisan, bipartisan trip we are making here, I understand there are a lot of Democrats present, too." After that he made little effort to disguise the nature of the trip.

The trip began badly. Homemade signs: IKE FOR PRESIDENT! HARRY FOR VP! blared his low standing. Boss Jake Arvey did not bother to welcome Truman to Chicago nor turn out crowds for him.

Nebraska was a disaster! In Omaha, poor advance work brought only 1,000 persons into a cavernous auditorium. Press photographs showed Truman staring at rows of empty seats. Staffers did not recognize state chairman William Ritchie and threw him off the Ferdinand Magellan. He angrily told reporters, "I'm convinced that he cannot be elected. He has muffled the ball badly. He seems to prefer his so-called buddies to the persons who have done the work and put up the money for the party."[164] Ritchie announced that he would walk out on Truman at the national convention.

In Seattle, Truman spoke to half empty stands where Wallace had drawn 6,000 at a $1 each three weeks before. The ADA's northwestern organizer called the President's Seattle appearance "a first class flop. He was just a little man in a big stadium."[165]

Truman stuck his foot in his mouth in Eugene, Oregon. In private, Truman thought of Stalin as just another political boss like Tom Pendergast. Perhaps too relaxed with his new spontaneous style, he announced: "I like old Joe. He's a decent fellow, but he's the prisoner of the Politburo. He can't do what he wants to." Newsman covering the trip gaped open-mouthed that the President of the United States could make such an inane remark. The tart tongued Clare Boothe Luce blistered him: "Good old Joe! Of course they like him. Didn't they give him all Eastern Europe, Manchuria, the Kuriles, North China, coalitions in Poland, Yugoslavia, and Czechoslovakia?"[166]

But the trip ignited flashes of hope. His aides had been stocking up the political ammo: how Congress had rejected his requests to expand Social Security to cover 20 million more persons and boost old age insurance benefits 50%; raise the minimum wage; approve $300 million in federal aid to education; save price control and accept his anti-inflation recommendations.

Relying on the local matters his staff had compiled, he tried to strike regional chords. In the Northwest, for example, he emphasized his support for reclamation and public power and he charged the Republicans had no interest in developing the West. He ended with a familiar refrain: If you vote Republican "you are bigger suckers than I think you are."[167]

His blasts extended beyond the normal workday, in numerous late night speeches from the back platform. At least twice he appeared in pajamas and a bathrobe. "I understand it was announced that I would speak here," he told the gaping crowd. "I'm sorry that I had gone to bed, but I thought you might want to see what I look like, even if I didn't have on any clothes." Once he appeared in a blue dressing gown and a young girl asked him if he had a cold. He shook his head. She persisted, "You sound like it." He grinned impishly and said, "That's because I ride around in the wind with my mouth open."[168]

Harry Truman had started his westward fight for the White House yelling, "If I felt any better, I couldn't stand it." Politicians and reporters could not figure out Truman's ebullience because it was so clearly genuine. His stamina amazed newsmen. They echoed the words of the mayor of his hometown of Independence: "He can fall harder and bounce back further than any man I ever saw."

Eventually, his spirit and stamina either became infectious or at least promised a good show. Reporters noted the effect. "Whether or not the President fell flat on his face, as he sometimes did, or hit out at the Republican in his new slam bang oratory, as he occasionally tried to do, he was getting a reaction from the public which a few weeks earlier had only yawned." His new campaign personality, "a blend of Will Rogers and a fighting cock," had emerged.

The trip became an icon of political Americana by an off hand remark from Robert Taft, who criticized Truman for "blackguarding Congress at whistle-stops all over the country." The Democratic National Committee asked mayors and Chambers of Commerce in thirty-five cities visited by Truman to comment on Taft's insult. They branded it a slur, and the Democrats happily distributed their indignant replies. In Los Angeles, where an enormous throng welcomed Truman, he grinned and shouted, "This is the biggest whistle-stop!" A few hours later, he accepted a basket of eggs in San Bernadino and, when someone suggested that he throw them at Taft, replied, "I wouldn't throw fresh eggs at Taft." [169]

On June 18, the day the Allies introduced their new currency in Germany, he returned to Washington. Taft's whistle-stop remark had pushed the "I like old Joe" remark off the front pages and let the trip end on a high note. Truman had been away two weeks, covered 9,504 miles through 18 states, and presented 76 speeches in cities, towns and villages, including major addresses in five strategic cities. But not everyone liked his tone.

TIME concluded, "Whatever happened in 1948, Harry Truman had started the fight." The Washington Evening Star reported, "The President in this critical hour is making a spectacle of himself on a political junket that would reflect discreditably on a ward heeler."[170] Newsmen tagged many of his words "irresponsible." The Republican Chicago Tribune wrote on page 1, "Thanks to The Tribune, the people of the nation know Mr. Truman for the nincompoop he is."

~

CHAPTER SEVEN

THE REPUBLICAN CATFIGHT

THE NEW HAMPSHIRE OPENER

In 1948's first primary, New Hampshire, on March 8, Dewey netted six of the state's eight delegates. Stassen won only two but considered it a draw in Dewey's back yard. Wisconsin, the next primary state, had a large Scandinavian population. More importantly, its senator, Joseph McCarthy, was one of Stassen's key supporters. There, Dewey would be the outsider.[17]

WISCONSIN

Four weeks before the Wisconsin primary, Douglas MacArthur elaborately announced his availability: "In this hour of momentous importance . . . I can say, and with due humility, that I would be recreant to all my concepts of good citizenship were I to shirk . . . accepting any public duty to which I might be called by the American people."[172] Within two weeks, he jumped from 5th to 2nd place in GOP polls. Dewey held 1st place with 34%, but 18 points below his 1946 peak.[173]

The Wisconsin contest now appears surreal. MacArthur was the front runner because he claimed to be a native son. He had gone to high school in Milwaukee and had secured his appointment to West Point from Wisconsin; but he had not set foot in the United States, let alone Wisconsin, since 1937! As an active duty officer, he could not actively campaign. MacArthur, who held a legendary view of his own epochal importance, oversaw the campaign from his gray carpeted, leather chaired office on the sixth floor of Tokyo's Dai Ichi (No. 1) building. He let others campaign for him.[174]

Dewey conceded the state to MacArthur and had a skeleton staff. He did not even visit the state until five days before the primary and spent only forty-eight hours there at that. [175]

The experts predicted that MacArthur would win at least 14 of the 27 delegates. On March 29, The New York Times even bannered a headline: MACARTHUR VICTORY DUE IN WISCONSIN. In this, an early call of the election year, they would be as wrong as they would be on the last.

Veteran politicians had written the young, out-of-office Stassen off. But he had become the most tireless campaigner in history. Since declaring his candidacy in December 1946, Stassen had journeyed more than 160,000 miles, visiting 42 states plus 19 countries on a two month trip to Moscow and back, making no fewer than 325 major addresses and hundreds of lesser speeches in 476 days. Mencken called him a "western wind machine." To add the personal touch, he had the innovation of a question and answer period after each prepared address and had raised handshaking to an art form. He visited Washington 13 times, New York City 20 times, the Twin Cities 20 times, and most important, Wisconsin no fewer than 10 times.

On the last night of his Wisconsin campaign, Stassen gave a small dinner party for newsmen, then drove to his home in St. Paul, Minnesota. Next day, Tuesday, April 6th, he slept late, napped in the afternoon, and played chess with his son. After a quiet family dinner, he clicked on the radio and listened to the returns. By 10 p.m., he knew he had scored a stunning upset. By pure hard, face to face work, he had confounded the experts.

Stassen won nineteen delegates, MacArthur eight, Dewey none. The usually dour McGrath gleefully told reporters, "This leads me to the conclusion that to insure the election of the Democratic ticket in November, we need only have the commentators united in predicting defeat."[176] To explain their error, the New York World Tribune crabbed, "We suspect political observers devote too much of their time talking with each other, and too little talking with voters."

Dewey had returned to New York on April 2, resigned to losing - but to MacArthur. He expected possibly two delegates for himself. Stassen's triumph stunned him. The same day he won ten first-ballot votes from Oklahoma, but he and any knowledgeable observers realized the danger. A Herblock cartoon showed a car crash with MacArthur, corncob pipe in his mouth and crumpled hat, on one side of the road and Dewey on the other, having just been run over by the Stassen steamroller, with Dewey yelling, "Hey Mac--which way to Nebraska?"[177]

The humiliating defeat burst MacArthur's dream of a triumphant procession to the White House. Besides Stassen, only Taft had something to gloat about. He had sat out the Wisconsin primary and saw Dewey's debacle as a clear boost to his campaign.

Primaries can break a man easier than they can make him. At the Wisconsin primary four years earlier, Dewey's effortless victory had eliminated Wendell Willkie. Now, Wisconsin almost finished Dewey. It was as stunning as Joe Walcott's flooring Joe Louis twice in December. Everyone waited for the rematch.

NEBRASKA

The next primary was Nebraska's, a week away, on April 13th, Stassen's 41st birthday. Stunned into action, Dewey went to Nebraska to confront Taft as well as Stassen. Taft did not want to enter any primaries except Ohio's where he was a favorite son, but he had to run in Nebraska. The state party had placed all the candidates on the ballot, except for Eisenhower whose refusal was unequivocal. Dewey campaigned three days, Taft, four. Stassen, in Nebraska often for two years, came back for the final days.

Once again, a Stassen upset, with an amazing 43%. Dewey came next with 35 percent and Taft a weak third. Taft's poor showing after a strenuous campaign cemented the perception of his poor voter appeal.

Dewey fared better than in Wisconsin and even won two delegates. Newsweek said he had regained much lost ground "by putting on a show of warmth and humanity which offset his supposed indifference and aloofness." Working the crowds, he "got his hair tousled as if it had been caught in a thresher." But such compliments meant nothing in the face of the Stassen steamroller.

The same Gallup Poll that showed Truman's popularity had nose-dived to 36% revealed that Dewey lagged behind Stassen for the first time. In its April 17th issue, Business Week began its Washington News Page with "Your next President: Harold Stassen. Two months before Philadelphia, six months before election day, it looks as if you can say that."[178] In May, the Gallup poll showed that Stassen would beat Truman 56% to 33%, with 5% for Wallace.

The May 3 Newsweek prophesied that Stassen's success at the polls might revolutionize long established methods for seeking the nomination and end much of the traditional coyness of aspirants. In the future, more candidates might frankly announce their intentions well in advance of the election year and work openly for delegates as Stassen had done for 18 months.

When the Nebraska primary was just as disastrous, MacArthur had his name withdrawn from future primaries. MacArthur's campaign evaporated while Dewey's hyperventilated. Joseph Alsop pitied Dewey's plight: "The rat leaving the sinking ship is a loyal old slowpoke compared to the delegates fleeing from the weakening candidate." The liberal magazine, The *Nation*, agreed: "Although he is not a popular figure, there is an element of tragedy in his collapse as a leading contender. He has a good mind and considerable administrative talent. But he has pursued such a cautious course and been so clearly motivated by ambition that he stands for nothing and has no real friends."[179] The opinion was premature in May but dead on in November.

Dewey and the other contenders braced for a Stassen stampede at the convention. The next battleground would pit Stassen against Taft in Ohio, Taft's home.

OHIO

Confronting a favorite son in his home state wasted time and money. Flouting this unwritten rule, Stassen had declared on January 25 that he would run in Ohio, challenging Taft for twenty-three of fifty-three delegates. Stassen's move was unconventional, rude, and absolutely essential. He was not a favorite of the party machinery and, as an out of office candidate, had no hold on the party regulars. So his only hope was to win enough primaries to prove that he had vote getting appeal and concurrently to crush his rivals in any head to head contest. By thus showing his strength and their weakness, he could stampede the convention to him. What better way for Stassen to prove he was invincible than to beat Taft in his home. If he won,

Taft would be finished and he would have an unstoppable momentum to steamroll Dewey in Oregon. So, Stassen, a champion rifleman, took aim at Taft.

Stassen was no fool. He did not contest every district, but only twenty-three seats concentrated in the industrial centers and ran only one statewide candidate against nine for Taft. Shrewdly, Dewey did not contest Ohio. He let his rivals maul each other.

Taft went all out. From April 17 until primary day, May 4, he worked 17 hour days, speaking 8-10 times daily. Taft was worried, angry at Stassen's effrontery, and philosophically opposed to his criticism of Republican policy. Stassen won only 9 district races and his candidate for delegate at large finished last. Stassen's feared invincibility was dashed, although he had maimed Taft who had merely survived a bloody internecine war in his home state. Both Stassen and Taft tried to put the best "spin" on the vote, by claiming victory, but James Reston saw through it. "One more 'victory' like this would be the undoing of both candidates."[180] Taft's debacle energized the Dewey campaign as it limped toward Oregon, where Stassen's string of victories had opened an early 5 to 3 lead.

OREGON

Oregon was Dewey's last chance. If Stassen beat him again, he would go to the convention as a tourist. Dewey would not let that happen without the fight of a lifetime. Vowing "to win or else," his staff moved to Oregon to patch together a campaign that would decide whether they would live the next four years in upstate New York or Georgetown.[181]

Only a few weeks before Nebraska, Dewey had declared he was too busy to address the Young Republicans of Oregon. Nothing frees up a schedule better than the fear of oblivion. So, on May 1st, Dewey told reporters on the tarmac of Portland's airport at 6:45 a.m. that he had come west for "some good old campaigning, which I love." [182]

Besides freeing his schedule, fear transformed him. Gone was the aloof, snobby, eastern aristocrat. The man who arrived at Portland's airport was as folksy and personable as a cousin at a family reunion.

TIME reported that Dewey's admirers had criticized Stassen for "campaigning like a county sheriff." Now, in Oregon, "Dewey was running like an alderman who wanted to meet all of Oregon's 630,000 voters personally." He exhibited a burning interest in everything Oregonians did - where they lived, how they worked, what they ate. Crisscrossing the state from the big cities of Portland and Salem to hamlets of Sweet Home and Klamath Falls, to barber shops and hamburger stands, he shook hands at a manic pace. One journalist called Dewey the greatest explorer of Oregon since Lewis and Clark.[183]

In Dewey's first week in Oregon, he was seen by 35,000 people. At the end of three weeks, he had traveled some 1950 miles and spoken to 100,000 people from platforms, busses and cranes. Dewey copied Stassen's bus-stop campaigning and often worked grueling sixteen hour days.

In Cheyenne, Wyoming, the previous summer, he had disappointed many of his supporters by refusing to don chaps and a cowboy hat. Now, no stunt was too corny. He posed in a ten-gallon hat and in an Indian headdress. He let the Coos Bay Pirates Club prick his arm and draw blood with which he might sign their guest book. At Grants Pass, he allowed a band of local pageant "cavemen," wearing tattered furs and carrying clubs, to "ambush" his party. Dewey gnawed on a bone handed him by the half-naked "neanderthals."[184] Joseph Alsop, so recently eulogizing Dewey's campaign, now hailed his "remarkable fight."[185]

Besides the personal touch, Dewey rained money on Oregon. His cash was running low and not being replaced, but it was now or never. Oregon businesses feasted on the bonanza that reached an estimated quarter of a million dollars, an astronomical sum in 1948, and more than three times Oregon's prior record. As if to prove that politics makes strange bedfellows, Taft forces helped Dewey battle Stassen.[186]

The issue of domestic Communism most sharply split Dewey and Stassen. Stassen wanted the Communist Party banned. His strong stance had won him Richard Nixon as a supporter. Dewey ridiculed Stassen's party-banning scheme. Clear the dust from your eyes, he insisted, and the confusion from your brains. "You can't shoot an idea with a gun."

Needing a dramatic confrontation to assure victory, Dewey accepted Stassen's challenge to debate that one volatile issue: "Shall the Communist party be outlawed in the United States?" Stassen took the affirmative, aided by his second, Senator Joe McCarthy; Dewey the apparently riskier negative.

At 6:30 p.m., Pacific time, May 17, a radio audience of 40 to 80 million switched from the *Carnation Contented Hour* and Fred Waring to hear the first ever presidential debate, broadcast live from Portland's KEX to some 900 stations around the country.

Radio was Dewey's medium. Dewey stood five feet eight inches, average build. Stassen towered 6 ft. 2-1/2 inches tall, 226 pounds of bone and muscle. Posing together, they looked like a home run slugger and the bat boy. (By convention time, Dewey had acquired elevator shoes.)[187] The radio audience could not see the short, gap-toothed, immaculately dressed and coiffured man on the wedding cake. Instead, it heard the rich baritone voice of the gang busting former prosecutor articulately and eloquently take Stassen apart. "There is no constitutional right to take away all constitutional rights."[188]

The debate turned the tide. Dewey won the primary by a shade under 10,000 votes, 53 percent of the vote. He won by showing the voters a new rough and tumble candidate in "surprising contrast to the stiff, overstylized candidate of 1944." [189]

HANDICAPPING THE FIELD

Oregon derailed Stassen's bandwagon. He no longer loomed as the nominee but could be the spoiler or one of several spoilers. Stassen disagreed and predicted that he would win on the ninth ballot.

Dewey had regained his momentum, re-establishing himself as the front runner, but he was clearly beatable. His defeats in Wisconsin, Nebraska and Pennsylvania showed that spirited campaigning could whip him. [190] Gallup reported a subtle but more fundamental problem. Less than a year before, half of the registered Republicans preferred Dewey. Now they fancied the relatively unknown Stassen, 37 percent over the 1944 candidate's 24 percent.[191] Such a drop of support should have shown his bedrock support had the consistency of ice cream.

Dewey went to Philadelphia with a commanding lead in the delegates, 331 to 219 for Taft, but he needed 548. A stop Dewey alliance was certainly possible. As TIME noted: "The balance of power rested with the uncommitted and favorite son delegations--and they would not make their final choice until the balloting had begun." The outcome of the convention was so cloudy that TIME had six separate covers waiting, but the front runners were Dewey, Taft and Vandenberg.

Immediately before the convention, Taft performed yeoman service on the international front. When the House wanted to cut funding for the Marshall Plan, Taft kept the Senate in session until the House caved in. [192] The ERP bill passed on Friday, June 19, but Glen Taylor filibustered against the military draft, proposed by Truman in his March 17 speech. Taft's forces broke the filibuster and the Senate voted 78-10 for the draft, including Taft who recognized that the Czech coup and the Berlin crisis mandated a strong military. The regular session of the 80th Congress finally adjourned on 7:15 a.m. on Sunday, June 21 after 44 consecutive hours in session, the second longest in American history. Taft and his wife immediately drove to Philadelphia for the convention.

For those hectic last days of the session, the Capitol dispensary had stockpiled digestive remedies and sedatives. Congress sent 263 bills to Truman for signature, including one that slipped by during the mad race to adjournment while everyone focused on the Marshall Plan and the draft. That one bill would cost the Republicans the election.

Every one of the 1,094 power hungry GOP delegates who converged on Philadelphia could taste victory in November. They would have their pre-victory festival before the largest audience ever to see a convention.

TELEVISION - THE CUB REPORTER

What the 1924 political conventions were to radio, 1948's was to television. The 1948 conventions were the first to be televised. Television exacted one concession. The Democrats, Republicans, and the Progressives agreed to hold their conventions in one east coast city where the farthest reach of the coaxial cable could bring live transmission to 18 stations strung between

Boston and Richmond.[193] Thus, Philadelphia became the political nerve center of the U.S. from mid June to mid July.

The lectern in Convention Hall could be seen on some 400,000 TV screens in the East.[194] The estimated 10 million viewers comprised the biggest audience television had ever had, although later in the week, the broadcast of the Louis - Walcott fight matched the record. Never before had so many seen an event as it occurred. One viewer was especially interested. At the White House, a new console 12-inch screen Dumont television sat in his office, against the wall to his left. Harry Truman could watch his vilification.[195]

More than 300 technicians assembled $1,500,000 worth of equipment to televise the Convention. On the Convention floor, CBS, NBC, ABC, Dumont, and New York station WPIX set up 4 cameras that could focus on any part of the huge arena. Other cameras roamed the Bellevue Stratford Hotel to be handy to its smoke filled back rooms. Also strategically placed were tela newsreel cameras whose film would be sent to TV stations outside the range of the cables that connected Boston and Richmond. So 5 million others as far west as Los Angeles could see telefilm versions a mere 3 to 24 hours after it happened.

Ten 10,000 watt lamps in the galleries focused on the speaker stand. A little above and directly in front of the stand glared ten more 5,000 watt bulbs. The extra lighting caused H. L. Mencken to write, "I began to go blind, so the rest of my observations had to be made from a distance and through a brown beer bottle."

RCA advertised, "Look before you vote--with television" and emphasized that with television at both conventions, "The candidate will be televised as he looks into the camera--talks to the people, face to face. His appearance, smile, gestures, combined with the sound of his voice, and his message, to complete the transmission of his personality. You have a new opportunity to know your man!"

The candidates recognized the promise and raced to polish their "image" even before that word came into vogue. Newsweek observed: "Although this year's televiewers are not numerous enough to elect a President, the

1952 campaigns may tell a different story. As Harry Truman had to be tutored in speech reading . . ., so a presidential candidate four years hence may have to take a course in dramatics."

TV impressed even the cynics. "An unpolished but very promising reporter," TIME said, adding: "The television camera was more important than a good political slogan--and more frightening than a powerful political enemy."

THE REPUBLICANS CONVERGE FOR A CORONATION

The Republican convention opened on a sweaty Monday, June 21, in Philadelphia's mammoth grand dame, Convention Hall.

Taft's forces encamped on three floors of the Benjamin Franklin Hotel. Dewey headquartered at the Bellevue Stratford Hotel which made 6,000 rooms available at an average of $12 a night, double the usual rate.[196]

The keynote speaker, Governor Dwight H. Green of Illinois, triumphantly proclaimed, "We are here to nominate the thirty-fourth President of the United States." The delegates ate it up. As H.L. Mencken observed, "Most of the delegates and alternates have been pining and panting for office for fifteen long years and their pulses race every time they hear that succor is at hand."[197]

On Tuesday night, the convention roared as the former Congresswoman from Connecticut, Claire Booth Luce, pronounced: "Mr. Truman's time is short; his situation is hopeless. Frankly, he is a gone goose." She declared the Democrats were split into "a Jim Crow wing, led by lynch-loving Bourbons . . ., a Moscow wing, masterminded by Stalin's Mortimer Snerd, Henry Wallace . . . and a Pendergast wing run by the Wampum and Boodle boys . . . who gave us Harry Truman in one of their most pixilated moments."[198]

The real action, however, took place blocks away. The primaries depended greatly on charisma. Here what counted was organization, deal making and years of painstaking preparation. This was Dewey's third convention as a major contender and the experience showed.

Dewey's forces took nothing for granted. They had gone into the 1940 convention, also in Philadelphia, expecting to win. He had won in the Republican primaries and had led all year in the polls. But they had overestimated their first ballot strength and not understood how conventions worked. Ambitious and arrogant, but not schooled in politics, they lost to Willkie on the sixth ballot.

Since then, Dewey and his lieutenants had mastered the art and squashed Willkie in 1944. They had improved even more in the last four years. His forces simply out-planned, out-maneuvered and out-spent the opposition in a blitzkrieg that would honor Rommel.

"The CIA were amateurs compared to the Dewey people," lamented one Taft aide. "They knew where your bank loans were, who you did business with, who you slept with." Dewey Campaign Manager Herb Brownell saw it less melodramatically. To him, this was the culmination of eight years of wining and dining, sending birthday cards and taking visiting Republicans to Yankee games and Broadway plays.[199]

At conventions, perception is half the battle. If delegates believe you have the necessary votes, it's easier to get the votes. So, twice a day, Brownell summoned newsmen to Room 816 of the Bellevue Stratford to report new gains and slyly hint of second-ballot conversions. These announcements, duly reported by the press which became Brownell's echo chamber, scared favorite sons into throwing their weight behind the Dewey calliope. If he clinched the nomination without them, they could kiss any later favors goodbye.

Modern conventions enjoy split second timing because the abundance of today's primaries and caucuses have already annointed the nomineee. So both parties strive to avoid the internecine warfare that is broadcast live to the electorate and which means death in November. Now, people and the networks know exactly not only the night of the nominee's acceptance speech but even what time, down to the minute, the speech will start, to ensure the largest possible prime time audience. Not so in 1948.

On Wednesday night, nominations began but did not end until 4:30 a.m., as long winded orators and over zealous demonstrators droned on. On the first ballot, Dewey won 434 votes, Taft 224, Stassen 157, Vandenberg 62, Warren 59; favorite sons and fringers had the rest. Dewey crept inexorably closer on the second ballot as both he and Taft won more votes:

Dewey 515, Taft 274, Stassen 149, with minor candidates bringing up the rear. Thirty-three votes stood between Dewey and the nomination. The anti-Dewey forces jumped to their feet to force a recess.

The recess gave Dewey's opponents one last chance to perfect a coalition. The problem with any "stop the front runner" campaign is that it requires several ambitious super egos to quit and anoint an often hated rival. The Dewey opposition was no exception. Neither Taft nor Stassen would accept the second spot to the other. Thus, the "Stop Dewey" movement was stillborn - a victim of blind ambition and ideological rigidity.

An avid reader of detective stories, Taft knew how this mystery would end. When Stassen refused to budge until one more ballot, even though he had already lost votes on the second ballot. Taft left the group to write his concession on yellow legal paper. A few minutes before the session reconvened, Taft announced "Simple arithmetic" made it impossible to go on.

When the convention reconvened on Friday, John Bricker of Ohio read a gracious concession from Taft releasing his delegates and urging them to vote for Dewey "a great Republican [who] . . . will be a great Republican President." In quick succession, Warren, Stassen and Vandenberg also withdrew. The battle ended on the same day the Berlin Airlift began. Dewey's convention performance glided so impeccably that people forgot that six weeks earlier, he had faced political oblivion.[200]

Dewey won by steering a course between the two wings of the party: the Taft Old Guard and the Stassen internationalists. He could do it because of a general lack of agreement as to where exactly he stood on most issues. His strength lay in his administrative ability, ("America's greatest administrator"[201]) not the substance of his policies. He had become the acceptable center that pulled in votes from all sides.[202]

Gone was the Oregon dynamo when he faced the convention that evening. Instead of coming out slugging, his acceptance speech lulled the audience to sleep. Dewey's main theme was unity and he beat it to death citing the need for political and national unity nine times. "The unity we seek is more than material. It is more than a matter of things and measures. It is most of all spiritual."

It was mercifully short--less than fifteen minutes--and dignified, more like an inaugural address. Not once did he mention Truman, the Democrats, domestic Communists, botched foreign policies, the Palestine debacle, inflation, the housing shortage, nor outline the programs he would pursue if elected. When it ended, the hall responded warmly but not wildly. The delegates did not know it, but they had heard a speech whose core would be repeated, with only slight variation, dozens of times over the next four and one half months.[203]

THE VICE PRESIDENTIAL BEAUTY CONTEST

Now he must pick a running mate. In Room 808 in the Bellevue Stratford, Dewey aides hashed out a list of acceptable candidates.

Shortly after 4 a.m., Dewey offered the job to Earl Warren. Warren asked for time to think it over. At 11:30 a.m., Warren telephoned his acceptance. At 11:35, the door to Dewey's suite opened and the press were informed.[204]

The nomination of Warren scored a political bull's-eye - a dream ticket - the governors of two states which alone provided almost one fourth of the required electoral votes. Moreover, it would defeat any Democratic plans to make hay of Republican failures to push through reclamation projects in the West. Warren was the most spectacular vote-getter in California's history with its 25 electoral votes. Unlike Dewey, the 57-year-old Warren had never lost.

This remarkably moderate (liberal for Republicans) and internationalist platform seemed invincible. Ernest K. Lindley wrote: "Only a miracle or a series of political blunders not to be expected of a man of Dewey's astuteness can save Truman, or probably any other Democrat, from overwhelming defeat." Picking Warren made up for Dewey's lackluster speech and allowed delegates to leave euphoric. Several Republicans, knowing they would be members of the new administration, went home via Washington, to buy good houses at bargain prices before November.[205]

Truman's reaction differed. The morning after the Republicans adjourned, Truman told a Secret Service agent that the Republicans had made a mistake in not nominating Taft, who he respected: "He was deserving of it and he is an honorable man... He would be a very much tougher opponent for me than Governor Dewey." He then added: "Before this campaign is over, I will take the mustache off that fellow, you can be sure of that."[206]

Amidst the Republican euphoria lay some similar discontent. On July 6, Richard Nixon astutely wrote, "Dewey lacks the warmth needed for a national campaign." The impression multiplied. One familiar quip was, "I don't know which is the chillier experience--to have Tom ignore you or shake your hand."[207] The New York Star's political cartoonist, Walt Kelly, who in 1948 would create the comic strip, Pogo, depicted Dewey as a small robot with a human head.[208]

CHAPTER EIGHT

THE DEMOCRATS RELUCTANTLY PICK A LOSER

THE PRE CONVENTION MANEUVERING

Two weeks before the Democratic Convention, Truman had assembled a group to help pick his running mate. The group chose Supreme Court Justice William O. Douglas, but Douglas refused. He would have gladly run with FDR in 1944, but he would not give up the Supreme Court for an almost sure loss. Besides, he told others, he did not want to be number two to a number two man.

So the Democrats went to Philadelphia unhappy with the top and whoever wound up at the bottom of the ticket. They resembled not enthusiastic followers of a charismatic leader but lemmings in what they instinctively felt was a suicidal parade.

The Democrats still tried to woo Eisenhower. A Roper poll showed that Ike as the Republican candidate would overwhelm Harry Truman. If he were the Democratic candidate, he would soundly beat any of the leading candidates. Conversely, the Public Opinion Quarterly showed that Dewey had a 12% lead over Truman.[209]

Southerners horrified at Truman's civil rights program, liberals distrustful of his commitment to the New Deal, and organization Democrats who feared that the party could not possibly win with him, rallied behind one goal, the nomination of Eisenhower who, Newsweek said, "paradoxically enough, supposedly is a Republican."

Over the July Fourth weekend, James Roosevelt, the chairman of the California delegation, persuaded eighteen other prominent party leaders to send a telegram to each of the 1,592 delegates to the convention, urging them to come to Philadelphia two days early for a special caucus to select "the ablest and strongest man available" as the party's candidate, Dwight Eisenhower.[210] The *New York Times* found more than 200 southern votes awaiting Ike. On July 4th, New Jersey Democratic leaders pledged its thirty-six votes to Eisenhower.

It was up to Ike. ADA members ringed his home on the Columbia campus with signs, "Ike, You're A-1 with Us, Be 1-A in the Draft," and "Ike, You Favor the Draft, We Favor It for You."[211] On Monday night, July 5th, Eisenhower made it again abundantly clear that he "could not accept nomination for any political office" or participate in a partisan political contest.

Florida Senator Claude Pepper sent a telegram designed to permit Eisenhower to coyly remain available without saying yes. Pepper wired his "opinion" that the convention should draft Eisenhower as a totally "national" candidate and let him write his own platform, with no party obligations. The Democratic Party would limit its activities to Congressional and local contests. At the end of the telegram, Pepper slyly asked for silence: "I neither expect nor desire either an acknowledgment or a reply."[212]

Eisenhower, however, did respond - in Shermanesque language. His July 9 telegram closed any semantic loopholes: "No matter under what terms, conditions or premises a proposal might be couched, I would refuse to accept the nomination." Ike squashed the Draft movement.

When Eisenhower sent his unequivocal refusal, Boss Frank Hague crushed out his cigar and with the disappointed recognition of the inevitable sighed: "Truman, Harry Truman. Oh my God!" He spoke for the entire convention.[213] It was Truman, not by acclamation but by default.

When Truman's train reached St. Louis after midnight, reporters wanted Truman's comment on Ike's refusal. He snipped, "General Eisenhower is an honorable man." In private, Truman fumed and called Eisenhower a "shitass" because the boom lasted so long. Truman was unfair and short-sighted. He was unfair because Eisenhower had tried to kill the movement. His letter in January and his announcement in March were both clear and unequivocal. The fact that the enthusiasm of his supporters proved harder to kill than Rasputin was not Eisenhower's fault.

Truman was being short-sighted, because if Eisenhower had killed the boomlet in January or March, party dissidents had time to coalesce behind another candidate. As it was, when the boomlet finally ended, they were stuck with Truman.

THE DEMOCRATS GATHER FOR A WAKE

With Eisenhower gasped the last spark of enthusiasm for the convention. Many reporters echoed the theme the Associated Press observed on July 12: "The Democrats act as though they have accepted an invitation to a funeral."[214] "There is no enthusiasm, no jubilation, no confidence," wrote John C. O'Brian of the Philadelphia *Inquirer*; "rather, a 'what else can we do?' air of resignation." "What is so strange about it all is that the heirs of Jefferson and Jackson . . . seem to have given up the fight even before it has started--and this in a year of roaring prosperity," marveled Edward Folliard of the Washington *Post*. " [215]

Bernard Baruch called it the "dullest, dreariest, most dispirited gathering ever assembled ... to pick a President."[216] The New York Times wrote: "An atmosphere of despondency...and a spirit of defeatism [translated into a] confession that President Truman seemed to have little chance of election."[217]

So with that inauspicious background, more than 3000 delegates, alternates, guests, reporters (press, radio and TV) assembled.

The Democrats met in the same auditorium three weeks after the Republicans, on July 12. The bunting and flags from the Republican Convention still hung in place. Contributions were so meager that Secretary of the Treasury Snyder had to ask Bernard Baruch for $2500 for balloons and noisemakers for the Convention. Delegates flinched at the usual banners "All 48 in 48" and "KEEP AMERICA HUMAN WITH TRUMAN". More common were signs like "To err is Truman" and "I'm just mild about Harry." From a baneful beginning, it went downhill from there, descending into racism, separatism, comic absurdity right out of a Marx Brothers movie, before ending on the high note of Truman's acceptance speech.

The party tried to appease the South by giving two Southerners the headline jobs at the convention. Senator Alben Barkley of Kentucky would give the keynote address and Sam Rayburn would serve as permanent chairman, the highest honor the convention could bestow.

Regarded as the best story teller on Capitol Hill, Barkley's oratory had made him the keynoter at the 1932 and 1936 conventions, chairman in 1940 and one of Roosevelt's nominators in 1944. His experience came in handy. Philadelphia had spent $250,000 refurbishing Convention Hall, but none went for air conditioning. The short stocky Barkley, with thinning gray hair, wilted. "Perspiration ran down his nose and dripped from his chin, and his elegant Palm Beach suit looked more and more like a wet towel."[218] Barkley's original speech would have run at least 2 hours, but the heat made him cut it to one hour and 7 minutes.

Barkley evoked the spirit and past glories of the Democratic Party. His spirited speech galvanized the crowd with anti Republican fervor. But he omitted the most common theme of a keynote - the loud unequivocal claim of victory: "We shall not follow the example so egotistically set by our opponents from this rostrum three short weeks ago, by announcing the result of the contest four months in advance." Most amazing of all, he mentioned the name of the incumbent Democratic President, and the man sure to be the nominee, only once and rather casually at that.

At the end of Barkley's speech, a Missouri delegate said, "This convention reminds me of a funeral we had back home. The man we were laying to rest was a ne'er do well, and nobody came to the grave to say anything nice about him. Just as they were getting ready to lower the body, the town barber stepped up and said: 'I noticed no one has said a good word about this man. Before he is covered, I want to say one thing. He was an easy man to shave.'"

Barkley was a rarity, especially for 1948 - an ambitious 70-year old! At an age when his contemporaries were retired or dead, he had been hoping for a boomlet to propel him as the presidential candidate, but arithmetic doomed that. Barkley then passed the word that he was available for the vice presidency. "I am willing . . . It will have to come quick; I don't want it passed around so long it is like a cold biscuit." Barkley himself was a cold biscuit. He had first run for the vice presidency at the 1928 convention, receiving nearly 100 votes, and been available at every convention since. Nevertheless, he was as good a choice as Truman had (peddling the vice presidency had not been successful) and the deal was made.

In contrast to the dream GOP ticket, the Democrats had picked a clinker. The Republicans had youth, big electoral states plus geographic diversity - New York to California. The Democrats had married Missouri and Kentucky with the oldest ticket ever. Barkley was 6-1/2 years older than Truman's 64 years.

THE BATTLE OVER CIVIL RIGHTS

To keep peace in Philadelphia and to consolidate the party, Truman had agreed to a brief innocuous civil rights plank that avoided specifics, including the administration's program. It collided with the Americans For Democratic Action who proposed a more forceful plank. So, the third night was going to be an ugly fight for the soul of the party.

Minneapolis Mayor, and Senate candidate, Hubert Humphrey would spearhead the ADA crusade. As Humphrey sat on the convention platform waiting to speak but expecting to lose, Ed Flynn, the Democratic boss of the Bronx, beckoned him over. "I hear you kids have a minority plank on civil rights." Flynn read Humphrey's minority report and told him, "Young man, that's just what this party needs." He sent runners to the floor for three other big-city bosses: Jacob Arvey of Chicago, David Lawrence of Pennsylvania, and Frank Hague of New Jersey, all of whom agreed to support Humphrey. Civil rights meant Negro votes.

Humphrey's ten minute speech was not merely eloquent; it was inspiring and was the first convention speech of the twentieth century worth comparing with William Jennings Bryan's famed "Cross of Gold" speech in 1896.[219] Speaking through bursts of applause, he built to a climax:

> There are those who say to you--we are rushing this issue of civil rights. I say we are a hundred and seventy-two years late.

> There are those who say--this issue of civil rights is an infringement on states' rights.

> The time has arrived for the Democratic Party to get out of the shadow of states' rights and walk forthrightly into the bright sunshine of human rights.

Southerners offered amendments to "preserve party unity." On the closest one, the ADA plank won by 651 1/2 to 582 1/2 - a shift of 35 votes would have defeated it.

Expecting an alphabetical roll call of the states for the final vote, Alabama chairman Handy Ellis awaited recognition so he could announce his delegation was walking out on the Democrats. Rayburn, a Truman supporter, knew that Alabama would lead the walkout when called on to vote. So instead, he ordered a voice vote. The convention, moved by Humphrey's rousing speech, shouted its approval.

Banging his gavel, Rayburn simply announced the plank's adoption; then declared that he would entertain no other motions than a motion to recess. The floor microphones then went dead. Fearing the loss of their dramatic walkout, the Alabamians and other southerners were apoplectic. Furious, Ellis turned to fellow delegate Bull Connor, the Birmingham Police Commissioner. "Raise some hell, Bull," he said.

Connor did. Sweaty, with no necktie, in shirt sleeves with buttons undone, Connor hopped on the seat of his chair and waved the Alabama placard furiously, braying: "Mr. Chairman! Mr. Chairman! Mr. Chairman!" Rayburn looked the other way. "Damn thing won't work--they cut it off-- Mr. Chairman!" Connor howled. Rayburn looked right at Ellis, ignored the shouts, banged the gavel and announced adjournment.[220]

Humphrey's plank prevailed partly because Harry Truman looked like such a loser in November. Since the party was going to lose the White House anyway, the walk out of the South did not scare the big city bosses like Hague and Flynn who needed the votes of Negroes and other minorities which could be decisive in their states. Actually, the move was a blessing in disguise. The Democrats could not have a tent big enough for racists and Negroes. Someone had to leave. The civil rights plank caused the Liberal Party and Negroes to stand firmly behind the Democrats when they might have set out the campaign or joined Wallace. Humphrey's bold defiance meant more to Truman's election than anyone realized. [221]

Alabama finally got a live microphone later that evening. Chairman Ellis announced that Alabama's electors had pledged "never to cast their vote for a Republican, never to cast their vote for Harry Truman, and never to cast their vote for any candidate with a civil rights program such as that adopted by the Convention." They held no malice for fellow Democrats, but they were leaving. "We bid you goodbye!" cried Ellis, leading the way to the door with

George Wallace, a young alternate, waving a placard. Most of the Alabama and Mississippi delegates followed, waving the battle flag of the Confederacy. For the first time since 1860 when the northern and southern wings of the Party split, permitting the election of Lincoln, the South walked out on the Democratic party, all but dooming Truman's chances.[222]

The President's train pulled into the Philadelphia station shortly before 10 p.m. Truman thought he would go straight to the podium. He could not; the nominating speeches were just starting. Suffering from a gastrointestinal upset, he waited four hours sweltering offstage, seated in a straight backed wooden chair in a small bleak room under the platform.[223] Truman was put in nomination around midnight by Governor Phil Donelly of Missouri. The first speaker to tout Truman as a leader, Donelly ticked off the accomplishments of the administration and its heritage from the New Deal. Donelly did the unexpected - he put some life into the tired, hot, discouraged delegates. A snake dance erupted in the aisles accompanied by the traditional hooping and yelling that seemed genuine.[224]

At 12:42 a.m. on Thursday, July 15, the President was finally nominated, on the first ballot, 947 1/2 votes to 362 for Georgia's Richard Russell and half a vote for a former governor of Indiana. Then Dixie inflicted the final indignity. Because the South would surely and publicly balk, Rayburn skipped the call for the usual extra round of voting to make the nomination unanimous. So for the first time, the traditional courtesy of acclamation was denied to an incumbent Democratic president. The delegates nominated Barkley by acclamation - emphasizing the insult to Truman.[225]

McGrath went downstairs to see if Truman wanted to accept the nomination immediately or wait until the next day. Truman refused to wait. So at 1:45 a.m., the ticket finally appeared on the platform to the strains of "Hail to the Chief." While Truman's advisers waited in the wings, a sweating LIFE photographer came in and said, "They won't let me photograph those dying pigeons." They did not know what he meant, but they soon learned.

All evening a floral Liberty Bell, a gift from the host city, had stood by the podium. Now a woman presented it to Truman, or tried to. As a sudden swishing under it erupted, she just had time to stammer "doves of peace" before 48 doves who had been cooped up for hours burst out and frantically flew to all corners of the cavernous hall, flapping their wings, bumping into people and things and all the while spraying the assemblage with droppings. Rayburn yelled, "Get those goddamned pigeons out of here." When one flew into a fan and fell dead upon the convention floor, a delegate remarked "a dead pigeon, just like Truman." To their surprise and pleasure, that moment of slapstick released the delegates' tension and jolted them awake.[226]

So, Harry Truman stood to address a party in more pieces than a $5 jigsaw puzzle over civil rights and foreign policy. Resplendent in a white Palm Beach suit, Truman began as people still fanned themselves to relieve the stifling heat. It was not a polished speech. His enunciation was sometimes so blurred that "foreign policy" sounded like "farm policy."[227] His timing was often off and he lapsed into technical specifics. But probably because their expectations were so low, he amazed them with his spirit. He opened with a taste of the defiantly fighting optimism that would permeate his campaign. "Senator Barkley and I will win this election and make the Republicans like it - and don't you forget it... We will do that because they are wrong and we are right." Until then, no one had promised victory in November. Truman followed that rousing opener with short punchy sentences, from an 18 page outline. [228]

Stabbing the air with quick, awkward gestures, he appealed to the warring elements of FDR's old coalition. "Labor's had but one friend in politics, and that was the Democratic Party and Franklin D. Roosevelt. Farm income has increased from less than 2-1/2 billion dollars in 1937 to more than 18 billion dollars in 1947.... Never in the history of any republic or any kingdom or any other country were farmers as prosperous as farmers of the United States, and if they don't do their duty by the Democratic Party, they are the most ungrateful people in the world." Later he broadened the plea to: "If the voters don't do their duty by the Democratic Party, they are the most ungrateful people in the world!" "I need your help," he blurted out.

His aides had recommended an unprecedented gambit to offset the Republican dream ticket:

> The election can only be won by bold and daring steps calculated to reverse the powerful trend now running against us. The boldest and most popular step the President could possibly take would be to call a special session of

Congress early in August. This would: (1) focus attention on the rotten record of the 80th Congress . . . (2) force Dewey and Warren to defend the actions of Congress . . . (3) keep the steady glare of publicity on the Neanderthal men of the Republican Party, which will embarrass Dewey and Warren; (4) split the Republicans on how to deal with such major issues as housing, inflation, foreign policy, etc., and (5) give President Truman a chance to follow through on the fighting start he made on his Western tour.[229]

Truman seized the chance. His staff had painstakingly scrutinized every line in the Republican platform, such as promises to end the housing shortage, trim inflation, and increase social security benefits. He then crunched an uppercut right on the chin of the GOP:

> On the twenty-sixth day of July, which out in Missouri we call 'Turnip Day,' I am going to call that Congress back in session, and I am going to ask them to pass some of these laws they say they are for in their platform, ... to pass laws to halt rising prices, to meet the housing crisis--which they are saying they are for in their platform.

> At the same time I shall ask them to act upon other vitally needed measures, such as aid to education, which they say they are for; a national health program; civil rights legislation, which they say they are for; an increase in the minimum wage, which I doubt very much they are for; extension of the Social Security coverage and increased benefits, which they say they are for; funds for projects needed in our program to provide public power and cheap electricity.

> Now, my friends, if there is any reality behind the Republican platform, we ought to get some action from a short session of the Eightieth Congress. They can do this job in fifteen days, if they want to do it.

He had called the Republicans' bluff, the political equivalent of "put up or shut up!" Truman pounded a wedge at the GOP faultline - between those itching to repeal the New Deal and those who wanted to end the party's heartless, "eat less" image by accepting but transforming New Deal programs.

The crowd ate it up! Truman had to shout into the microphone at the end to make himself heard because the loudest, longest ovation had already started. The previously dispirited Democrats stood on their chairs and roared approval. As one delegate said, "You can't stay cold about a man who sticks his chin out and fights."[230]

The New Republic wrote: "It was fun to see the scrappy little cuss come out of his corner fighting . . . not trying to use big words any longer, but being himself and saying a lot of honest things. Unaccountably, we found ourself on top of a pine bench cheering."[231] A 15-year-old student attendee agreed, "He's really quite dynamic. I hadn't realized it before."

Truman's fighting speech let the Democrats depart on a high note but the finale could not mask the dissension. In a New York World Telegram cartoon, an elephant sat bemusedly in his corner while a donkey pummeled itself continuously with the caption, "Take that and that--you bum!"

The first Gallup Poll after the conventions showed no post convention bounce for the Democrats - Dewey/Warren in front 48% to 37% for Truman/Barkley, Wallace/Taylor 5%, but showed no drop despite the walkout of the Dixiecrats.

POLITICIANS AND TELEVISION ADAPT TO EACH OTHER

Despite snafus, television served the Democratic convention better than the Republican one. The Democratic National Committee had sent mimeographed warnings to speakers and state chairmen: "Millions throughout the country can see as well as hear all convention activities. . . . We must not forget that millions of curious eyes are on us at all times, as well as many more millions of ears turned to the broadcast. Our attention to these points means votes."

Unlike the Republicans whose men came across as unshaven thugs and women as lipless ghosts, the Democrats' makeup artists had plastered on enough pancake to make them look natural in the new medium.[232]

Television cameras caught some historic moments. When the clerk called for vote of the Mississippi delegation which had walked out, the shot of the empty chairs and the coat draped over the abandoned floor mike encapsulated Truman's dilemma. The audience concluded that the new art was here to stay whether viewed in the comfort of home or a noisy tavern.[233]

When Rayburn pounded the gavel to adjourn early on the morning of July 15th, he sounded the end of the old convention, focused solely on the delegates. Future conventions would play to the cameras and the millions of viewers. Television had become not just a medium for reporting the news but for helping to create it.

~

CHAPTER NINE

DIXIECRATS, PROGRESSIVES, CIVIL RIGHTS AND THE TURNIP SESSION

DIXIECRATS

The official name of the departed Southerners was States Rights Democratic Party, but the Charlotte, North Carolina News labeled them – "Dixiecrats." The name stuck. At their one day convention in Birmingham, the day after the Democratic convention adjourned, keynoter Governor Frank M. Dixon of Alabama cursed Truman's civil rights program as a plot "to reduce us to the status of a mongrel, inferior race, mixed in blood, our Anglo-Saxon heritage a mockery." [234]

Condemning the Democrats' "infamous and iniquitous program of equal access to all places of public accommodation for persons of all races, colors, creeds and national origin," the Dixiecrats tried to expand their platform by arguing not racism but states rights against unconstitutional Washington intrusions. One wag said that the motto of the Dixiecrats was "If at first you don't secede, try try again."

They nominated Strom Thurmond for president and Governor Fielding Wright of Mississippi as vice president. Governor Wright had told the Negroes of his state that if they expected "equality" they had better "move to some state other than Mississippi."[235] In his acceptance speech, Thurmond said, "We believe that there are not enough troops in the Army to force the southern people to admit the Negroes into our theaters, swimming pools, and homes."[236]

The Republicans mischievously cheered on the Dixiecrats when possible. In Indiana, for instance, GOP staffers prepared the petitions used to put the Dixiecrats on the ballot, but political realism doomed the Dixiecrats. Regardless of what happened to Truman, southern members of Congress were elected for life because the South really had a one party system. While in Congress, they accumulated seniority that allowed them to stonewall progressive legislation. If they bolted the party, Southerners would lose that seniority and their influence. Moreover, electing Dewey could be doubly disastrous. The Republican platform went even further on civil rights than had Truman, and Dewey had established the nation's strongest civil rights program in New York. So Dixie's solid line soon began to crack.[237]

But as with Wallace, whatever damage inflicted was more than Truman could survive. A Democrat had never won the presidency without the Solid South. Labor became more important than ever as Truman avoided the Deep South.

WALLACE SELF DESTRUCTS

As if the Republicans and Dixiecrats were not making Harry Truman's nights restless enough, Henry Wallace was still thundering from the left. The New Republic of April 19th stated that, buoyed by the Isacson victory, the new party had decided to try for 20 million votes.[238] The Alsop brothers forecast that Wallace would be "wrecking the Democratic Party, at least temporarily . . . and electing the most stodgily conservative Congress in a great many years."[239] In reality, the Progressives were convulsing.

The Czech coup, Berlin crisis, and Truman's shift to the left on domestic issues gutted Wallace's appeal. His keystone appeal had always been that the Soviets were not really the enemy and that only paranoia caused the anti-Soviet hysteria. Stalin's actions, especially the attempt to starve Berlin, corroded Wallace's message.

Charges of communist influence persisted and were largely substantiated. The Americans for Democratic Action (ADA), composed mostly of former high New Deal officials, and the American Federation of Labor (AFofL) and Congress of Industrial Organizations (CIO) condemned his candidacy and repudiated him. The Executive Council of the AFofL even denounced Wallace as a "front, spokesman and an apologist for the Communist Party"[240]

Virtually all prominent New Dealers had deserted them. H.L. Mencken described those who remained as a motley blend of "grocery store economists, money professors in one-building universities, editors of papers with no visible circulation, preachers of lost evangels and customers of a hundred schemes to cure all the sins of the world."[241]

Rowe's memorandum had recommended branding Wallace as a Communist - the kiss of death in 1948. Truman played his role to the hilt. At the end of his statesmanlike March 17 speech in New York, he assumed the role of candidate. "I do not want and I will not accept the political support of Henry Wallace and his Communists. If joining and permitting them to join me is the price of victory, I recommend defeat. These are days of high prices for everything, but any price for Wallace and his Communists is too much for me to pay. I'll not buy it."

On March 29th, Truman ad-libbed that Wallace "ought to go to the country he loves so well and help them against his own country if that's the way he feels."[242]

After that, Truman ignored Wallace but the label stuck as Rowe knew it would. The label brought an often violent response, especially among one of Wallace's primary targets - labor. Internal power struggles against Communists had wracked many labor unions, turning many of them virulently anti-Communist and therefore anti-Wallace. [243]

Wallace helped curdle his appeal. Discussing rural electrification in Salem, Oregon, Wallace announced, "The government should buy up land which can't be served by electricity. If people insist on living on such land, then the government should not let them have children." Soon, after horrified aides had taken him aside, wearing an embarrassed grin and nervously twisting his lapels, he asserted that he really hadn't meant to say what he did. "I have no idea of interfering with anyone's desire to procreate."[244]

So by May, Wallace's campaign gasped and wheezed with conviction - its initial steam and support long gone.

THE PROGRESSIVE CONVENTION

Ten days after the Democrats adjourned, Wallace's Progressive Citizens of America arrived in Philadelphia. Large portraits of Wallace and Taylor replaced those of Truman and FDR.

The convention seemed hell bent to alienate voters. The keynote speaker said that the United States had thrawted Russia's hope for peace. The platform committee repudiated the Marshall Plan, in virtually the same language used by the Communist Party's convention earlier that summer, and then drove away any business support by calling for the nationalization of basic industries.

Wallace himself wanted America to abandon beseiged Berlin, denigrated the Marshall Plan,[245] and accepted a formal endorsement from the Communists. "I would say that the Communists are the closest things to the early Christian martyrs," he said at a press conference. Wallace told reporters not to ask him to repudiate Communist support because he wouldn't -- "so you can save your breath." A Gallup Poll showed that 51% of the voters believed that Communists ran Wallace's party; only 21% disagreed. As Truman remarked, "Poor Henry. He doesn't know what's happening to him."[246]

Commentator Howard K. Smith suggested, "American liberals might consider abandoning the effort to recapture the Democratic Party and start trying to recapture the Progressive Party."[247]

THE FIGHT FOR CIVIL RIGHTS

Truman was caught between Dewey and Wallace wooing Negro votes on one side and southern hotheads on the other.

Truman's proposal for universal military training and a revived draft ran smack into the war against segregation. As one returning Negro corporal explained, "I spent four years in the Army to free a bunch of Frenchmen and Dutchmen, and I'm hanged if I'm going to let the Alabama version of the Germans kick me around when I'm back home. No sirree-Bob! I went into the Army a nigger; I'm coming out a man!"[248] A. Philip Randolph and other Negro leaders grabbed this opportunity to press for military desegregation.

When Congress passed the Selective Service Act without an anti-discrimination clause, Randolph formed a league for nonviolent civil disobedience that vowed to persuade Truman to issue an Executive Order desegregating the armed services before the new act took effect in August.[249]

Many Democrats wanted Truman to forget about civil rights until the campaign ended. He had stalled the legislation to avoid hindering the Marshall Plan. He should do the same with the Executive Order for the sake of the party's chances. Wallace and Randolph would not let him.

Wallace taunted: "If the President's message was more than an attempt to woo votes with lip service, he will issue that Executive Order, and he will issue it without further needless delay."[250]

On July 26, 1948, Harry Truman, the nephew of a Confedrate soldier, whose own mother still condemned Republicans as abolitionists,[251] issued two Executive Orders. E.O. 9980 established the Fair Employment Board to combat discrimination in the hiring, retention and promotion of civil service employees. The more dramatic and more successful E.O. 9981 ended segregation in the armed services. To understand the significance of that order look at the military it changed.

In 1948, the Army had 931 Negro officers, only one senior officer. The Navy had four black officers while 80% of all Negroes were serving as mess attendants. There were no Negro Marines.

Nineteen of the 22 southern senators resoundingly condemned the Orders. Georgia Senator Russell denounced them as an "unconditional surrender . . . to the treasonable civil disobedience campaign organized by the Negroes." The Chicago Defender countered that the Executive Orders were "unprecedented since the time of Lincoln." The newspaper declared that the people would not "permit Mr. Truman to be crucified on a cross of racial bigotry."[252]

THE TURNIP SESSION

The same day Truman dramatically issued his Executive Orders, Congress' special session opened. In contrast to his decisive action, Senators spent 11 minutes in actual session that day.

Not since 1856 had a President called an emergency session of Congress in a presidential election year and never before from a party convention. Republicans groped for appropriate condemnations. Congressman Hugh

D. Scott Jr. of Pennsylvania deplored "the act of a desperate man who is willing to destroy the unity and dignity of his country and his government for partisan advantage after he himself has lost the confidence of the people." Newspaper columnists and editorial writers denounced it as a gross abuse of the Presidential prerogative and dared impeachment. Many found it galling that Truman felt the need to recall Congress, since he was the one who had traipsed around the country for three weeks on his supposedly nonpartisan jaunt while Congress was laboring mightily.

When Truman appeared before the special session the next day, July 27th, Speaker Joe Martin offered the shortest introduction on record: "The Chair presents the President of the United States." Truman urged a broad legislative agenda, similar to the State of the Union Address and received even more icily. Some members did not even stand up as Truman entered and left the chamber. Soon after Truman left, the Republicans announced, "Our efforts will be devoted to completing this session as soon as possible."

While the Turnip Session could not have passed all Truman's measures if it had sat for a year, Newsweek thought that Dewey would have Congress pass some of the GOP platform pledges, including the civil rights program to boost his campaign and further aggravate the southern revolts. Instead, Truman's Turnip Session widened divisions between Taft and Dewey from wary collaboration to barely concealed mutual repulsion.

Vandenberg, Brownell, and Scott wanted to placate the ethnic vote by liberalizing the Displaced Persons Act and to secure the farm vote by passing the international wheat agreement that would provide an export market for 185 million bushels of wheat annually. But Taft said "No! We're not going to give that fellow anything!" [253] If they did, Truman would take the credit. If they did not, it was more fuel for Truman. Truman's move was a political mousetrap - a stroke of political genius.[254]

Taft had the best mind in Washington, until he made it up. After that he gave new meaning to the phrase hardheaded! So resolved was he not to cave into such political blackmail that Taft even fought against his own public housing bill when liberals reported it to the floor.

The Turnip Session lasted 12 days, half of that wasted in a Southern filibuster against a bill outlawing the poll tax. Nothing of consequence was accomplished except authorizating a $65 million loan to finance the building of the permanent headquarters of the United Nations in Manhattan, some controls on credit, and some assistance for housing construction.[255] The Chicago Sun Times editorialized that "Republican strategy was based throughout on the assumption that the voters are stupid and have short memories."[256]

At a press conference on August 12, Truman picked up a reporter's phrase and agreed it had been a "do-nothing" session of a "do-nothing" Congress. The catch phrase of the campaign was born!

The combatants were now all identified and the issues fairly established. At the end of August, Truman boarded the Presidential yacht Williamsburg for a leisurely 9-day cruise in the Chesapeake and Delaware Bays. Even there, he was heckled. As he eased into the dock at Yorktown, Pennsylvania, the boat was overtaken by a small runabout carrying a dozen teenagers shouting "Harrah for Thurmond," and singing Dixie. Unperturbed, Harry Truman resumed his last rest before the most remarkable campaign in American history.

∾

CHAPTER TEN

DOMESTIC COMMUNISM AND THE HISS CASE

A CLAMMY FEAR

Americans in 1948 suffered an almost choking fear of Communism - not just the phobia of Communism abroad, aggressive and expansive, but Communism at home, overt but most ominously covert.

Such molten passions ignited an atmosphere of paranoia and mistrust in which every one was suspect. Anti-Communist militancy swirled through the country egged on by rumor-mongers, and various ad hoc "patriotic" organizations,[257] that columnist I.F. Stone called "the paid hounds of slander." Joe McCarthy merely gave his name to a movement that permeated the postwar era.

1948 witnessed modern witch trials in which paranoid neighbors and co-workers told equally paranoid investigators of suspicious activities. The National Educational Association, the country's leading organization of teachers, voted that Communist teachers should be barred from all schools.[258] In June 1948, the University of California required its four thousand faculty members to swear that they were not Communists. A year later, one hundred fifty seven professors were fired for refusing to take the oath.

To his credit, Wallace stood up for the First Amendment. "The defense of civil rights of the Communists is the first line of defense of the liberties of a democratic people."[259] But it did no good. He was damaged goods arguing on behalf of other damaged goods.

The August 9, 1948, Newsweek reported that in New York's courts, Edmond Kokalas sought to regain custody of his 2 year old daughter from his ex-wife on the grounds that Mrs. Kokalas was a Communist sympathizer. Judge Bertram Newman stated, "If this charge of Communist influence were established, we could not hesitate to change custody. It would be our duty to do so. This child is entitled to be reared as an American under American influences." However, the charge of Communist sympathies was not proven so the mother retained custody. Then, after he stepped off the bench, reporters asked if he would take a child from pro Wallace parents.

He stated firmly, "I believe I would."

A few days later, in New York City, a gray haired Soviet school marm, seeking to avoid return to Russia, gave the West its biggest break in the 3 year propaganda war.

Oksana Stepanovna Kosenkina taught chemistry to children of Soviet officials. Ordered to return to her homeland, she protested to the American authorities. On August 7th, the Soviet Consul General announced that Oksana had been brought to the Consulate "willingly" for her protection. Ignoring a Writ of Habeas Corpus to produce her in court, he alleged the U.S. wanted to kidnap her and, alternatively, that he was rescuing her.

On August 12th, Mrs. Kosenkina proved who did the kidnapping. In a third floor room of the Russian Consulate on 61st Street, she opened a window and jumped. Her body hit some telephone wires, then plunged to the cement courtyard with the wires still wrapped around her legs. Ignoring Russian protests that their own doctor would take care of her, the police took her to Roosevelt Hospital.

Her plunge happened next to the office of Manhattan TV Station WPIX. She plummeted out of the window at 4:19 p.m. WPIX had the film in the cutting room at 6:00, and put part of it on the air at 7:00, and showed the whole film on the 7:30 newscast. Just three hours and eleven minutes after Kosenkina jumped, the station showed a startled audience the biggest national scoop ever scored by video - the complete events from almost the minute of the plunge to her rush to the hospital. The riveted audience saw her lying against an iron grill in the courtyard; the Russians and two New York police officers running to the scene. From her bed she begged to stay in the U.S.

THE HOUSE COMMITTEE ON UNAMERICAN ACTIVITIES

Fearing that Communists had infiltrated the Truman administration, Truman took drastic action. On March 21, 1947, Executive Order 9835 required loyalty boards to screen all federal employees. Political beliefs had become the object of government inquiry. The American Civil Liberties Union called the loyalty program "the most outrageous, undemocratic measure that could possibly be conceived."[260]

Witch hunters could find a great many witches if they defined "Communist" broadly enough. During the 1930's, Stalin's Russia was touted and perceived as the Worker's Paradise rather than the Gulag it was. Many well intentioned Americans found Communism especially attractive because the Great Depression had soured many on capitalism. In the later 1930's, many applauded Russia's standing up to Hitler while the West remained silent. That applause ended abruptly with the 1939 Russo-German Non-Agression Pact, but by then many had already flirted with the temptress.[261]

Intellectual curiosity during the 1930's ended many careers as investigators dredged up old memberships in now suspect groups. The Loyalty program forced the firing of more than 200 individuals and caused the resignation of over 2,000 others on "evidence," often innuendo and anonymous charges, which today shocks the conscience for its lack of due process. Columnist I.F. Stone captioned the most absurd example "The Case of the Legless Veteran," in which membership in one such group got a hapless double amputee veteran fired.[262]

The House UnAmerican Activities Committee (HUAC) became the American version of the Spanish Inquisition. Confusing criminal deeds with free thought, HUAC condemned any deviation from correct American thinking.

The most venomous members, the Chairman, Parnell Thomas (R-N.J.), John Rankin (D-Mississippi) and Karl Mundt (R-South Dakota), abused and harassed witnesses unmercifully. Thomas and Mundt, being partisan Republicans, relished the chance to skewer any past or present Democratic officials. A Democrat, Rankin so hated Negroes and Jews that he grabbed any opening to disparage both, regardless of party affiliation. By comparison with those three, the others members seemed restrained. TIME described HUAC member, Richard Nixon, as "a lank, earnest Quaker attorney" while another reporter called him the "handsome, strong-jawed Republican freshman from California."

In many ways, Truman had instigated this Red-baiting atmosphere. His efforts to "scare the hell out of the people" to enlist their support for his foreign policy, however necessary, had contributed to the anti-communist paranoia.[263] The Loyalty program had put the imprimatur of Presidential concern on the entire movement and legitimized guilt by association. His branding of "Henry Wallace and his Communists" had driven into the Nation's consciousness the fear that Communism was lurking even in the highest levels of the government. If a former vice president, chosen by FDR himself, could become a Communist, then who was safe or, more importantly, who could be free from suspicion.

PRELUDE TO THE HISS CASE – THE COMMUNIST MATA HARI

All these vituperations were mere prelude to the most politicized confrontations in our history.

If the Democrats took over the House, they planned to abolish the HUAC. The Republicans did not tremble at that remote possibility but why take chances? The Committee decided to kill two birds with one set of hearings: show the committee's value by exposing Communists in government and embarrass the Democrats and help win the election in the process.

HUAC used the Turnip Session for a public relations coup. The FBI had offered the Republicans a prime attraction - Elizabeth T. Bentley. Reveling in the most shameless yellow journalism, newspapers pronounced her "blond, beautiful, glamorous," the "Beautiful Blonde Spy Queen" or "the nutmeg Mata Hari." They expected a statuesque Valkyrie. They got a dowdy fireplug. Bentley was rather plump, plain, dumpy, and with a receding chin. She wasn't even blond, but she had been a spy.

She began her soft voiced testimony, her plainness accentuated by the artificial roses pinned in her light brown hair. Her love for a Russian spy ensnared her as a courier in his spy ring in 1941. She collected information from Communists and sympathizers throughout Washington, even the White House. After her lover died late in the war, she ended her treason. [264]

She implicated a Who's Who of about thirty names of Washington insiders. Bentley was the first of two witnesses who would rock the headlines. The second was a paranoid, pudgy ex-Communist. Whittaker Chambers is the most enigmatic figure of 1948.

WHITTAKER CHAMBERS - THE CHARGE

Just three days after Bentley testified, Chambers, a senior editor of TIME, appeared before the committee. He had read Dostoevsky's Crime and Punishment at age 11. That was fitting because Arthur Schlessinger, Jr. labeled him "a figure out of Dostoevsky."[265]

Born on April Fool's Day, 1901 in Philadelphia, Chambers had been an unwanted baby. His mother raised chickens, which Chambers slaughtered, and vegetables, which Chambers peddled, to eke out the family's income. His bisexual father had deserted his mother, a neurotic, for a male lover when Chambers was 9. Two years later, his father returned, but to continued estrangement in an upstairs bedroom. The troubled household also included a demented grandmother, who wandered about the house shouting from windows that they were all trying to gas her. This bizarre family produced two tormented sons. Whittaker formed a suicide pact with his younger brother, Dick. Dick went through with it; Whittaker backed out.

In his rambling and searching youth, Whittaker had been a passionate Communist, but his ardor later cooled. Chambers had begun writing book reviews for TIME and had come to the attention of owner Henry Luce who eventually made him a senior editor. Despite his present enviable job, Chambers remained an anguished neurotic whose thoughts often turned to suicide.

On Tuesday, August 3, 1948, a hot sultry Washington morning, he testified in a wrinkled, baggy, untidy blue serge suit, made even more rumpled because he kept an old pipe in the pocket. Nixon thought Chambers was the most disheveled man he had ever seen. The shy, moon-faced, sad-looking awkward man, with narrow darting eyes, looked at the floor more than the questioner.

A pile of neuroses shoveled into a bad suit, in a droning monotone, Chambers named members of his Communist cell in the 1920s and 1930s, including Alger Hiss, a former high official of the State Department and now president of the Carnegie Endowment for Peace.

The next day's newspapers blared, "TIME editor charges Carnegie Endowment head is Soviet agent." Sam Rayburn moaned, "There is political dynamite in this Communist investigation. Don't doubt that."[266]

ALGER HISS REBUTS

Probably no other cause celebre of the twentieth century swiveled so completely on the credibility of the two antagonists. They became symbols of their convictions. The novelist Arthur Koestler wrote that the Hiss case suffered from "bad casting." The lean Hiss, always arrayed in a tailored suit with a fresh white handkerchief in the breast pocket,[267] was as opposite to Chambers as imaginable. The journalist Murray Kempton, a Harvard classmate, wrote: "I remember Alger Hiss best of all for a kind of distinction that had to be seen to be believed. If he were standing at a bar with the British ambassador and you were told to give a package to the ambassador's valet, you would give it to the ambassador before you gave it to Alger. He gave you a sense of absolute command and absolute grace."[268]

Besides style, Hiss carried impeccable credentials. After graduating cum laude from Harvard Law School and its famed Law Review, he earned a fledgling lawyer's dream job, clerk to the revered Justice Oliver Wendell Holmes.

He entered private practice, then became counsel to the Nye Senate committee investigating the munitions industry. Later, Hiss served in the Department of Agriculture under Henry Wallace, and in the Justice and State Departments. After organizing the Dumbarton Oaks conference and the United States side of the Yalta Conference, he was secretary-general of the San Francisco conference that organized the United Nations in 1945. Hiss resigned from government in 1947 to head the prestigious Carnegie Endowment for Peace. John Foster Dulles himself, the GOP's foreign policy expert, selected him for the Carnegie post. When Hiss left the State Department, Dean Rusk, later Secretary of State under John Kennedy and Lyndon Johnson, replaced him.

So tainted was HUAC's reputation that many of Hiss' friends recommended that he ignore Chambers' testimony and it would soon be forgotten. Others urged him to utter a simple denial but not to force HUAC's attention. HUAC's Republicans were in a spot. Further investigation could embarrass not only Dulles, anointed as the next Secretary of State, but Dewey, his patron. Unfortunately for Hiss, he ignored the advice.

Hiss telegraphed HUAC an ardent denial the day the story appeared in the papers. He asked to appear before the committee and deny the charges publicly. HUAC agreed; so Hiss testified on Thursday, August 5.

The morning Hiss appeared, a Herblock cartoon in the Washington Post portrayed an innocent man in an arena being attacked by a vicious tiger labeled "smear statements," while caricatures of the HUAC members, including Nixon, watched gleefully from the stands.[269]

Hiss cloaked himself as a personification of history who had helped draft some of the Yalta documents. In his brilliant and eloquent testimony, Hiss' denial blended outrage and bafflement.

> I am not and never have been a member of the Communist Party. I do not and never have adhered to the tenets of the Communist Party. I am not and never have been a member of any Communist-front organization. I have never followed the Communist Party line, directly or indirectly. To the best of my knowledge, none of my friends is a Communist. . . .

> To the best of my knowledge, I never heard of Whittaker Chambers until in 1947, when two representatives of the Federal Bureau of Investigation asked me if I knew him and various other people, some of whom I knew and some of whom I did not know.

When asked, "You say you have never seen Mr. Chambers," Hiss replied, "The name means absolutely nothing to me."

When he finished, the credibility of the committee was tattered. It had not expected Hiss' immediate and brilliant denial nor how poor a witness Chambers looked in comparison. When it retired to an antechamber, they all stood in silence until Mundt groaned: "We're ruined!" [270]

HUAC faced two problems. Not only had Hiss' performance been masterful, but that same day, Truman adopted a phrase which entered the political vocabulary. A reporter had asked, "Mr. President, do you think that the Capitol Hill spy scare is a red herring to divert public attention from inflation?" He replied: "Yes, I do."

But forearmed with leaks of other allegations in Hiss' file, Nixon detected Hiss' hair splitting. Hiss did not actually deny that he knew the man who had testified against him nor did he definitely state he did not recognize the photo of Chambers. He simply did not recognize the name "Whittaker Chambers."

NIXON GRABS THE OPPORTUNITY

The Hiss case became a battleground on which two great armies grappled. The case pitted liberals against conservatives in a drama that transfixed the nation. Richard Nixon used Hiss' prostrate form as a steppingstone to the White House, but earned the enmity of the liberal community. The liberals mobilized first, growing bolder after Hiss' bravado performance. They publicly rallied behind him - believing HUAC's foolhardy move in pitting the buffoonish Chambers against the stalwart Hiss would end its influence. As skeptical of Chambers as the liberals, conservatives hesitated to rally around him. They did so only because Nixon forced the issue. Once so mobilized, each side planted its flag beside its champion and pledged to fight to the death.

Nixon had swept the primary in June and was guaranteed re-election. That freed him to investigate the matter. With the zeal of a headline seeking prosecutor, he kept the Hiss case alive when others wanted to drop it like a hot potato. Nixon chaired a subcommittee to grill Chambers in closed session to learn all he knew about Hiss.

On August 7 in Room 101 of the deserted Federal Courthouse in Foley Square New York, Chambers ticked off detail after detail about Hiss, his family and household. Nixon's sixth question was critical. [271]   Did Hiss knew him by the name "Whittaker Chambers?" "No. He knew me by the party name of Carl."[272]

Assuaging the committee's concern that he was motivated by some personal hatred of Hiss, Chambers described Hiss as "a man of great simplicity and a great gentleness and sweetness of character." Chambers related that the Hisses were amateur bird watchers (a fact noted in several biographical reference books), but he added a tantalizing specific. He recalled, "Once they saw, to their great excitement, a prothonotary warbler," rare in the Washington area. Much of Chambers' testimony was wrong or readily available. But he knew enough to convince Nixon. [273]

Fearing that Dulles and the other Republican heavyweights on the Carnegie Endowment Board of Trustees would issue a vote of confidence in Hiss, Nixon raced to New York and showed Dulles the transcript of the supposedly secret interview. Dulles read it and concluded, "It's impossible to believe, but Chamber knows Hiss." He told Nixon that under the circumstances, HUAC would be derelict if it dropped the matter.

Still worried, Nixon drove to Chambers' farm in Westminster, Maryland, on the afternoon of the 9th to verify the facts. He and Chambers talked for more than 2 hours in rocking chairs on the porch of the small farmhouse.

Realizing that his political life could depend on it, Nixon again drove to Chambers' farm on Sunday, August 15th, with Bert Andrews of the New York Herald Tribune. A Pulitzer Prize winning journalist, Andrews had written "Washington Witch Hunt" earlier that summer criticizing HUAC and the unfair firings of State Department employees. Nixon was gaining a neutral observer plus securing a favored partner who would make Nixon a household name by year's end. Chambers' unperturbed answers convinced Andrews of his truthfulness.

At HUAC's executive session the next day, August 16th, no longer coolly self assured, Hiss griped about newspaper leaks of Chambers' supposedly secret testimony and that Chambers, "a confessed former Communist and traitor to this country," should be given credibility.

A dramatic turning point came when the committee asked: "Did you ever see a prothonotary warbler?" Hiss replied, unaware he was corroborating Chambers: "I have, right here on the Potomac."

After a recess, Hiss abruptly stated he thought he could resolve some of the mystery. Both Nixon and Chambers believed that in that brief recess, and especially after some incredulous questioning by F. Edwards Hebert, the committee's most reasonable and respected questioner and a fellow Democrat, Hiss decided that he had denied too long.[274]

After dredging his memory for anyone who could fit Chambers' claim to have lived in Hiss' house during the 1930's, he remembered a ne'er-do-well free-lance writer named "George Crosley." In 1935, Crosley sought information from Hiss, then a Senate counsel, for an article on the munitions industry. Hiss both liked and pitied the man. Because Hiss and his wife were moving at the time and the leases overlapped, they let Crosley, his wife and small child stay in Hiss' apartment a few nights during their move to Washington, lent them some furniture, and let them use a run-down 1929 Ford. The acquaintanceship ended when Crosley never paid rent on the apartment nor returned several small loans.

Hiss again demanded to confront Chambers but emphasized that even if Chambers were Crosley, he never knew him as a Communist agent. The committee promised the long-sought confrontation would occur nine days later.[275]

The next day, Hiss received a cryptic telephone call telling him to report to Room 1400 of the Commodore Hotel in Manhattan for unspecified reasons. Once Hiss arrived, Nixon directed that Chambers be brought into the room.[276]

With the styfling August heat, the committee sat with its back to the windows overlooking 42nd Street. Hiss sat on a chair near the door and Chambers took a seat on a sofa to the side and slightly behind.

Hiss had not looked at Chambers when he entered. Once directed by the committee, the two men stared at one another - Hiss thinking that "I saw Crosley in the added pounds and rumpled suit," but unsure until he heard him speak.[277]

Nixon told Chambers to state his name. Hiss then wanted to hear more of Chambers' voice. Nixon handed Chambers a Newsweek *magazine*, and he began reading aloud. Eventually, Hiss announced he could "positively" identify Chambers as the man he had known as Crosley. And he dared

Chambers to repeat his charges outside the libel-proof forum of HUAC: "I challenge you to do it, and I hope you will do it damned quickly."[278]

Nixon leaked the supposedly secret testimony almost immediately. Newsweek announced that on one vital point clearly it was not Chambers who was lying - Hiss had admitted that he had known Chambers but under a different name.

On August 25th, Dulles asked him to resign from the Carnegie Endowment. That same day, Hiss confronted Chambers in the first major Congressional hearing ever to be televised.

THE PUBLIC CONFRONTATION

More than an hour before the hearing opened, the line of spectators outside the big caucus room circled the rotunda 3 and 4 abreast and stretched far down a corridor. 1,000 managed to squeeze in before the Capitol police shut the door. At 10:15 a.m. HUAC's counsel snapped, "Mr. Hiss, kindly stand up." Hiss rose stoically from the witness chair. "Mr. Chambers, will you kindly stand up too." Hiss turned and glared at Chambers, then Stripling asked, "Mr. Hiss, have you ever seen this individual?" "I have," Hiss replied. "I have identified him." Nixon then seized the questioning and hammered away for 9-1/2 hours, first of Hiss and then Chambers.

Hiss took the offensive by listing the famous people he had worked with in the State Department and especially at the Yalta and the San Francisco conferences. He cited Secretaries of State, Senators, Congressmen, Stassen and Mrs. Roosevelt. By wrapping himself in their eminence, he raised the stakes immeasurably and placed the Hiss case at the center of the nation's attention for years to come. Unspoken but perceptible was the fear that if Hiss were a Communist, then much of post war American foreign policy must be re-examined and, by implication, those who had made it. They were either accomplices or dupes.[279]

After so substantially upping the ante, Hiss fared poorly. TIME's reporting was typical. Hiss "knowing better than anyone that a possible perjury charge hung on his every word, almost never offered a flat yes or a flat no. His favorite phrase, as he fenced tediously with the Committee, was 'to the best of my recollection.' He used it and similar phrases 198 times."

After his first testimony on August 5, Hiss was swarmed with well-wishers. After his August 25 testimony, he stood alone.[280] Public opinion rallied around Chambers.

To regain momentum, Hiss again challenged Chambers to repeat his charges where Hiss could sue him for libel. On August 27, Chambers said ten fateful words on radio's, "Meet the Press," "Alger Hiss was a Communist and may still be one."

Having issued the challenge, Hiss now hesitated. A libel suit can blow up in your face by adding exposure to the original charges. When he did not sue immediately, the Washington Post reminded him he had created "a situation in which he is obliged to put up or shut up," adding "each day of delay [in filing] . . . does incalculable damage to his reputation." [281] The New York *Daily News* asked, in a one-sentence editorial, "Well, Alger, where's that suit?" Newsweek asserted that every day, people were asking, "If Hiss wasn't a Commie, why hasn't he sued Chambers?" Hiss finally sued on September 27th, 1948.

The tide then shifted to Hiss. Truman attacked HUAC's "reckless disregard for the Bill of Rights [which] has injured the reputations of innocent men by spreading wild and false accusations." [282] More importantly, Chambers did not fare well in the pretrial depositions. Hiss' lawyers jackhammered his credibility: spotlighting inconsistencies, inaccuracies and outright lies in his testimonies and effectively questioning his motives, his sordid past, and even his sanity. Chambers' lawyers warned him that if he had anything of Hiss' to buttress his word he had better get it.

Chambers traveled to the home of his wife's nephew. From the shelf of an unused dumbwaiter, he retrieved an envelope "densely covered with the clotted cobwebs and dust of a decade." [283] Within lay a cache he had hidden as a "life preserver" when he broke with the Communist Party. The material included documents and microfilms of papers from the State Department's Trade Agreements Division, in which Hiss had worked. [284]

He split them. The microfilms he hid on his farm, in a legendary hiding place. The papers he took with him.

On November 17th, at a pretrial examination in Baltimore, Hiss' lawyers scoffed: "Do you have any documentary proof of your assertions?" Calmly, blandly, Chambers said: "Only these." He handed over 65 single spaced typed pages of diplomatic cables and cable summaries, and four memos in Hiss' hand summarizing other cables.[285]

The lawyers numbered each document and, for identification, read a few words at the start and the end of each set of papers into the record. "Paris: to the Secretary of State, strictly confidential . . . Signed Bullitt; Rome: To the Secretary of State, I learned in strictest confidence . . . Signed Philips." After an hour of "stunning itemization," Hiss' lawyers sat aghast.[286] The documents disclosed America's 1938 intelligence apparatus.

THE PUMPKIN PAPERS

To discover any more bombshell evidence for himself, Nixon ordered HUAC investigators to Chambers' farm late the night of December 2 with a subpoena. Chambers guided them by flashlight into his pumpkin patch where he fumbled about for a moment, and then pulled out what came to be known as "the pumpkin papers" – five rolls of microfilm wrapped in wax paper, each no larger than a spool of thread. He had hidden them that morning thinking who would ever look in a pumpkin in a pumpkin patch.[287]

Reproducing only part of them created a pile of documents almost four feet high. Several documents bore the notation, "This telegram must be closely paraphrased before being communicated to anyone." The phrase meant that any foreign power that got the exact text of the coded message might break the State Department's most secret Code D.

Displaying an unusual mastery of political intrigue and maneuvering for a freshman congressman, Nixon became front page news. By prearrangement, HUAC staffers flashed the news to Nixon on a cruise ship in the Caribbean where he and his wife were vacationing. Soon at 10:35 a.m. on December 5th, the cruise ship's lifeboat transported Nixon to a Coast Guard amphibious plane in a calm sea. When he landed at Biscayne Bay, Florida at 2:10 p.m, the press had been alerted, so his picture jumping from the plane appeared in newspapers the next morning.

The pumpkin papers skewered Hiss' credibility; as one of President Truman's political intimates remarked years later, "Had Chambers stuck his hand in that pumpkin before the November election, we'd've had Tom Dewey for President."[288]

THE GRAND JURY

Hiss spent eight days, off and on, before the grand jury. The FBI had tracked down Hiss' Woodstock typewriter that had typed the documents disclosed on November 17, along with two of Hiss' personal papers typed on it in 1938. Prosecutors asked Hiss how he could explain the matching typewriter evidence which corroborated Chambers' testimony. Hiss weakly suggested that Chambers had somehow gotten into his home and typed the copies himself. The jury did not believe him.[289]

As a light snow fell outside the New York Federal Courthouse, on the last day of their tenure, the grand jurors trooped to Judge John Clancy's courtroom. The jurors considered Chambers unstable and abnormal, as one prosecutor confided to a Hiss lawyer, but by a majority of one, they indicted Hiss on two counts of perjury.

The next morning, dressed in pajamas, Hiss opened the door of his Manhattan apartment, with his 7-year-old son Tony following him. At the door stood a group of newsmen. Tony asked his father, "Who are all these men? Why do they keep coming?!" Hiss replied, "I wish I could explain it."

At the first trial, the jury failed to reach a verdict, but a second trial convicted Hiss at in January 1950. At both trials, Chambers' sanity was a predominant issue. Hiss was sentenced to five years in prison and was paroled in 1954, still maintaining his innocence.

AFTERMATH

Despite the Hiss triumph, HUAC had a so-so year. The November election slashed its GOP members but even those re-elected did not fare well. Two days after Parnell Thomas' re-election, a federal grand jury summoned him on charges that he had demanded kickbacks from his employees. While running HUAC, Thomas was often frustrated by witnesses who invoked the Fifth Amendment right against self-incrimination. In August, HUAC had proposed limiting that right. On November 4, he himself refused to testify on the ground that it might incriminate him and stomped out of the jury room. Indicted four days later, he was soon convicted of receiving kickbacks and for conspiracy to defraud the government. Sent to the Federal Penitentiary at Danbury, Connecticut, Thomas joined other figures that HUAC had ruined.

Hiss' guilt or innocence is irrelevant from a national historic view. What matters most is the case's impact on the country. Most Americans had traditionally griped about government officials, questioning their intelligence and even their honesty but never their patriotism. The citizens' view of their government was forever changed.[290]

~

CHAPTER ELEVEN

1948 – THE TELEVISION YEAR

THE DECLINE OF RADIO – THE ADVENT OF TELEVISION

As the year began, radio was king with 75 million sets in use. Not every home had electricity, but those that did had a radio around which the family gathered for news and entertainment. Radio was national then, and the whole country tingled to the croonings of its favorite singers, roared with its favorite comedians, and shuddered to its favorite dramas.

Television was hardly a blip on the screen, for two reasons. First, television sets were expensive, approximately 10 percent of the average annual wage. Second, for those brave souls willing to shell out such a princely sum, there was not much to see. Vast areas of the country had no reception. In 1947, television had been a truant, with prime time blank for days.

In January, NBC prophetically took out full page ads in newspapers and magazines announcing "1948 - TELEVISION'S YEAR" and described it as the greatest mass communication device in history. Radio did not realize it, but 1948 was its transition year. Rarely does one year encompass so clearly the time in which a dominant technology is so completely dethroned by an upstart.

Inaugurating its television section on May 24, TIME predicted: "Chances are that it [television] will change the American way of life more than anything since the Model T." Television's enthusiasts boasted that it would eventually make radio as obsolete as the horse--and empty all the nation's moviehouses. Children will go to school in their own living rooms, presidential candidates will campaign from a television studio. Housewives will see on the screen the dresses and groceries they want, and shop by phone.

Nothing showed the transition better than what happened to Bob Hope. His top rated radio show had become stale – still heavy with a World War II theme. He revamped the show, adding singer Doris Day and comedian Hans Conreid.[291] His new show won great reviews, but it premiered on the same Tuesday that Milton Berle became the permanent host of TV's Texaco Star Theater.[292] Hope's ratings suffered mightily.

Hope's and the other top rated radio shows - Jack Benny, George Burns and Gracie Allen, Duffy's Tavern, Perry Como, Amos and Andy, Ozzie and Harriet - all soon shifted to TV. Radio's The Candid Microphone of Alan Funt soon became TV's Candid Camera. The shows that premiered on radio that year soon sequed to TV, where they became part of the nostalgia of the baby boomers: "This is Your Life" with Ralph Edwards, "Our Miss Brooks" with Eve Arden, and "My Favorite Husband" with Lucille Ball and Gale Gordon which evolved into "I Love Lucy."

Radio would survive but differently. Television changed where radio came from and where it went, dislodging it as the premium entertainment medium and relocating it physically from the center of the home to the beach and the car. Moreover, its days as a national system ended. It became an outlet for local shows and commercials.

Watching TV was almost certainly a communal experience. Most Americans first experienced TV, other than the glance in the window of the appliance store, at an affluent neighbor's house or at the local tavern. Owners of appliance stores scored big as people clustered around their store windows to watch TV. Downtown theater owners were the big losers.

FEARS

Although radio and TV were both vying for the same audience, no institutional animosity split the two. Individual radio performers like Fred Allen might snipe at the new medium, but radio's owners were TV's biggest fans, because the same people, NBC, CBS, and ABC, owned both the radio and the TV networks. They would like nothing better than for TV to succeed. It was the film industry that feared this new rival. Since the film industry was headquartered in Hollywood and the radio/TV industry sprang from New York, a bicoastal rivalry developed.

Movie stars spurned TV for two seemingly opposite reasons: fear of failure and fear of success. The stars feared that the new medium would flop and taint them. The movie studios worried that having their stars appear would boost TV's success and kill its theater market. For that reason, TV viewers would not see fresh, first class Hollywood films anytime soon.

A survey confirmed that people's habits drastically changed once they bought television sets. 92.4 percent listened to less radio; 80.9 percent cut their moviegoing; 58.9 percent read fewer books, 48.5 percent fewer magazines; 23.9 percent even cut back on newspaper reading. (But over 70 percent reported more visitors.) [293] One publisher's counsel groaned that television had become "a devastating competitor" to books in particular and to all culture in general.

Experts debated whether TV would eventually put the movies out of business. Some suggested that movie houses show TV in place of the second feature in order to survive. But others believed that the tube would boost business for Hollywood as a hawker and as a customer. A movie executive predicted, "Through television broadcasts, we will come into your home to show you just enough of a picture to make you hungry for the rest of it." The Television Research Institute estimated that TV would need "3 to 4 times the total annual input of the U.S. film industry."[294] Eventually Hollywood might have to spend at least half its time on films that television could afford. That would be a long time coming, however. Television's purse could not match its appetite.

In 1948, TV stations ran on shoestring budgets. By mid-year, only one American in ten had seen a television program. So, advertisers shied away from the new medium. That created a double whammy, because the TV technology was very expensive and required remodeling to remake an old theater into a television studio. Such financial constraints meant that, as one critic complained as the year began, TV programming was "ill conceived, awkward and dull."

Take Truman's State of the Union speech. TIME magazine in its January 19 issue described what had been on TV that day under the title "A Day with Television." [295]

Live coverage began with Truman's address on three major networks - NBC, CBS and DuMont. During the speech, the camera focused on Truman's face, with only occasional glimpses of his audience. When he finished, NBC and

DuMont signed off for the rest of the afternoon (daytime programming was rare), while CBS switched to a supermarket in Jackson Heights, Queens, for a shopping show called "Missus Goes A-Shopping," highlighted by children imitating animals.

At 5 p.m., the other networks returned with kiddy fare. NBC presented "Playtime," with a woman, "Popit Hostess," dressed as a clown who introduced short films, a picture tour of Italy, a lesson in how to make beanies out of felt, and a marionette show. DuMont offered the popular "Small Fry Club."

From 7:30 to 8 p.m., NBC presented classical music but no picture except for the station's name and cards advertising coming attractions. The musicians union barred its members from being shown on television. At 8 p.m., NBC featured "Americana" a quiz show. DuMont switched to a grade B movie. NBC rebounded with "Kelvinator Kitchen," which demonstrated how to prepare Oysters Rockefeller. Actually, the show was really a quarter hour commercial as the cook prominently used Kelvinator products the entire time. Few other ads appeared throughout the day.

From that kinetic blend of clowns, hucksters and B movies, by the end of the year, television muscled itself into a major force in entertainment and politics.

Originality was risky and expensive. So producers searched for shows that were popular, cheap and ideally suited for the fledgling technology - one stationary camera could catch all the action confined within a small area, something like a boxing ring!

TV AND SPORTS

Boxing, wrestling, tennis and other sports that are contested in a small area could be almost as good on the screen as on the spot. So boxing became a staple of television, airing on NBC on Monday nights, 9:00 to conclusion; on Tuesdays on DuMont from 9:00 to 11:00; on Wednesdays on DuMont from 9:00 to 11:00, and on Fridays on NBC from 9:30 to conclusion. Many fights were high caliber; others featured two tomato cans who bled from the first punch onward. One fight and one fighter was a must see event.

On June 25, Joe Louis defended his heavyweight championship against "Jersey Joe" Walcott. Champion for a record 11 years and 3 days, the legendary Louis had won a split decision over Walcott on December 5, 1947, but only after Walcott had floored him twice, to the astonishment of the crowd. The rematch was billed as Louis's last fight.

For the most part, the fight stunk. As TIME said, "The only thing that saved it from being the worst heavyweight championship fight in history was the 11th round." In that round, Walcott flung a left and a loop right and that gave Louis the opening. He partially paralyzed Walcott with a right on the temple. Walcott backed into the ropes. Then time seemed to stand still as the aging champion, for a few seconds the Louis of old, hit him at will and dissected him with a flurry of lefts and rights. Walcott pitched forward on his face. It was Louis' 22nd knockout victory and 25th title defense.

Only 42,667 people saw the fight from their seats at Yankee Stadium but 86.6% of all TV sets in the 7-city East Coast NBC network were tuned into the fight. Six million homeviewers and bar flies totaled the biggest fight audience in history. [296]

Wrestling pinned down more and more fans thanks to a flamboyantly effeminate extrovert. A good wrestler but a great showman, George Wagner so preferred the ring name "Gorgeous George" that he had it legalized. Exuding vanity, sartorial splendor, and swishiness, Gorgeous George not only revived a languishing sport, he sold an enormous number of sets. He wrestled almost every night, so set buyers got plenty of return on their investment. [297]

Gorgeous George and his imitators took the nation by storm on four networks. Wrestling began in earnest on July 30, when it premiered on Fridays on the DuMont network from 9:00 until it concluded. It became so popular that ABC showed it on Wednesdays from 9:30 until its conclusion. Not to be outdone, NBC aired it on Tuesday in October from 10:00 to conclusion, and Dumont put it on Thursdays from 9:00 to conclusion. Soon gladiators like Gorgeous George, Argentina Rocca and the Mighty Atlas became household names.

Sports enticed bars and grills to be television's first major customers. Bars could use the expensive sets to draw thirsty sports hungry patrons. Bar TVs generally turned on at 7:00 p.m. when network programming began and business improved. Bartenders reserved screenside seats for regular customers. By late 1947, an estimated 12,000 sets glared at drinkers in Manhattan alone. Fred Allen quipped, "There are millions of people in New York who don't even know what television is. They are not old enough to go into saloons yet." [298]

That wasn't always true. In Patrick Radigan's Hoboken saloon before 6 p.m., he shooed the drinkers out and waved children in. They climbed on the bar stools, or sat on, around, under the tables to watch Radigan's television to see DuMont's Small Fry Club, WATV's Junior Frolics and others. At 7, he swept out the children again and let the profitable customers return. Unfortunately, the New Jersey Beverage Control Commission ruled that he was not licensed to run such a nursery and stopped it.

MILTON BERLE

Sports events and shows that gave scores, commentary, and interviews with star athletes proliferated. Sports occupied a quarter of television's programming, not because it was good, but because everything else was so bad. As the year progressed, the variety on TV improved - Thanks primarily to a middle aged vaudevillian. The Modern Age came in the form of Uncle Miltie.

On May 19, 1948, the William Morris Talent Agency placed a two page ad in the Entertainment Trade Weekly Variety:

> "Vaudeville is back.
>
> The golden age of variety begins with the premiere of the Texaco Star Theater on television, Tuesday, 8:00 to 9:00 p.m. E.D.T., starting June 8th on NBC and its affiliated stations in New York, Washington, Boston, Philadelphia, Baltimore, Richmond, and Schenecktady. WANTED-- variety artists from all corners of the globe. Send particulars to the William Morris Agency."[299]

Since the right host was vital, the network decided to test several through the summer. On Tuesday June 8, 1948, Milton Berle was the first host, followed in the summer by Henny Youngman, Morey Amsterdam, Jack Carter and others, but clearly Berle was the best. He became permanent MC in September. Newsweek had been prescient. In June, it wrote that big name stars were moving into video very slowly and mostly experimentally. "This week, NBC is putting the Texaco Star Theater on its six station east coast network. . . . Little more than an hour long vaudeville bill, in its first four weeks it will be MC'd by an old vaudevillian, Milton Berle, whose facial antics were, of course, invisible on radio but may be a natural for television."

Berle began performing as a toddler and by the age of 8, in 1916, had appeared in over 50 films. He broke into vaudeville and at 21 became the youngest person to headline at the Palace Theater in New York, but he had never hit it very big in radio or the movies. He had brought down the house at an auction televised by Dumont on April 7th. Encouraged, Berle sought the Texaco Master of Ceremonies job.

The first comedian to have a show on national television in prime time, Berle was so unsure of television that while he did his TV show Tuesdays, he did a weekly radio show Wednesday nights just to be safe. Read that last sentence again because you probably missed its significance. Berle was worried not only that he would bomb, but that television would flop. Today we view TV's success as inexorable. On the contrary, Berle and many others, whose livelihood depended on their judgment of the public's taste, had qualms. TV was expensive, not very good and potentially dangerous. Americans feared the glare and magazine articles reported that the radiation might be fatal. Big stars would not risk going on TV. Only someone like Berle, still hungry, would!

Reviewers hailed his June 8th opening as "television's first real smash." TV and his personality had meshed perfectly. His split second ad libbing, audience rapport, and infallibly hammy showmanship clicked. He forced the medium to expand. Cameramen told him to stand still for long periods, then move to a prearranged mark, and then stand there. Realizing that he would be the one hailed or ruined by the show, not the cameramen, Berle told them, forget the "marks." "You follow me wherever I go as I react to the audience."

Pioneering close camera positioning, the show placed the camera on stage, not out in the studio audience. TV viewers loved the resulting close-ups that theaters could not match. Camera positioning also changed the performance. The monitor-less studio audience had to look around the cameras to see the performers. With those obstructions and without any applause signs to cue the studio audience, Berle had to exaggerate his actions to make sure the audience saw them and laughed. The public loved the extra hamminess.

Soon 80.7% of home televisions were tuned to the Texaco show. No one in radio had ever reached such numbers. So many children stayed up to watch his show that, in response to parents' pleas, he spoke to the kids. "Listen to Uncle Miltie. Go to bed right after the show." Uncle Miltie was born!

He so owned Tuesday that theaters and restaurants sat empty. People who did not have television sets visited those who did.[300] In Detroit, officials discovered water reservoir levels took a drastic drop on Tuesday nights between 9:00 and 9:05 p.m. Everyone waited until the show ended before going to the bathroom. A theater manager in Ohio hung a poster in the lobby: "Closed Tuesday. I want to see Berle too." A laundromat at Brighton Beach installed a TV set and advertised: "Watch Berle while your clothes whirl."[301] By November, 94.7% of all the TVs in use at that time were tuned to Milton Berle.

Berle doubled the sale of TV sets in a year. Fellow comedians turned green with envy. Joe E. Lewis carped: "Berle is responsible for more television sets being sold than anyone else. I sold mine, my father sold his, . . ."[302]

ED SULLIVAN

On June 20, 1948, 12 days after Berle debuted, Toast of the Town premiered, on CBS on Sundays from 9:00 to 10:00, with Ed Sullivan, a newspaper and radio gossip columnist

Headlining Dean Martin and Jerry Lewis, the new talent that the show sought, the show was broadcast over six stations. NBC competed with Senator Taft in a preconvention interview from Philadelphia.

Viewers liked the show, but no papers bothered to review it. Eventually, John Crosby wrote a review in the December 31, 1948 New York Herald Tribune. He liked the show but not Sullivan, asking, "Why is Ed Sullivan on [TV] every Sunday night?" "The CBS show is marked by an elegance that the Texaco Star Theater doesn't have and doesn't seem to want. You find upper class night club acts on Toast of the Town, where Star Theater sticks pretty closely to good old rowdy vaudeville."

Obviously, the nation liked the high brow stuff too! Sullivan followed with ballet, opera, plays, jugglers, magicians. People who had never ventured further than their county seat could now view the best of Broadway, the Metropolitan, or London from the comfort of their easy chair. Later renamed the Ed Sullivan Show, it lasted twenty years. Like Berle on Tuesdays, Sullivan dominated Sunday night and altered the nation's habits. He was not a performer and had awkward gestures, a high pitched New York accent, a strange stance, and body language that defied description but which would keep impersonators busy for decades. It took Fred Allen, the radio impresario, to put his finger on the reason for Sullivan's success: "Ed Sullivan will stay on television as long as other people have talent."[303]

OTHER LEGENDARY BEGINNINGS

It is a truism that the first renditions of a new technology look like the old. Just as the first automobile looked like a carriage, the first TV programs looked like radio shows. Simulcasts were born. CBS began broadcasting simultaneously the radio performance of Arthur Godfrey's Talent Scouts, Monday 8:30 to 9:00 EST. Simulcasts were cheap but usually failed. This one came off because, although lacking musical, singing and acting talent, Godfrey had a natural television personality.

An easy going conversationalist and raconteur, he became a welcome guest in millions of homes for years and not just once a week. He achieved the near impossible - two top rated shows at the same time: one in prime time, one in daytime.[304] In the beginning, however, Godfrey realized his priorities and kept his radio show. "40 million people listen to us on the radio. We're not going to louse that up in order to please a few thousand who can see us."

On December 24, the Chesterfield Supper Club with Perry Como premiered in the Friday 7:00 - 7:15 time slot. One of the hottest properties in show business, Como had a four-year string of hit records and an NBC radio series to his credit.

As it did with Godfrey, the network simply simulcast Como's popular radio show and made few concessions to the new medium. Cameras simply showed the performers in front of the microphone, scripts and all. The basic format remained Perry's easygoing crooning, often of his latest hit record, with interludes by regulars and assorted guest stars.[305] Como stayed in the top ten for years.

Aside from such jewels, television mostly offered a bland smorgasbord: man on the street interviews, cooking lessons, charades, fashion shows, illustrated weather forecasts, other simulcasts, and faded old B movies. Quiz programs proliferated where prizes and antics reached a fever pitch.

CHEAP SHOWS

Radio was terrific for sound based entertainers such as singers and joke telling comedians. Sight based performers, such as dancers, jugglers, magicians, and slapstick comedians had been shut out. Television unleashed the video equivalent of the Oklahoma land rush, serving a kinetic stew of visual based performers.

Variety shows proliferated. Many were talent scout shows, such as Ted Mack's The Original Amateur Hour, because established stars were reluctant to appear. So star wannabees were cheap (free) and plentiful.

Original stories were rare, so writers adapted plays, books and short stories to television's physical limitations and its thirty to sixty minute format. The fear of established stars to appear, plus television's voracious appetite, was a godsend to young unknown actors such as Paul Newman, Walter Matthau, Julie Harris, Rod Steiger, Charlton Heston, and Marlon Brando.[306]

News and public affairs shows also sprouted, not because the nation had become high brow but because these talking heads were cheap. Reporters reading headlines from wire service copy needed only a chair, a table and an occasional map, cartoon, or still photograph. All the networks had regular news shows in 1948, normally only 10 or 15 minutes long.

TV AND CHILDREN

Newsweek reported, "Wherever there is a television set, there usually is also a child. And as the past generation grew up accepting radio as standard fare, so is this generation accepting video." The Architectural Forum announced that a television set was better than hashish in calming active children. Television had treated its young viewers far more responsibly than radio ever did, developing real children's programs.[307]

The first smash success in children's video was the Small Fry Club on DuMont, Monday through Friday, 6 to 6:30 p.m. EST. Run by Big Brother Bob Emery, this gentle show stressed education and interaction rather than mindless prattle. Brother Bob mixed slides, silent films which he narrated, a puppet who taught lessons on good behavior, safety, drinking more milk, etc.; sketches by a studio cast of actors representing different animals, and whatever else Emery thought would tickle and sometimes inform his children. It was simple, friendly, sprinkled with commercials, and the kids loved it. His young listeners flocked to obtain official membership cards, wrote him letters, during which he would gleefully show their pictures, sent pictures and drawings, and joined in contests.[308]

Right behind the Club in popularity came a show that got an unusual boost. Remember that mammoth snowstorm I talked about in Chapter 1? That helped make Howdy Doody a household name.

Puppet Playhouse premiered at 5:00 p.m. on Saturday right, after Christmas, 1947. It started to snow on Friday and didn't stop for 24 hours. The following Tuesday, a review in Variety catapulted it to fame. The storm kept hundreds of thousands of people indoors. For those with a TV set, Puppet Playhouse had mesmerized their children at what is normally the most boisterous time of the day. As Variety noted, "In the middleclass home, there is perhaps nothing as welcome to the mother as something that will keep the small fry intently absorbed and out of possible mischief. This program can almost be guaranteed to pin down the squirmiest of the brood." By the end of January, the show was so popular that it began broadcasting on Thursdays and Saturdays. By the end of March, the show was on Tuesdays, Thursdays and Saturday.

The show lacked sponsors so NBC paid for the show itself. Despite the show's success, it took three months for ads to appear. The first touted a Polaroid television filter, a plastic screen to place on the television set to cut down the glare. Then Colgate Corporation signed on, then Continental Baking, makers of Wonder Bread, then Ovaltine, then Mars Candy. By April 1948, the program was sold out for two years ahead, with two sponsors every day. Colgate even advertised an adult product, Halo Shampoo, on the show, because it was selling more of the product on Puppet Playhouse than on the Colgate Comedy Hour.

The show became the Howdy Doody Show to capitalize on the name recognition. To tie in with the election, on March 4th, Howdy decided to run for "President of the kids" against the mysterious Mr. X, Howdy's twin brother--Double Doody. As the election progressed, the show taught children about the country. It talked about cheese-making in Wisconsin and the coal mines of Pennsylvania, while host Buffalo Bob Smith would explain what a democratic election was all about.

On March 23rd, Smith offered a Howdy Doody campaign button to anyone writing to one of the five stations that carried the program. The next day, 6,000 letters inundated the mailroom. NBC's affiliates received 8,000 letters in Philadelphia, 6,000 in Baltimore, 3,000 in Washington. Five more offers in the next 10 days brought another 35,000 requests. A week later, the total had reached 60,000, and the mailroom refused to accept any more. Elated, NBC boasted to sponsors that 60,000 requests represented one-third of the estimated working television sets. Meanwhile, so many stores had been flooded with requests for a Howdy Doody doll that manufacturers contacted the studio. The first tie-in of TV and merchandising was born.

COMMERCIALS

The year began with General Foods Corporation announcing it would increase its television advertising. But how to do it? In mid February, TIME magazine reported that television commercials' primitive or prosaic attempts to combine eye-catching and ear-catching produced a strange blend of sight and sound. The camera focused unblinkingly on a bar of Ivory Snow while an announcer extolled its fragrant virtues and foamy lather. Oranges cracked jokes, penguins smoked cigarettes, cigarettes danced. Disembodied hands proliferated, pouring a cup of tea or snapping on a Ronson lighter. TIME described live mishaps like the woman who extolled Lipton's Tea while she brewed a pot with the sponsor's Tender Leaf.[309]

The $10 million paid by television advertisers still paled along side radio's $447 million; but TV steamrolled forward. In November, NBC announced that in the previous 90 days it had doubled its TV sponsors. The number of sponsors jumped nearly 800% in one year.

TECHNOLOGY

For TV to succeed, not only the programming had to improve. Prices had to drop and reception had to clear up. Television prices began the year around $300, but elaborate mahogany consoles could retail for $4,000. With median family income just over the $3,000 mark, not many families could spend a tenth of their annual earnings on an unproven, nonessential appliance. Soon RCA came out with a seven-inch set for $180, which put television within the reach of at least the upper middle class. The crude technology made the "snow" on many pictures so bad it might as well have been broadcast in an actual blizzard. Most television pictures were only five inches wide so their subjects looked like mug shots. To switch a camera from long range to close up, often the cameraman would manually shift the lens on live TV. Fred Allen quipped, "I haven't bothered much about television . . . I think the men who used to take passport pictures are now the cameramen."

The technology was so primitive as 1948 began that any development substantially advanced the art. Television improved primarily because of the political conventions. TV producers had the lead time to set up, and because all three conventions would be held in the same city and the same hall - they could go to more effort than usual.

The proof of the progress came in December. Some 2 million people in Boston, Baltimore, Philadelphia and New York saw ABC's telecast of the

Metropolitan Opera's Othello. None of the many cameras involved could obstruct the view of the audience, so to get enough light in the darkened opera house, special infrared "black light," invisible to the audience had to be installed. The New York World Telegram gushed: "It was an experiment on a grand scale, and it succeeded beyond all hopes."

GROWTH

After years of promise, television had joined the airplane and radio as the 20th century's third major contribution to communication. The networks raced to match the public's demand. Each week brought new stations, new programs, and new types of receivers. In the early spring, 26 commercial stations were on the air but 16 of them east of the Alleghenies. Of the 325,000 sets in the nation, half were clustered around the New York metropolitan area. In May, the New York area gained its fourth television station while Boston gained its first. TV moved west. The August 9, 1948, Newsweek reported that 31 stations now aired in 20 cities, with 24 more due by the end of the year. Chicago's new station WGN opened. ABC TV announced its new station in Detroit. In November, Seattle had its first commercial broadcast.

NBC dominated television, operating a six station network in the east and in September, NBC's Midwest coaxial cable network began operating connecting Chicago, St. Louis, Detroit, Milwaukee, Toledo, Buffalo, and Cleveland. NBC planned to have regional television networks operating by late fall and coast to coast telecasts in early 1949. A new east-middle west network would begin functioning January 12th.[310]

The epidemic demand had manufacturers scrambling to keep TV sets on the market. Television makers had dreamed of making 600,000 sets but turned out 800,000. By year end, they were working at a 2 million a year clip. Radio production dropped 24% under 1947. By November, 718,000 sets glared in homes and bars and more were being installed at the rate of 1,000 a day. One million television sets were sold in 1948, 7-1/2 million in 1949. [311] Only 2.9% of the people owned TVs in 1948, the first year statistians kept count. The next year it soared to 10.1%.

Not only the programming expanded; so did the hours. Except for some ball games and kiddie shows, television had been a nighttime operation. In the fall, DuMont, weary of all the wasted daytime hours and the lost advertising revenue, announced that in October its New York station would run from 7 a.m. until after the wrestling matches Monday through Friday. Station owners would now be able to amortize their capital costs over more shows.

Televison benefitted from better shows, better technology and the baby boom. With infants and toddlers at home, parents had to stay home more than they otherwise would. (The word "baby-sitting" doesn't appear in dictionaries of the time [312] although the practice was starting - $.25 an hour was considered a generous rate.)[313] This self-imposed confinement harmed the downtown movie theaters but increased the appetite for TV. The move from the farms to the cities and suburbs concentrated people so TV could more easily reach them. A number of hotels already had installed televisions and hiked their room rates as much as $3 a night. Out of town familes sat mesmerized in front of the screen.

THE RESULT

Everything about television loomed large including its losses. In 1948, the entire industry lost $15 million. Not one station made a profit. NBC's network lost an estimated $13,000 a day. But with all that, television continued to snowball. The combination of improved programming and cheaper sets meant more people wanted and could buy sets. That increased demand sparked the desire for more stations on which sponsors fought for air time. As the stations multiplied, the cost of the technology decreased. Its eventual profitability was obvious. An unstoppable momentum had begun.

In one year, TV had elbowed its way up the entertainment ladder. No other force changed the nation's habits so quickly: how Americans got their news, spent their evenings, scheduled their events. Viewed from any angle, 1948 marked the beginning of a long quick descent of radio against the spiraling ascent of television, even though the latter was still unavailable to much of the country.

In Chicago in mid December, Mrs. Ruth Wellborn divorced Orin Wellborn. The settlement awarded her the family television set. This was the first

Chicago court recognition of video's cultural position. Had the Wellborns been divorced 6 months earlier, the set, if any, would probably not have been contested. As its first big year ended, television had left the toy or luxury class for the necessary appliance category.[314]

Radio columnist John Crosby wrote in his concluding column for the year, "All in all it's been a turbulent year, 1948. If I weren't mildly suspicious of the word, I'd say it was the beginning of an epic and the end of another."

CHAPTER TWELVE

THE BERLIN AIRLIFT - CONFRONTING STALIN

THE INTERNATIONAL POLITICAL SCENE

Truman worried over what would later be called the "Domino Theory." Ironically, so did Stalin. While the Truman Doctrine, the Marshall Plan and the planned reforms for Germany upset Stalin, he was apparently more concerned about an incipient revolt from behind the Iron Curtain by Tito of Yugoslavia. A loyal Communist but also a devout nationalist, Tito had liberated his nation from the Nazis without Stalin's help and approval. He saw no need for them now.[315]

Stalin called a special Cominform meeting that denounced Tito and his Yugoslav comrades. It warned them to end their anti-Soviet opinions or face expulsion from the party and office for "taking the route of nationalism." The Yugoslavs responded by giving Tito a vote of confidence and expelling all Cominform supporters. Stalin threatened: "I shall shake my little finger and Tito will be no more." But Stalin's attempt to overthrow him failed.

So in June, while Stalin was trying to choke dissent within the Iron Curtain, the Allies challenged Soviet control in Germany. Stalin reacted in Berlin with the blockade and in Eastern Europe with bloody purges to exterminate would-be Tito's. [316]

Meanwhile, in the House of Commons, on June 30, Foreign Minister Ernest Bevin stated: "We cannot abandon those stouthearted Berlin democrats who are refusing to bow to Soviet pressure."

> We recognize that, as a result of these decisions, a grave situation might arise. Should such a situation arise, we shall have to ask the House to face it. His Majesty's government and our western allies can see no alternative between that and surrender, and none of us can accept surrender.[317]

No one knew better than the Berliners the severity of the Soviet threat and

147

the precariousness of their plight. Their hopes depended on pilots and planes that only a few years before had bombed Berlin.

THE AIRLIFT GATHERS STEAM

On July 5, ten Sunderland flying boats of the RAF joined the transport fleet. Shuttling to Lake Havel adjoining Gatow Airfield, neither fog nor floating debris kept the Sunderlands from flying over 1,000 sorties, carrying in 4,500 tons of food and taking out 1,113 starving children until ice floes on the lake halted operations on December 15th. They also presented one other intangible but real benefit. Seeing these flying boats land and take off boosted the morale of the Berliners, who visited and picnicked at the lake just to see their operations.[318]

In the first 19 days of Operation Vittles, about 350 flights daily had flown in more than 13,000 tons. More planes continued to arrive. After two Navy C-54 squadrons landed, within three weeks, the U.S. total had risen to over 1,500 tons a day. Air Force officers sported calling cards labeled "LeMay Coal & Food Company," guaranteeing "round the clock service via the Airlift."

Ingenuity cut the load. Loaves of bread were one third water so the allies just sent flour; boning meat sliced weight by a quarter. These proxies plus dried eggs, dried milk and other substitutes cut minimum daily food requirements from 2,000 to 1,000 tons and became staples of the Berlin diet.[319]

Potatoes permeated the German diet but were bulky and heavy. The airlift substituted dehydrated potatoes or POM, used by the British Army, and saved 780 tons a day. When mixed with water, POM turned into a creamy substance close enough to potatoes to make a nourishing soup.

Berliners willingly accepted the substitutes. Many women had bitter memories of 1945, when the invading Russian soldiers had demanded "woman-come" as the foreplay to a rape. So the expression in 1948 was "better POM than 'Frau, komm.'"

Nevertheless, on July 9th, the New Statesman and Nation in London stated: "But every expert knows that aircraft, despite their immense psychological effect, cannot be relied upon to provision Berlin in the winter months." [320]

On July 10th, Clay again asked to ram his armed column through but was denied. Secretary Forrestal pointed out that the nation's ground troops amounted to slightly over two divisions, of which only one could be committed with any speed. So any attempt at a land threat would be instantly dismissed as a bluff. The trump card would have to be the atomic bomb, used immediately.

To "up the ante" and insure the Soviets would not risk shooting down the planes, on July 15th, Truman ceremoniously transferred to England sixty B-29 super fortresses, the planes that could carry the atomic bombs. The B-29s could not break the Berlin blockade, but they dramatically increased the threat of Allied retaliation.

THE BERLINERS

On the night of July 24, a C-47 hit a roadblock along the approach to Templehof and crashed on the doorstep of an apartment house in downtown Berlin, killing the two airmen crew. The Russians milked the tragedy's propaganda value, decrying how the Airlift endangered the inhabitants. But the crash pained the fiercely independent Berliners who felt a personal loss. The mayors of the six boroughs in the U.S. sector personally expressed their condolences. Tagesspiegel editorialized that "An airman who crashes in the course of supplying Berlin is more than a transport pilot who has died in an accident; he is a man who has given his life for a free world, for the same world which we choose every day when we put up with discomfort, chicanery, threats, and worse."

At the site of the crash, a Berliner put a plaque: "Two American flyers became victims of the Berlin blockade here. You gave your lives for us! The Berliners of the West Sectors will never forget you." For weeks, Berliners reverently placed fresh flowers at the plaque. At 11 a.m. on August 1st, some 4,000 Berliners prayed at a memorial in the American sector as planes roared overhead. [321]

Early in the Airlift, 25 percent of Berliners thought the Allies would leave and the Soviets would just walk in as the Allies retreated; only a third expected the Airlift to succeed. Optimism soon grew. By the end of July, 89 percent of the people believed that the Americans would stay in Berlin as long as they stayed in Germany--16 percentage points more than two months earlier. [322]

On July 11, more than 10,000 Berliners in the American sector wept and cheered as they heard Reuter, the socialist mayor kept from office by the Russians, pledge, "Berlin will be the German's Stalingrad that will turn back the tide of Communist pressure."

Opinion in all of Germany also gelled. In July, the people of Melsungen, an old world city, only 22 miles from the Soviet zone's border, were awakened by the town criers, "Come to the schlosshof and give aid to our beleaguered countrymen." When the crowd assembled, a speaker pointed to the overcast skies. "Up there" he cried, "the American people are showing their faith in the cause of our Berlin brothers every hour of every day. Yet we--their countrymen--have done nothing. Now we must act! There is not much food for us here in Melsungen, but let us share with those brave Berliners what little we have." To yells of "Ya," the town agreed to contribute four freight trains of grain, dried fish and fresh vegetables to be flown to Berlin. Hamburg donated a day's rations to Berlin. All over West Germany much the same thing was happening as cities fasted to donate the saved food to their countrymen in Berlin. [323]

The next 11 months transformed the world via the indomitable human spirit displayed. The pilots, "Clay's Pigeons," and all their support personnel displayed courage, stamina, ingenuity, and heart warming generosity. The Berliners displayed amazing courage in the face of tremendous hardships and a ruthless enemy who could easily have crushed them before the Allies could react. People spent days in bed to keep warm while fire departments hauled off those who had died from starvation or freezing. Housewives fried pancakes in engine oil from their mechanic husbands. Arnold Toynbee observed, "Russian folly has turned Berlin into the heroic symbol of liberty."

The July 19, 1948, Newsweek reported that the lights were going out all over Berlin. With street lighting cut 75%, the capitol looked as it did right after the war—a Halloween tableau of dark and menacing ruins. Most big power plants stood in the Russian sector. Only one lay in the West. That caused erratic power. Berlin housewives did their chores in the middle of the night during the brief periods with power. Streetcars and subways stopped running at 6 p.m. Only 13 of 18 theaters could stay open. Nightclubs sat practically empty.

Newsweek chronicled a day in the life of Erika Neumann, a recent bride. Because of electricity reduction and the lack of raw materials caused by the blockade, she rose each morning to make her husband's breakfast and lunch. With the gas allotment now half the pre-blockade amount, she used coal briquettes from the last allotment in April plus the wood that her husband picked up every evening on his way home. At almost all hours, U bahn (subway) and S bahn (elevator) trains filled with men, women and children carrying satchels, sacks or boxes loaded with scavenged wood. Berliners gleaned coal bits at the airfield and tore up wooden paving blocks.

Daily, Erika would pick up the bread ration, shop for vegetables, collect fat, cereal, and sugar rations the 1st, 10th, and 20th of each month, and tend her miniature vegetable garden in a debris cleared lot 3 blocks away. In Berlin, every day became turnip day by harsh necessity. Tilling any vacant land, 2 million Berliners desperately tried to supplement the food flown in.

At noon, she and her mother each ate 2 slices of bread. She ironed between 4 and 6 p.m. or 1 and 3 a.m. She often went to hear the 6:15 broadcast from the American radio station over a lautsprecheraagen, three of which circulated through the western sector because home radios sat useless without electricity. Groping in the dark, she heard the same drone of planes as in the war but now without a dread. [324]

The Soviets had not succeeded in intimidating Berlin. The outrage of West Berliners had reached the boiling point.

While mass meetings had become common, the assemblage at the Reichstag on September 9 reached a different order of magnitude. The Berliners crammed into the square in front of the Reichschtag, at the boundary between the British and Soviet Sectors. TIME wrote: "The people arose some 300,000 strong to shout their defiance of the Reds in one of the greatest voluntary mass meetings in German history." "Even Hitler didn't get crowds like this," said one gray-haired man in shirtsleeves.

Displaying the Berliners' increased confidence, one speaker chided, "The blockade has failed, and now the Communists can only wait for the help of General Hunger and Generalissimo Winter. Again, they will fail." By the time the speakers had finished cataloging the Soviet atrocities in a fiery rhetoric, the crowd pulsed at a fever pitch. [325]

Several thousand people going through the Brandenberg Gate on their way home in the Soviet Sector spontaneously began stoning Soviet police trucks. Soon Russian troops and police reinforcements arrived and fired into the crowd, fatally wounding a 15-year-old boy in the groin. A tall dark youth then climbed to the top of the Brandenburg gate and began pulling down the red flag as the crowd shouted "Anbrennen! (burn it)" Two more youths tried, and a third finally sent it fluttering to the street. The crowd tore the flag apart and burned it. A 12-yr. old German boy marched off with a 10 ft. section of the flagpole, poignantly explaining, "I'm taking it to my uncle. We need fuel for the stove."

The potentially disastrous cauldron cooled only when British military police arrived and positioned themselves between the crowd and the Russians. The 15-year-old was the only fatality, although 23 others were injured, mostly by thrown stones.[326]

AN ASSEMBLY LINE APPROACH

In the beginning, the airlift was fueled by the adrenaline of pilots bored stiff by peacetime flying, after the exhilaration of wartime bombing and strafing. The high energy made up for the lack of planning and inadequate equipment. During the early weeks, the pilots worked virtually non-stop. Neither they nor the machines could continue at this pace for long, nor, for all their efforts, could they meet the minimum tonnage needed.

An operation of this magnitude demanded an experienced commander. General William H. Tunner, who had led the Himalaya airlift, earning the nickname "Willie the Whip," looked like he had been cast by Hollywood - handsome, strong jawed, tall, erect and with a pilot's jaunty arrogance. His ability matched his looks as he drove his subordinates beyond what they thought were their limits. They did the impossible, because he inspired them with his infectious determination, that they could not let Berlin fall, and because they knew he worked harder and longer than any of them.

On July 26, Turnip Day, when Tunner took over, he found an operation long on personal bravery and enthusiasm but short on long range planning and coordinated effort. He immediately began changing that.

ASSEMBLING THE PLANES

Two more squadrons of the C-54s flew in with Tunner. Six more came in August. How fast they came shows their urgency.

On Sunday July 26, Lieutenant Colonel Forrest Coon landed his C-54 at Bergstrom Field, Texas after a long flight from Guam. He had just arrived at the base swimming pool when the loud speaker announced that all personnel had to report to Operations. A few hours later, Coon and forty seven other officers and eighty eight airmen of the 48th Troop Carrier Squadron were flying to Frankfurt.

The 54th Troop Carrier Squadron, home based in Anchorage, departed so suddenly that they simply followed their standard procedure and brought their snowshoes - required for Alaskan tundra flying. They wound up as a decoration at the 54th operations room at Rhein-Main. One plane of the 19th Troop Carrier Squadron had even farther to go. Home based in Hickham Field in Honolulu, it had flown to Brisbane, Australia and had just landed when it was ordered back to Hickham immediately. The other eleven planes had already left when it landed. So it refueled and immediately flew on to Rhein-Main. Twelve more planes from the 20th Troop Carrier Squadron were already in the air from the Panama Canal Zone.[327]

By the middle of August, the C-54s committed to the Airlift hit 161. The tonnage also rose steadily. From June 26th to July 31st, 8,117 sorties toted 41,988 tons; in August, 9,769 sorties and 73,632 tons; in September, 12,905 sorties and 101,871 tons. At the end of that month, Tunner withdrew all C-47s as Operation Vittles became exclusively a C-54 operation except for 7 other isolated aircraft. 225 C-54's eventually replaced the smaller planes.

Berlin desperately needed coal. Barges and trains had hauled tons of it on each trip before the blockade. Now coal was almost 70 percent of the planes' cargo. The West Berliners received a weekly ration that they lugged in their shopping bags.

On July 31st, American and British planes set a record with 594 flights to Berlin. They brought in a record 3,469 tons of supplies, including 1,337 tons of badly needed coal.

To celebrate Air Force Day, its first birthday on September 18, LeMay had called for a special 24-hour effort. Special loaded planes - really winged pack mules - would carry coal into the city. At noon, after 24 hours, loudspeakers barked out the official scores, 652 flights had carried 5,582.7 tons of coal. In the same period, the British had toted 1,405.3 tons of food and other supplies in 244 flights, a British airlift record. So, the Allies landed a total of just under 7,000 tons in 24 hours. Each family in Berlin with small children enjoyed 25 pounds of coal.

By October 1, the Allies were landing more than 3,640 tons a day, including 2300 tons of coal, 200 tons above the emergency minimum and stocks had grown to a 47 day supply. Food reserves had grown from a 34 to a 38 day supply. Flyers even delivered 2000 rubber hot water bottles for a hospital. TIME Magazine praised the airlift's "genuine Bunyonesque flavor."

PERSONNEL

An estimated 10,000 Americans (Air Force, Army Transportation Corps and Army engineers) and 7,000 British had formed a remarkable team. The Airlift personnel became so cohesive that they had their own newspaper, the Task Force Times.

Pilots had flown the 270-mile grind into Berlin for over 5 months. The typical pilot flew two or three times to Berlin during each period of duty, flying between 6 to 8 hours, plus another 6 to 8 hours on standby for loading, unloading, maintenance. After this 12 to 16 hour tour of duty, pilots had to do it again in another 12 and 20 hours. Most pilots worked 7 days a week with very little leave, and many flew for 4 or 5 months without any leave at all. Hell-raising bachelors lived like monks. Even their free time helped the Airlift. One pilot bagged a 10 point stag on a hunting trip in West Germany. He flew the 290 pounds of meat to a hospital in Berlin.[328]

To train crews, the Air Force had built a duplicate of Berlin's air corridor at the Air Force base in Great Falls, Montana, chosen because its winter temperature sometimes dropped to 40 degrees below and was snow swept like Berlin.[329] The planes were the same, the airfield even had a huge smokestack on its approaches like the hazardous brewery stack near Templehof, but instead of coal and potatoes, the planes were loaded with drums of cold Montana sand. The "little airlift" graduated some 116 three-man crews, 2 pilots and one engineer every month and immediately shipped them to Germany within a few hours.

Former Air Force pilots, unable to get flying jobs with the fledging airlines, were clamoring to go. Confident in their training, in October, the Air Force called upon 10,000 veterans to reenlist at their old ranks for immediate reassignment to Operation Vittles.

GROUND CREWS

Besides assembling and flying the aircraft, loading and unloading supplies became an international and interservice operation. The Army's Transportation Corps railroad lines ran from the port at Bremerhaven to Frankfurt along with a web of truck convoys every bit as intricate and timed as the airplanes. It had assembled a small army of loaders and unloaders in crews of twelve or fourteen displaced persons, normally from Eastern Europe - Serbs, Latvians, Estonians, Lithuanians, Poles but with numerous Germans, who labored 24 hours a day.

In October, Tunner grumbled, "The trouble with all airplanes is that they spend too much time on the ground." To speed up the loading and unloading, a competition developed between the displaced persons. The best times won cartons of cigarettes.

Experts scrutinized every phase of loading and unloading, refueling, briefing and dispatching the planes on the ground. Constant experimentation plus better management techniques had cut times drastically. The transport chief at Templehof devised constant improvements in unloading and transferring cargo to trucks and waiting freight cars. These included swivel ramps on the rear of trucks which could be hoisted to fuselage doorways or freight cars and special platforms on rollers for unloading planes and moving cargo to freight cars. Such devices cut unloading time from 24 to 10 minutes. Refueling time shrank from 33 to 8 minutes.

The air crews did not go to the operations office; it came to them: a meteorologist and an operations officer in a jeep, a portable snack bar with a couple of German girls to sell coffee, cocoa and sandwiches. One pilot flew 190 trips into Berlin and never got more than 50 feet from the plane.

The planes did not necessarily leave Berlin empty. Often they would bring out the few manufactured goods. Other times they bore more valuable cargo. The Air Force flew out 1500 tuberculosis patients, while the RAF and USAF together evacuated 15,426 children. Planes from Gatow alone had carried 2,297 metric tons of freight, 3200 metric tons of German mail and 11,900 German children, sick, and aged going to Western zone homes. Once a RAF Dakota pilot approaching Wunsdorf with a planeful of kids suddenly found himself tail heavy as he readied to land. The teenager in charge of the children had suggested that they all visit the lavatory in the tail of the aircraft before landing. Fortunately, the children moved forward in time for a smooth landing. [330]

MAINTENANCE

Maintenance also vastly improved. To keep the planes and pilots flying required steady and reliable maintenance, but mechanics were scarce. The shortage of mechanics especially galled Tunner because a "no fraternization" rule prohibited using numerous competent Germans for anything but menial labor. Once Clay removed the edict, the task force hired ex-Luftwaffe Major General Hans von Rohden who called back dozens of experienced Luftwaffe mechanics.[331]

Airlift aircraft were flown to the United States for 1,000 hour inspection, since these could be done more easily there than by transporting large repair facilities to Germany.

AIR TRAFFIC CONTROL

The flight crews and the ground crews were only two legs of the three required. Someone had to manage this flying circus. Only four minutes flying time separated hundreds of planes shuttling into the city--a southern corridor for inbound planes, a northern corridor for those returning west. In the orange and white control tower, 13 GIs worked around the clock amid Coke bottles, cigarette smoke, and radio chatter.

The skies over Berlin became a cacophony of call signals and accents. A call sign into Templehof of 'Little Easy 25' translated as follows: Little meant a C-47. A C-54 would have been "big". "Easy" meant it was eastbound into Berlin. "Willy", would have meant westbound. 25 was the number assigned to the craft.[332]

Periodically, Russian fighters would fly beside the plane and perhaps do some simple aeronautics. Other airborne dangers were nonpolitical. In the fall, to ward off thousands of starlings that were flocking to Gatow and menacing the props of Airlift planes, the Allies brought in a squadron of falcons trained to clear airfields of such airborne pests.[333]

THE RESULT

On July 7th, the 17th day of the Airlift, the chief of Newsweek's Berlin Bureau flew to Frankfurt and back and found a mad scramble of planes, trucks and men, reminiscent of hectic wartime operations. Planes were stacked at 6 or 7 levels, ground control occasionally directed 2 planes to the same level.

On October 5th, after more than 100 days, he took the same flight and found, "Today Operation Vittles is Big Business, organized and operated with typical American commercial efficiency." All planes flew on a tight schedule maintaining 4 minute separation between each plane throughout the entire flight. When one pilot noticed that he was a minute ahead of schedule, he cut the speed from 190 to 180 mph for 18 minutes so he could arrive exactly on schedule.

The Airlift had become a logistical masterpiece - an aerial conveyor belt that stunned those who knew all it entailed. Stopwatches and statistical charts replaced the pure adrenaline of the early days. Each squadron had a "howgozit" chart to show what it had done vis-a-vis competing squadrons. At the end of June, the pilots had doubted they could reach 1500 tons a day. When the big C-54s arrived, it passed 3,000. Then the airlift began to hit 4,000 daily tons with some consistency. By the end of August, the combined British American daily tonnage exceeded 5,000, well over the survival minimum of 4,500. Moreover, the Berlin accident rate sank lower than the overall Air Force rate.[334]

The Airlift injected some extra self-respect into the American psyche. The New York Times wrote: "We were proud of our Air Force during the war. We are prouder of it today."

THE BERLINERS ADAPT

The roar of the airplanes became so routine for the Berliners that any pause sparked a brief panic that the Airlift had suddenly ended.

In an essay contest, three years after the blockade, virtually everyone recalled the noise. "The insistent roar of the planes reverberated in the bizarre stone yards of the hollow broken houses; from there it throbbed in the weary ears of Berlin's people who were bitter, afraid but not broken; it echoed in the intently listening ear of history. The sound meant one thing: the West was standing its ground and fighting back."[335]

Probably the greatest testament to the West Berliners is that during the early days of the Airlift, East Berlin had more vegetables, more food, more electricity. In the fall, the Russians offered West Berliners the chance to have East Berlin ration cards. In response, in one ration office, 20 persons had registered out of 285,000 eligible. Another had only 16 registrations. In several offices, nobody had shown up. Of 2.1 million West Berliners, only 20,000 accepted the offer and many of them later rejected it.[336]

As Emmett Hughes wrote: "No one knows how the Western powers are going to hold Berlin. In a deeper sense, the Russians have already lost it." Morally, it was now the West that lay siege to Russia.

THE SOVIETS TURN UP THE PRESSURE

The blockade had delayed everything. Because the incumbent Assembly had been elected in October 1946, a new election was slated for December 5. The Soviets would permit city elections only if the Western allies caved in to Soviet demands for control of the whole city.

To discourage votes, the Russian-controlled S Bahn "elevated" trains showered pamphlets warning, "Stay away from the polls. Don't endanger your future." The 150,000 Western sector residents who worked in the eastern sector were ordered to report at 8 a.m., the hour the polls opened, to put in an extra Sunday of work to stymie the voting. Transport workers replied by striking from 6 to 10 a.m., giving West Berliners a chance to vote before going to work.

In spite of all attempts at disruption and intimidation, West Berliners overwhelmingly dealt the Communists a major defeat. The December 5 election had been heralded with the slogan, "Every voter who stays at home casts a ballot for the Communists and for terror." Of approximately 1-1/2 million eligible voters, 83.9 percent voted for nominees of the three democratic parties.

Against such a backdrop of political courage, Western resolve stiffened. On the 112th day of the Airlift while Russian artillery boomed into the gray skies in "target practice," the Airlift was doing so well that Western Berlin's food rations were boosted by 15% from an average of 1,800 to 2,040 calories a day. That meant more cereal, fat, sugar and--for the first time since war's end--cheese.

Clay announced, "An almost unbelievable recovery." The Airlift had then carried 5,000 tons of food and fuel a day during good weather and 3,000 tons "under very bad conditions." That would keep Berlin supplied through the winter especially with the additional C-54s he had secured from Truman. In the 4 months since the currency reform began, West Germany's production had risen a staggering 35%. Annual steel production climbed from 2.5 million to 7 million tons; coal from 275,000 tons to more than 300,000 tons a day.

In the fall, Clay returned to the U.S. and met with the President and asked for 60 more planes that he believed were needed to sustain the airlift over the winter. Truman went around the table and each of the members of the National Security Council said no. At the end of the meeting, Truman asked Clay and Kenneth Royall, the Secretary of the Army to remain. Truman said: "You look pretty sad, General. Don't be. You'll get your planes."

Many still doubted, but Tunner was undaunted. "We are well along with our winterization program. We will fly Vittles as long as the United States government wants it flown."[337] Biting winds, gloomy skies, shorter days and falling leaves proclaimed that the city's long winter was coming.

THE WINTER

Berlin's weather is bad enough in the fall, it turns absolutely abysmal in the winter, as fog and sleet cover the city like a silvery shroud. What made it worse was the city's protection from the elements was perforated. Berlin had not recovered from the beating inflicted by Allied bombers, artillery and finally the block to block and house to house fighting that had snuffed out the Third Reich in May 1945. The buildings still standing had cracks, gaping holes, doors off their hinges, and windows with broken, and often irreplaceable, glass. Frigid air, wind, sleet and snow now seeped or raced through.

With the winter came ice, and ice on wings scared even the cockiest pilots. Not only could it be fatal, it could slow down the operation tremendously. To overcome that, Yankee ingenuity devised "a field expedient." A ground crew sergeant suggested that they put decommissioned jet fighter engines on small trucks and heat the wings with the jet exhaust as the trucks moved slowly along. It worked perfectly and cured the icing problem.[338]

Regulations called for a minimum 500 ft. ceiling and half mile visibility. But in the fall, twin truck-size vans appeared at Templehof and cut these requirements to a 300 ft. ceiling and quarter mile visibility. The vans housed CPN-4, the latest ground control approach (GCA) radar equipment--25,000 lbs. of cathode ray tubes, radar and other delicate devices. CPN-4 let planes land every 3 minutes at Templehof in almost any weather. Pilots boasted, "We flew when birds walked."

THE THIRD AIRFIELD

Berlin needed more landing room. Two new airstrips were built at Tempelhof and a third at Gatow, but a third airfield was vital. In September, the French offered an ideal site, near the Tegel Forest in their zone; but building the airfield required material, laborers and heavy equipment.[339]

The Allies had to find sufficient material that could take the constant pounding that the Airlift would inflict. Raw material lay everywhere. Allied bombs and shells had littered Berlin with bricks and cement from shattered buildings, streets and statues. Engineers decided to lay six-inch layers of bricks in the foundation, plus ballast from old railway tracks, pulverize them, compact them with rollers, and then penetrate the mass with an asphalt binding.

A runway 5500 feet by 150 feet with 500 foot overruns at each end required over 10 million bricks. Laborers would have to collect the bricks and haul them to the site. When the Allies offered 1 Mark 20 Pfennigs and one hot meal for each shift, over 20,000 Berliners volunteered to work three shifts a day, covering all 24 hours. Approximately 40% of the workers were women.[340]

Material alone was not enough to withstand the sledgehammer pounding of a fully loaded plane landing every 3 to 4 minutes, unheard of just a few months earlier. Producing a runway sturdy enough to withstand such a beating required heavy construction equipment. But the Russians had stripped Berlin of all such equipment, and such behemoths would not fit into the biggest plane in the Air Force fleet.

Then came one of the greatest field expedients. To build an air base in Brazil several years earlier, a civilian welder named H.P. Lacomb in Florida had sliced the large earth moving equipment with an oxyacetylene torch into components that would fit into the plane. He flew with his jigsaw pieces to Brazil where he reassembled and rewelded them into the original configuration. Someone in the Air Force remembered Lacomb. The FBI located him working at an airport in the Midwest. Overnight, he and his torches were shipped to Rhein-Main.

After drawing chalk-lines on a bulldozer, he donned his welder's mask and using his blue flame at the chalked sections, carved the machine like a turkey. When he finished, the disassembled parts fit into several C-82 flying boxcars brought in to fly the heavy machinery. Lacomb flew with the parts to Templehof and artfully reconnected the equipment with a welding rod. He then trained two crews, the cutting crew at Rhein-Main and the assembling crew at Templehof. Lacomb and his crews cut and reassembled 81 tractors, bulldozers, rollers and graders. [341]

Tegel had one problem. A transmission tower of a Berlin radio station obstructed the new runway. The tower stood in the French Sector but the Russians controlled its operation. General Jean Ganeval, the French commandant, had asked them to move the tower, but they refused.

A few days later, on December 16, Ganeval invited the American detachment to his office. When they arrived, he served refreshments. The perplexed Americans sat there drinking, while French engineers were placing explosives at three of the four legs of the tower. When the charges ignited, the Americans reached the windows just as the 200 foot tower crashed to the ground - in the Soviet sector. "You will have no more trouble with the tower," said Ganeval.

An enraged General Kotikov demanded of Ganeval, "How could you do that?" Ganeval answered literally, "From the base - with dynamite."[342] Ganeval's forceful act further boosted an already surging West sector morale.[343]

At the first planning session, his engineers advised Clay that the new airport would be ready in March 1949. Clay told them, "It would be complete in December." Work had begun on September 5 and the first plane landed on November 5.

Tonnage dropped in early November and the terrible weather continued into December, but the Airlift's daily average reached 4,500 tons. On December 23, the 50,000th Plane Fare landing put down at Gatow. Three days later, the Berlin Airlift marked its six-month anniversary. It had flown 96,640 flights, an average of 502 a day, carrying 3,800 tons a day of food, coal, raw materials and manufactured goods.

The Airlift kept surging - reaching 5,500 tons in January and February - the third field put Operation Vittles over the top. It was clear now that Berlin would do more than merely survive. By early spring, the Airlift was landing 8,050 tons a day, and one day put down 13,000 tons. Warehouses were crammed. Besieged Berlin was fast becoming one of the most affluent cities in Europe.

OPERATION LITTLE VITTLES

The third airfield was not the only Christmas present for Berliners. Operation Little Vittles, the inspiration of U.S. Lieutenant Carl S. Halvorsen, began. In the fall, Halvorsen had seen some children watching the American planes. He walked over and handed them two sticks of Wrigley's Doublemint through the fence. He told them that if they gathered at the end of the Templehof runway the next day, he would drop some gum and chocolate to them. But how to do it? He had gone to Germany with a barracks bag full of handkerchiefs for his stuffy head cold! Halvorsen converted them into mini-parachutes that he had his crew chief drop through the hatch. Gradually, the crowd of children grew larger and larger. Other pilots in Halversen's squadron joined in and then other squadrons enrolled. On the way in and out of Tempelhof, they parachuted bags of candy and toys to the children waiting below. The crews bought every toy, doll, piece of candy with their own money.

After Halvorsen had returned to the United States for a national radio show, crates of candy bars and gum flooded in to Rhein-Main from the U.S., eventually 23 tons worth! So the skies over Templehof filled with hundreds of tiny parachutes each carrying its goodies. Halvorsen, now nicknamed "Der Schokoladeflieger," the Chocolate Airman, received more than 4,000 cards and letters from the Berlin children at Christmas.

Children began calling the planes "Rosinenbomber" - raisin bombers for the boxes of raisins they dropped. For those who did not catch the mini parachutes, airmen delivered Hershey's raisin chocolate bars once a month to schools in the American sector. Teachers then dutifully had all children take at least one bite out of the bars to discourage their being traded on the black market.

In December, the airmen mounted Operation Santa Claus in which thousands of tiny parachutes floated down bearing gifts. The candy airlift's next high point came in the spring when the Airlift detachment at Templehof arranged a picnic for thousands of kids on Peacock Island in Lake Eggel with a mass candy drop.

THE END

On April 16, 1949 in the 24 hours ending at noon, the Air Force airlifted 12,940 tons of supplies through 1398 sorties. At that rate, General Clay announced, "We were able to bring in more food to Berlin by air than we brought in by rail and road before the blockade."

On May 8, 1949 the new Federal Republic of Germany adopted its constitution. 24 hours later, the Soviet military governor ordered that on one minute past midnight on May 12, the barricades would come down. The allies had done what the experts called impossible. The Soviets had been sure the Airlift would fail. Besides the sheer size of the task, the Soviets did not understand instrument flying so they felt that the dreary German winter and its continuous overcast skies would doom the Airlift.

Counting the first weeks of partial "little blockade" in early 1948, the siege had lasted fifteen months. America and its allies had logged 277,264 flights, hauling 2,343,315 tons of food, fuel, medicine, and clothing - nearly one ton for every citizen of Berlin.

On September 23, 1949, the crew of the last flight to Berlin from Lubeck had scrawled on the Dakota's nose: "Positively the last load from Lubeck, 73,705 tons. Psalm 21, verse 11." "For they intended evil against thee; they imagined a mischievous devise, which they are not able to perform." Perhaps the best description came fifty years later in a Boeing advertisement. "Disguised as coal, food and medicine, the right to vote, the freedom to speak and numerous other human rights were heroically airlifted into Berlin."

The Blockade marked the first time the superpowers confronted each other without surrogates. So, the Airlift marched shoulder to shoulder with the Marshall Plan. The Airlift allowed the Plan to succeed primarily because the blockade had been a reaction to the promise of the Marshall Plan. The Plan showed that America had good intentions and money. The Airlift showed it had backbone. Clay said that if we had not stayed in Berlin, there would have been no Marshall Plan and no NATO, because Europe would have lost all confidence in our ability and willingness to face down the Soviets for Europe's benefits.

The blockade forced European countries to realize how vulnerable they were to Soviet tanks. They took steps toward collective defense under American leadership

The cost of the Airlift in money was almost as staggering as the performance, nearly $500,000 a day for the United States alone. Yet, as Clay stated, "Measured in terms of prestige, measured in the courage which it has brought to millions of people who desire freedom, measured indeed in comparison to our expenditures for European assistance . . . and national defense, its cost is insignificant." [344] It was expensive in other ways. Between June 26 and May 12, 1949, 79 people, 31 American airmen, 39 British airmen and nine civilians, died. Nevertheless the Airlift went on.

Clay never asked approval for the Airlift; he announced he was going to do it and what he needed. His actions earned him worldwide fame. A U.S. observer in Berlin noted, "Two of the most important reasons why the West is still in Berlin and not at war with Russia are that Clay has forged a policy of firmness almost solely on his own initiative, and that in so doing he has avoided making any fateful blunders based on silly belligerence."[345]

Following his retirement from the Army in 1949, Clay managed several large corporations and published two books. He returned to Berlin in 1961 to represent President Kennedy during the crisis ignited by the building of the wall between East and West Berlin.

Buried at West Point, Clay has a simple headstone. It announces his rank and his position as Commander in Chief in Europe and Military Governor of Germany. The people of Berlin added a footstone. It states, in German, "We thank the defender of our freedom."

∾

CHAPTER THIRTEEN

THE FIRST ARAB/ISRAELI WAR

THE ARABS INVADE - BUT WILL THEY UNITE?

Things looked bleak for the Israelis. The Haganah, the official Israeli Army, was still forming. While later in the year, it would reach about 80,000, only 20,000 were combat troops. With no heavy supporting weapons, not enough small arms, and ammunition for only 3 days, the Israelis could arm only about three quarters of their Army. Initially, the rest had to rely on homemade devices, improvised farm implements, and an unconquerable spirit. The Haganah kept busy. Besides drilling farmers in marksmanship, in hidden workshops, they welded metal shields onto old trucks; then mounted light machine guns on them to produce "armored cars."

The two splinter terrorist groups also fought but not under the Haganah. The 3,000 member Irgun Zvi Leumi boasted 600 to 800 armed members who operated in small bands, which submerged into the populace whenever necessary.[346] The Stern Gang's 200 to 300 armed fanatics could swell quickly with reserves of up to 2,000 active supporters.[347]

Arrayed against them were the Arab regular armies, for the first time supposedly united against a common enemy and ready to overrun the Israelis. Those armies were gathering, but the real question was posed by the May 24th Newsweek with a cover of an Arab holding a rifle, "The Arabs: Will They Unite?"

On paper, those forces numbered well over 100,000, but really ranged between 70,000 and 80,000. Fortunately, for the Israelis, the sum of Arab soldiers actually sent, paled compared to the total promised.

The Saudis pledged 40,000 but sent only two companies, which operated under the control of the Egyptians. More followed but never more than two battalions of Saudis served in the war and as of October 1948, the force numbered only 700. Lebanon's 2000 troops were more policemen than combat soldiers. The Syrian Army totaled between 7,000 and 8,000 but sent far fewer. The Iraqis offered an armored brigade and 8 infantry battalions, a force of 10,000 men supported by 3 squadrons of aircraft, but its abysmal morale and inadequate training made it useless as a fighting force.

In May 1948, the Egyptian army's strength of approximately 50,000 was more paper than flesh. Only about 5,000 men served a full conscription each year and Egypt had trouble fielding 10,000 men for the invasion force. The Egyptians put 2 brigades in action and a third in reserve on the southern front. Egypt never mobilized more than 40,000 including Sudanese, Saudi Arabians and volunteers from other Arab countries.

TransJordan was Israel's most formidable enemy. So much so, that Golda Meir led a secret mission to persuade King Abdullah Ibn Hussein, ruler of the desert kingdom, not to take part in the Arab invasion. But, with his eyes on Palestine and the rest of the Middle East, Abdullah grabbed the chance to expand his territory at the expense of what would have been a Palestine Arab state and an internationalized Jerusalem.

What made TransJordan so formidable was the 6000 man Arab Legion, by far the most effective fighting force in the Arab world. Formed in 1920, to bring order to the desert frontiers under the mandate and trained by England, it served with the British during World War II. The Legion still drew a British subsidy, and had 37 British officers on duty with it. Sir John Bagot Clubb was the British commander of the Legion, Abdullah's right-hand man, honorary Pasha and latter day Lawrence.

On May 15, seven Arab armies of no more than 30,000 men invaded Palestine to destroy the state of Israel. The Arab Legion invaded first when its trucks and armored cars crossed the River Jordan at the Allenby Bridge on May 15th. It followed the path Biblical scholars believed the Israelis took after the capture of Jericho. Together with Iraqi troops, the force then marched the route towards Jerusalem taken 2,000 years ago by the Magi.[348]

During this phase, the attacking Arabs made impressive gains but lacked command and control and failed abysmally at logistics. The Arab Liberation Army split itself into the Northern, the Eastern, the Western and the Southern Commands, which barely spoke to each other. No general strategy dictated the opening moves, just each country's perceived advantage.

After the first two weeks of fighting, the invaders had seized all of Arab Palestine, but unexpectedly stiff Israeli resistance had halted the Arab onslaught.

The vastly outnumbered and outgunned Israelis could not mount a counter-offensive but took selected targets. Acra, the old crusader's fortress in the North, fell to the Israelis on May 18th. The next day, they took Sarafand, a huge former British military camp in which they planned to house 20,000 immigrants.

The Arab onslaught forced the Israelis to unify. On May 28th, Israeli Defense Order No. 1 formally established the National Army giving Israel the advantage of a central authority to issue orders and plan strategy.

THE TRUCE

On May 20th, the Security Council elected Count Folke Bernadotte of Sweden, president of the Swedish Red Cross, as U.N. mediator in Palestine. In World War II, he had negotiated the first exchange of German and British prisoners of war in 1943. Later, he persuaded the Nazis to send some 14,000 Norwegian and Danish hostages to Sweden. As Bernadotte prepared to leave his American wife and family, he estimated his chances of success as 1 in 100. The task was also highly dangerous. On May 23rd, snipers killed Thomas Wasson, U.S. Consul General in Jerusalem and Chief Radioman Herbert Walker during the fighting in the Holy City.

In three weeks, Count Bernadotte shuttled nearly 10,000 miles in a white Dakota plane with six red crosses and the words "United Nations" painted on the wings and body. In a typical day, he cajoled the Egyptian foreign minister at Cairo, the TransJordan foreign minister at Amman, and the Israeli foreign minister at Haifa.

Finally, Arabs and Jews had accepted Bernadotte's laboriously worked out plea for a four week cease fire. The truce began at June 11, 6:00 a.m. Greenwich time under the supervision of Count Bernadotte and his staff of Swedish, French, Belgian and American officials. To enforce the truce, a token unit of 49 uniformed U.N. guards, the nearest thing to an international armed force the U.N. had yet produced, left LaGuardia Field on June 20th, carrying 38 caliber Smith & Wesson revolvers--but no ammunition.

Both sides violated the truce somewhat but basically obeyed. The Israelis especially welcomed the time it gave them to assemble and train their armed forces and to field the war material that was beginning to pour in from their global efforts.

The Arabs did not need the truce as badly but they needed it. The Arabs could use the breathing space to recover from the unexpectedly harsh defenses and to consolidate, train, and resupply their troops. Logistically, they sagged on the ropes, with few replacements and meager supplies. Clubb wanted an armistice to consolidate the Arabs' substantial goals, especially TransJordan's, but the Arabs fell victim to their own hype. Having whipped their people into a frenzy, only Jewish annihilation would be politically acceptable. That was a fatal mistake. The first truce marked the high water mark for the Arabs. Israel emerged from the truce much better organized, supplied, armed, and led. The Arabs just emerged with far more problems. On July 8th, Count Bernadotte reported from his headquarters that the war in Palestine raged again.

THE WAR RESUMES

The next phase again began with Arab attacks. The Arabs boasted that their blitzkreig would erase the new state in ten days. To make driving the Jews into the sea easier, they ordered an Arab exodus from the cities. But the Arab armies soon retreated when the Israelis counterattacked.

Not only were the Israelis better supplied, but their tactics had improved. Besides coordinating their infantry, armored, and artillery attacks, they bombed strategic targets using newly smuggled Flying Fortresses, manned by U. S. pilots who had flown during the war. While the Arab Legion remained formidable, the soldiers of the other Arab armies fought ineffectively, when they fought at all.[349]

During this phase, age-old rivalries temporarily papered over in the union against Israel suddenly resurfaced. By late summer, the fractures in the Arab world had become chasms. Napoleon had said, "Give me a coalition to fight." And this coalition was riddled with distrust and jealousy. King Abdullah proclaimed to his Legion that TransJordan's "army has preserved the holiness of Jerusalem. We and the others went into this fight jointly. We are here. Where are the others? We have fought and progressed, but we have not seen this progress made by others."

One bitter Palestinian Arab, Musa Alami, wrote, "In the face of the enemy, the Arabs were not a state, but petty states; groups, not a nation; each fearing and anxiously watching the other and intriguing against it. What concerned them most and guided their policy was not to win a war and save Palestine from the enemy, but what would happen after the struggle, who would be predominant in Palestine, or... how they could achieve their own ambitions."[350]

The August 16th issue of TIME, with Ben Gurion on the cover, said it bluntly. "The Jews beat the Arabs. Out of the concentration camps, ghettos, banks, courtrooms, theaters and factories of Europe, the Chosen People had assembled and had won their first great military victory since Judas Maccabeus beat the Syrian Nicanor Adasa 2,109 years ago... It was time to stop wondering whether there would be a Jewish state and start asking what kind of nation Israel was."

The U.N. ordered a second truce - the first time the U.N. invoked that portion of its charter that provides for the imposition of sanctions to halt the threat of war. The Jews and Arabs soon agreed. Unlike the first truce, the second truce/cease fire was a blessing for the bloodied Arabs.

The second truce began at 5:30 p.m. local time on July 18th with Count Bernadotte's observers spread throughout the area. Really a cease fire, the combatants merely stayed in place, on alert and ready to resume hostilities immediately.

Under the original partition resolution, Israel would receive the Negev, a desert in the south ranging north from the Gulf of Aqaba to a line from the southern end of the Dead Sea to the Mediterranean, passing just south of Beersheba. To secure a permanent settlement, Count Bernadotte's peace plan would transfer the Negev to Transjordan, thus giving it a land bridge to Egypt. Also Israel would return Lydda and Ramleah to TransJordan although Lydda would be a free airport. In exchange, Israel would receive western Galilee. Jerusalem would be a separate and protected city under the United Nations and Haifa would be a free port.

The other Arab nations disliked the plan, because it gave the choice territory to King Abdullah's TransJordan. The Israelis despised it.

BERNADOTTE - MAN ON A TIGHTROPE

Both sides distrusted Bernadotte's efforts and motives. His peace proposal confirmed the suspicion of the Israelis that Bernadotte was against them and it verified the paranoia of the fanatics that he was really conspiring with the Arabs. To retaliate for his July 12th report on truce violations naming the Israelis, as the more aggressive party, the Stern Gang publicly threatened to kill him.

He had braved Allied air raids on Berlin in November 1943 to negotiate with Heimlich Himmler for the release of concentration camp prisoners (he saved 20,000 in all). He sat through a raid at Lupeck in April 1945 to discuss Himmler's surrender terms and dove into a ditch to escape Allied strafing of a Danish airfield while heading back to Germany, shortly after receiving the Allied reply.

On September 17, he went to Jerusalem for an inspection tour before leaving for the U.N. meeting in Paris. He began to tour Israeli-held sections in a three car convoy. At the foot of the Hill of Evil Counsel (where, the legends say, Satan tempted Jesus), the convoy was halted by an Israeli army-type jeep set in an abandoned road block. Two men in Israeli army uniforms strode along the convoy, carrying sten guns--a cheap but highly effective little submachine gun of the type the Allies parachuted to European guerrillas during the war. As they came to Bernadotte's limousine, the driver leaped out and grappled with one who fired ineffectually in the front seat. Meanwhile, the second assassin recognized Bernadotte, thrust his gun through a window ventilator and fired a burst at the back seat.

One of Bernadotte's companions, General Aage Lundstrom, was uninjured. The other, Colonel Andre Serod, a French Air Force truce observer, was riddled by a fusillade of 17 bullets and died instantly. The rest of the bullets went straight through the ribbons on Bernadotte's uniform. He died before they could reach the hospital.

His 13 year old son heard the news when he switched on the radio in Sweden. One U.S. captain on the truce mission spoke for many when he said, "I am in the country where Christ was born, and I wish to Christ I was in the country where I was born."[351]

At the funeral, the presiding Lutheran pastor took for his text Isaiah 6:8:

"Also I heard the voice of the Lord, saying whom shall I send, and who will go for us? Then said I, here I am; send me."

DIPLOMATIC MANEUVERS

Meanwhile, the U.N. met at the Palais de Chaillot in Paris to address the Palestine issue again, along with Berlin.

When news came of Bernadotte's murder, the U.N.'s blue and white flag slumped to half staff. Bernadotte's successor, his assistant, Dr. Ralph J. Bunche of America, submitted Bernadotte's 150-page report. With posthumous irony, it urged the world and the Arabs to recognize that "a Jewish state called Israel exists."

Count Bernadotte had strongly recommended giving the Negev to the Arabs rather than Israel because, at the time, Arabs controlled most of it. The Israelis argued that their battlefield victories made those lines irrelevant. They had now repulsed the Arabs and captured new territory which they planned to keep.

Soon, the Israelis on the battlefield made the peace plan being discussed in Paris irrelevant. In October, the Israelis launched two offensives, one against the Egyptians in the south and a second against the Arab Liberation Army in Northern Galilee. The Egyptians took a terrible beating as their tactics and command failed. In Galilee, the Arabs simply collapsed. They failed to join together in their Holy War.

Before a new U.N. ordered ceasefire began on October 22nd, the Israelis isolated Gaza and captured Beersheba; re-established communication with the Jewish settlements in the Negev; and cut off Egyptian forces on the Jerusalem fronts from their bases. The Israelis strengthened their demand to revise the Bernadotte plan.

THE EFFECT ON THE PRESIDENTIAL ELECTION

Bernadotte's plan jolted the American election. When Marshall called the Bernadotte report "a fair and reasonable solution," the announcement outraged American Jews who thought that Israel should keep the Negev.

Breaking his pledge to keep Palestine out of the election, Dewey attacked Truman for supporting the plan.

Truman had approved Marshall's message, accepting the proposal. In fact, Marshall again cabled notice of this to Truman, and Truman did not object, if he ever saw the statement between whistlestops.

Fortunately, Israel's victories made the plan irrelevant and gave Truman a way out in favor of domestic politics. On October 24th, Truman promised an eventual lifting of the arms embargo and that the U.S. would sympathetically consider Israeli applications for economic aid.[352] This eased Jewish worries.[353] The next day he went further.

On Monday, October 25th, Truman reaffirmed the boundaries of the original partition resolution of November 1947. The Israelis would have to agree to any modifications. Three days later, Thursday, October 28th, Truman settled the debate over the Bernadotte plan by flatly renouncing it. "Israel," he said, "must be large enough and strong enough to make its people self-supporting and secure."[354]

THE WAR BLEEDS TO ITS INCONCLUSIVE CONCLUSION

On December 22, Israeli forces routed the Eyptians on their southern front and bombed Gaza and neighboring villages. A week later, the Security Council ordered a cease fire and withdrawal to the positions occupied before the October fighting. Ignoring the UN ceasefire, the Israelis drove the Arabs from the Negev and rolled up the Egyptian right flank, pinning their forces in the Gaza Strip and opening a path to Egyptian territory in the Sinai. They then invaded Egypt. The British demanded that the Israelis withdraw from Egypt, or they would attack them under a treaty with Egypt. With the election over, Truman sent a note to Ben Gurion so severe that Ben Gurion said, "It might have been written by Bevin himself." Truman demanded an immediate withdrawal as the minimum requirement to prove the Israelis' peaceful intentions. The Israelis complied under protest after three days.

Egypt and Syria teetered on the edge of collapse, shaken by psychological and economic shocks from the Israeli victories. Collapse menaced in other Arab states within the next several months. The Arab masses were just beginning to realize the disgrace in the Holy Land.

On December 28, a few minutes before 10 a.m. in the lobby of Cairo's Ministry of Interior, a young man in the uniform of a police first lieutenant saw Egypt's premier Mahmoud Fahmy Lel Nokrashy Pashy walking in. As Pashy approached the elevator, the young man saluted, pulled out a pistol and fired five bullets into the premier, killing him. The assassin, a member of a fanatical religious political organization, had blamed the premier for the loss of Palestine to the Jews.

On January 7, 1949, as Israeli troops readied another attack, Egypt asked for an armistice. The fighting ceased almost at once and the Arab Israeli War of 1948 ended. Without a permanent settlement, the cease-fire lines became the *de facto* boundaries of Israel, about 6,000 to 8,000 sq. mi. beyond the UN partition confines. So, of the more than 800,000 Arabs who lived in Palestine before 1948, only about 170,000 remained. The rest became refugees in the surrounding Arab countries.[355] King Abdullah of TransJordan annexed much of the proposed Palestinian Arab state, including the West Bank, and King Farouk of Egypt annexed the Gaza Strip on the Egypt-Israel border that sheltered 500,000 uprooted Arabs. The region became a flash point of global tensions ever since. On November 16, 1948, when the war was all but over, the Arab League declared that the Arabs would never agree to partition and would never recognize Israel or have any relations with it.

Before 1948, a compromise might have been reached. After 1948, it was impossible.

∾

CHAPTER FOURTEEN

THE CAMPAIGN TAKES SHAPE

WILL THE NEW DEAL CONTINUE OR BE ROLLED BACK

As August ended, the same heat that made Chambers and Hiss sweat at HUAC hearings steamed the country. A giant mass of tropical air drifted up the Mississippi Valley and spread from the Rockies to the Atlantic. Record breaking temperatures blanketed the nation. Dallas recorded 107, Chicago 98, Kansas City 100, Detroit 98, Cleveland 103, Philadelphia 101.2, 100.4 in Boston, 100.8 in New York, and 96 in Hell, Michigan. It inflicted unmitigated suffering on the Midwest and East, killing more than 150 people.

In the big cities, "Asphalt pavement softened to the consistency of taffy. Hundreds of factories and offices let workers off early. When they didn't, workers just stayed away." Detroit's automobile plants had 20,000 absentees on the day after the heat wave began. Women sitting under beauty parlor hair dryers stripped off half their clothes and donned toga-like sheets.

Farmers watched their chickens drop dead. New York had a rash of roaming wrench-waving gangs who turned on hundreds of hydrants. In Washington, the Daily News printed its masthead to resemble melting type and dated its issue "Fry Day."

What made such heat unbearable and deadly was the lack of air conditioning. Central air conditioning virtually did not exist. Window units had only come out after the war and just 74,000 units were sold in 1948. Only .3% of the population owned air conditioners. In Baltimore, the air conditioned Century Theater invited the public in after the last show to spend the night cooling off in upholstered seats. Most people had no place to go to escape.

Amidst that stifling atmosphere, the hot air of a presidential campaign was about to blow. Much has changed about political campaigns, but the essence remains the same. It is an ancient ritual of "audience flattering, enemy vilifying, name remembering, moon promising."[356]

A presidential campaign was not a contact sport. Between the conventions and election day, Truman and Dewey met only once, on July 31, at the dedication of New York's Idlewild (now John F. Kennedy) Airport. Dewey opened with, "I'm glad to welcome you here." Truman responded, "It's nice to see you again, Governor." Then Truman joked, "Tom, when you get to the White House, for God's sakes do something about the plumbing."[357]

From then on, the two candidates rarely if ever mentioned each other by name. Once in California, Dewey's train passed within four miles of Truman's. That was as close as they came.

THE PERSONALITIES - WHO ARE THESE GUYS

The contrast between the two men was obvious. Truman did not evoke confidence. Dewey did not evoke friendliness. For the first 30 or 40 years of his life, Truman was a failure professionally. I emphasize professionally, because he was a devoted family man with a loving wife, an adoring daughter, a reputation for honor and a stainless personal life. But, as a businessman, he was a bust. His haberdashery shop failed, as did his other business ventures, and he had enormous debts to pay. But as even his critic Alistair Cooke noted, "He is not a despondent man and one can admire the sigh and the plucky grin with which he has, throughout his life, tried to learn by his mistakes."[358]

Dewey on the other hand had known only success, becoming a national hero in his mid 30s. For that reason, he had a difficult time relating to common people. He exuded the arrogance that one gets by triumphing early in life.

Having labored in county politics, Truman always had his staff work with the local candidates for sheriff and aldermen. Dewey's staff paid scant attention to local politicians, perhaps because Dewey had never really been a local politician. As a result, many local Republican candidates felt no loyalty to him.

Dewey's voice was a cultured modulated baritone that he pampered by having it sprayed every morning during the campaign. He played that instrument superbly. One expert proclaimed Dewey's vocabulary and diction, "The most perfect type of American English." Truman answered with terrible diction, slurred words, and a flat and nasal voice, laced with a Missouri twang. He spoke as if he had a mouthful of grits.

An old man by 1948's standards, Truman occasionally carried a cane and wore trifocal glasses that gave him the look of a nervous owl. Whenever he faced newsreel or television cameras, he slipped on special spectacles that did not reflect floodlight glare. He wrote in 1948, "The head at 64 doesn't work as well as it did at 24."[359] When one woman at a whistlestop exclaimed, "You're close enough to see your dimples," he replied: "Not dimples, they are wrinkles. You don't have dimples at 64."[360]

At 46, eighteen years Truman's junior, Dewey was the first candidate for President born in the 20th century. Dewey's overly large head sported a wide gap smile, because he had lost some front teeth in a high school football scrimmage, and a black mustache in a time when Adolph Hitler had made mustaches unfashionable. Together with his conservative clothes, Homburg hats, and stiff bearing, the mustache made him look fastidious or, as Alice Roosevelt Longworth sniped, like the little groom on the wedding cake.[361]

Dewey also suffered from a portrait drawn of him in John Gunther's 1947 classic, Inside America. Gunther had spoken to many who had worked with Dewey. Almost all respected him but none liked him.[362] "He is unfortunately one of the least seductive personalities in public life."[363] People referred to his vindictiveness, the "metallic" and "two dimensional" nature of his efficiency, his cockiness and his suspiciousness. Other typical descriptive adjectives were "egotistical, lordly, overbearing, didactic, too cold to like easily, pompous, self-important, high-handed to the point of rudeness, astonishingly insensitive." [364] The contrast with the folksy Truman who typically introduced the White House butlers to visiting royalty made Dewey's vanities even more glaring.

Dewey's father edited a local newspaper in Owosso, Michigan. So you would think he would have a rapport with newsmen. Not so. The reporters on Dewey's train did not particularly like him but believed he would win. The reporters on Truman's train liked him, but did not think he had a chance.

THE UNDERDOG HAD TO FIGHT

Historically, a President seeking reelection had not actively campaigned lest he appear undignified. Only Presidents staring at an ignominious defeat, such as Taft in 1912, had ventured out of the White House.[365] Truman certainly met that criterion and he planned to fight. He became the first incumbent President to tour extensively, but he did more than that. As he wrote to his sister that fall, "It will be the greatest campaign any President ever made. Win, lose, or draw, people will know where I stand . . ."[366]

Since the Republican dominated press opposed him, Truman decided to see and be seen by as many voters as possible. Unknowingly, he agreed with Whittaker Chambers: "I believed then, and I still believe, that if the mass of people can hear a man's voice, listen to what he has to say and his way of saying it, they will, not invariably, but as a rule, catch the ring of truth, and pretty unerringly sort out a sincere man from an imposter."[367]

Truman had to do it in person. He was not a good radio speaker - his voice and style were not built for that medium. In the pre-TV era, there was no other way to be seen by the voters except by personal appearances, and the best way to do that was by train. William Jennings Bryan had first used a train to campaign in the 1890s. By 1952, the airplane dominated, but in 1948, the train was the presidential mode of travel. And it was the best, if not the only way to get to Pocatello, Idaho; Crestline, Ohio; or Beaucoup, Illinois. Truman did what TV would. He brought the election to the people.

Six times during the next two months, Truman's train clanked out of Washington's Union Station tugging the *Ferdinand Magellan*, a mobile White House, political headquarters, and press room. Truman sallied to Detroit and back on September 5-7; from September 17 and October 2, to California through eighteen states for 15 days of non stop speeches; October 6-8, a three day tour through Delaware, Pennsylvania, New Jersey, and Upstate New York; on October 9-16, ten northeastern and Midwestern states for 8 major speeches; October 18th to 19th, to Miami and Raleigh by air for two major speeches; on October 23, to Pittsburgh and its heavy labor vote through a final charge October 23rd to 30th, 10 states from Rhode Island and Massachusetts for 12 major speeches to the big population centers (Chicago, Cleveland, Boston, New York); and a trip home to Missouri that continued to Election Eve. He spent all or part of forty-four days away from Washington.[368]

TRUMAN'S STRATEGY - FEARMONGERING

Eisenhower was convinced that the public's concerns boiled down to two words: "Russia" and "inflation." [369] But Truman and Dewey avoided foreign affairs, because the policies had been so bi-partisan and both candidates believed that politics ended at the shoreline. Truman broadened the "inflation" issue.

Truman's strategy can be expressed in one word "Attack!" Truman had peppered the Congress with bills that he knew had no chance of success, but now he kept harping on what he had offered and what the Republicans had done.

Truman did not unfold a bold new vision of what America should be like. He meant to preserve the accomplishments of the New Deal by scaring the hell out of people that all would be lost if the Republicans seized both the White House and the Congress. He became a fearmonger. He planned to spend every minute strafing the Republican Congress.

ATTACKS ON THE 80TH CONGRESS

Truman and Congress loathed one another. He had vetoed 57 bills of the 80th Congress, 13 in the week before the Democratic Convention alone, and been overridden 6 times. Not since Andrew Johnson had any President been overridden so many times in one term.

It is ironic that Truman, the running mate Roosevelt picked because of his excellent bonds with Congress, would so antagonize not only the Republican 80th Congress but the Democratic 79th and 81st Congresses also. In the Spring of 1946, Truman had called the 79th Congress "the worst since [President] Andrew Johnson's Congress." [370] For the first two months of the 1948 session, he did not consult his Democratic leader in the Senate, Barkley, nor Rayburn in the House.

Ironically, many of Truman's defeats in the 80th Congress had been inflicted by Democrats who deserted him to vote with the Republicans. For example, Senate Democrats voted 27 to 10 to override his veto on tax relief. On the Taft Hartley law, 20 Democrats in the Senate and 106 in the House had made it possible to override his veto.

Amazingly, Truman accomplished much with the GOP Congress while he kept tearing into it. Besides the Greek Turkish Aid Plan, the Marshall Plan, the Vandenberg Resolution, the National Security Act unifying the Armed Services, and the reinstitution of the draft, it had passed the first long range agricultural bill enacting flexible farm price supports, the Taft Hartley Act, the Tax Reduction Act, the 70 Group Air Force, the Hoover Commission to study government reorganization, and the Presidential Succession Bill.

The 80th Congress submitted to the states the Constitutional Amendment limiting the President to two terms, but it excepted Harry Truman from its provisions. It established veteran's preferences for housing, set up a separate secondary market for GI mortgages to help private housing, and had appropriated more money for reclamation than the preceding Democratic Congress.

Congressional Democrats planned on touting the achievements of the 80th Congress in their re-election campaign. The Republicans were even prouder. During the campaign, Vandenberg said: "When history is written, the 80th Congress will be remembered for the record in foreign relations long after other relatively transient issues have been forgotten. I respectfully suggest that the record makes the 80th Congress ... not the 'second worst' in history as we sometimes hear in general attack, but the first best."[371]

The press agreed. LIFE Magazine gushed over such an industrious Congress that passed 1,000 bills.[372] The Washington Evening Star doubted whether Truman would get far with attempts to plaster the 'do nothing' label on the 80th Congress and thought the Republicans would "reduce it to an absurdity. . . . The 80th Congress achieved bi-partisan foreign policy accomplishments excelled by few if any earlier peacetime congresses."[373]

The Washington Post, a friend of Truman, stated: "The 80th Congress seems to be in little danger of falling to the level assigned to it by Mr. Truman in the ardor of his preconvention campaign."[374]

Truman is remembered for his decision to drop the atomic bomb, for which reaction was mixed, and two things for which he is universally praised and respected--his foreign policy and his victory in 1948. Because of that, the observation of Charles Halleck, the House Republican Majority

Leader during the 80th Congress, rings true: "It always galls me to think that Harry Truman won in 1948 by attacking the Congress which gave him his place in history."

DIRTY HARRY

No candidate since the torchlight days of Williams Jennings Bryan matched Truman's intensity and pitch. Some of his choice diatribes: "Wall Street reactionaries," "gluttons of privilege," "economic tapeworm of big business," "tools of the most reactionary elements," "silent and cunning men who would skim the cream from our natural resources to satisfy their own greed . . . who would tear our country apart . . . bloodsuckers with offices in Wall Street, princes of privilege, plunderers." [375] Truman accused the GOP of favoring "labor baiting, union hurting, yellow dog open shop contracts."[376] One Truman scholar has pointed out that there were several Trumans: one who could please almost anyone when it suited him, Truman the President who could conscientiously act as statesman, and dirty Harry who could both get mad and get even. Dirty Harry was most evident in the campaign.[377] As William Manchester wrote: "Much that Truman said was absurd or irresponsible, and some of it was mischievous."[378]

At virtually every stop, Truman blamed Congress for the high cost of living and every other domestic woe, except the weather! "The Republicans don't want any price control for one very simple reason: the higher the prices go up, the bigger the profits for the corporations," he yelled in Reading, Pennsylvania. "The real estate people have one of the most powerful, best organized, and most brazen lobbies in Washington. And the Republican Party has proved to be its faithful servant," he yelled in Buffalo.[379]

He targeted his venom. To consumers, he roared that the Republicans "have begun to nail the American consumer to the wall with spikes of greed."[380] To labor, he shouted, "The Republicans . . . voted themselves a cut in taxes and voted you a cut in freedom. The 80th Republican Congress failed to crack down on prices. But it cracked down on labor all right." To farmers, he argued for price supports. In the West, he harped on reclamation and power projects, arguing that the Republicans wanted to give the control of government efforts to develop power "into the hands of highjackers--so they can stick you with high prices."

Truman personalized his attacks. The tirade in Fresno, California was typical. "You have a terrible Congressman here in this district. He has done everything he possibly could to cut the throats of the farmer and the laboring man. If you send him back, that will be your fault if you get your throat cut." The Congressman lost in November.[381] He called Dewey, Wall Street's "me too" stooge, and obliquely attacked Dewey for not being a veteran. That was a cheap shot. Dewey had been 14 when America entered World War I and was 39 and a candidate for Governor of New York at Pearl Harbor. Besides, he was a veteran of a different kind of war.

TIME dismissed the tirades as proof that Truman was showing the strain of the election. It reported that some of Truman's advisers on the train felt that his harpish name-calling sank below the dignity of a President. They pleaded with him to put his case in more statesmanlike phrases.

The more they criticized and pitied, the more Harry Truman spat out the most virulent tongue-lashings ever uttered by an incumbent President. What most seemed to infuriate Truman was that Dewey was not rising to the bait and getting into a slugging match with him. Like a boxer with only a flicking jab, Truman was hitting his foe, with seemingly little effect. He could not land the knockout punch that he desperately needed to win.

The "Give 'em hell" campaign was a symbiotic relationship. Truman was feisty to begin with and the crowds often came to hear his explosive invectives and egged him, shouting "Give 'em hell" or "Pour it on, Harry."

A lively fellow, impulsive and given to eruptions of anger and spite, Truman never talked down to his audience, showed no hint of pompousness. He never had to remind his audience that he had been a farmer. Often at his speeches, newsmen snickered and politicians winced, but his audience smiled sympathetically when he stumbled over a phrase or a name. Truman came across as a bantam rooster, fighting a little recklessly perhaps, but always with courage and a high heart. Many of his diatribes horrified his soberer followers, but he seemed a simple sincere man fighting against overwhelming odds.

But Truman imposed some limits. "When I was in Michigan, they wanted me to light into Senator Vandenberg. But I wouldn't do it. He'd supported the Marshall Plan; if it hadn't been for him, it might never have been approved in the Senate, and I wasn't about to forget that and start attacking him. And in California I wouldn't say anything against Governor Warren because he was a friend of mine."[382]

WHY GIVE MONEY TO A LOSER

Another spur to Harry's diatribes was that often the Republicans and even Henry Wallace could afford radio time. He rarely could. Money always runs to the favorite. Dewey was flush with cash. Truman became a beggar, unable even to find a campaign treasurer. Cornelius Vanderbilt was expected to take the job after the convention to underwrite any losses. He declined. Joseph P. Kennedy and Bernard Baruch, normally deep-pocketed supporters, left their checkbooks untouched. Two others also refused the President of the United States before Washington lawyer Louis Johnson accepted.

The opening of Truman's campaign almost did not occur. His Labor Day speech in Detroit was to be broadcast by radio but, on Saturday morning, the network announced that it wanted the $50,000 fee by the end of the day, or it would cancel the Monday broadcast. The local unions did not have that much cash on hand, and only a frantic appeal to Governor Roy Turner of Oklahoma raised the money from wealthy Democrats in that state.[383] Often, checks had not been in the banks long enough to clear. So McGrath had to carry as much as $35,000 in cash to the radio studios to get Truman on the air.[384]

In Oklahoma City, on September 28, the cash shortage even stranded the train in the station. Once more, Governor Turner saved the day. He convened a fund-raising party aboard the train and raised enough cash to fund the rest of that tour. Eight times the train could not leave a station without frantic telephoning to raise cash.[385]

Party treasurer Louis Johnson called some wealthy Democrats to the White House, and Truman got up on a chair in the Red Room to beg for money or the "Truman Special" would not get beyond Pittsburgh. Two men immediately pledged $10,000, to get the train rolling.[386]

Louis Johnson believed having the President of the United States treated so shabbily offended people. In fact, several Truman broadcasts were cut off intentionally to dramatize the lack of funds. On one occasion, a broadcast representative turned to Johnson and said, Truman would be cut off in a minute unless Johnson agreed to put up more dollars. Johnson replied: "Go ahead, that will mean another million votes."[387]

THE POLLS

What made fund raising so vexing was the widespread belief that it would be money tossed down a rathole. The polls cemented that belief.

America had almost a religious faith in the pollsters. Roper had been off by only 1.1 percent in 1936 and by .3 percent in 1944. Such successes had anointed the pollsters as celebrities in their own right with their own radio and TV shows. TIME put George Gallup on its cover and described him as a "big friendly teddy bear of a man with a passion for facts and figures." At the end of August, that teddy bear had asked the company handling advertising for the Dewey campaign, "Why does the Republican Committee want to spend any money? The results are a foregone conclusion."[388]

On September 9, Roper announced: "Thomas E. Dewey is almost as good as elected" with virtually no chance of an upset. Roper continued, "That being so, I can think of nothing duller or more intellectually barren than acting like a sports announcer who feels he must pretend he is witnessing a neck-and-neck race that will end up in a photo finish or a dramatic upset for the favorite--and then finally have to announce that the horse which was eight lengths ahead at the turns is still eight lengths ahead." Roper would keep polling but "stop reporting . . . [results] unless something really interesting happens. My silence on this point can be construed as an indication that Mr. Dewey is still so clearly ahead that we might just as well get ready to listen to his inaugural. . . ."[389]

By mid September, all three major polls were proclaiming that Dewey's election was as sure as Uncle Miltie's popularity. Gallup gave him a 48.5% to 36.5% lead over Truman to 5% for Wallace. Archibald M. Crossley predicted that Dewey would win at least 304 electoral votes and perhaps as many as 397. President Truman could only be certain of carrying nine states. Roper announced 44.2% for Dewey, 31.4 for Truman, 4.4 for Thurmond and Wallace 3.6.

Dewey was still polling roughly the 44 percent he had at a similar point in 1944. What had changed, and dramatically, was the Democratic candidate's standing with traditionally Democratic voters in the South and large cities. Among Democrats, he was down 22 points from 1944. Among independents, too, Truman lagged far behind FDR's showing. The Republicans just had to avoid mistakes, pray no world upheaval erupted, and their election seemed assured.

To understand why Democrats were so pessimistic, consider two things. First, ever since the Civil War, the party winning the midterm election had gone on to win the presidency in the next election.

Second, in 1944, Dewey had come closer to beating Roosevelt than anyone. Against the popular wartime President, Dewey had garnered 45 percent of the vote to FDR's 53. The rest split among the numerous splinter parties. Even if Dewey did not do any better than that in 1948, and everyone believed he would against the unpopular and ordinary Truman, the Democratic vote itself would be fragmented three ways - Truman, Wallace and the Dixiecrats. Wallace and the Dixiecrats would take away enough key states, so Dewey would win comfortably. The Philadelphia Evening Bulletin ran a cartoon of the four candidates playing poker, with Wallace and Thurmond slipping Dewey aces under the table.

Yet even in Roper's numbers, nearly all of those who had voted for Roosevelt, but did not fancy Truman, chose Wallace, Thurmond, or the don't-know category. So far, the invincible Dewey had made no inroads into Democratic strength.[390]

No one seemed to notice. Never before or since has such unanimity of opinion reigned. As the first presidential candidate to have his own polling unit, Dewey mirrored the country's faith in the science of public-opinion sampling. In July, Stassen warned him that he faced a formidable foe, but Dewey pulled out an advance copy of Roper's announcement and said: "My job is to prevent anything from rocking the boat."[391] That exchange showed the tone of the campaign. Truman was trying to win. Dewey was trying not to lose.

CHAPTER FIFTEEN

UNION MEN, FARMERS AND THE TRAVELING MEDICINE SHOW

THE LABOR VOTE

With the deep South lost, the Democrats focused on Negroes, veterans, consumers, but especially labor and farmers.

Labor votes in many states could mean victory or defeat. With many political machines offering only tepid support, the unions offered the most efficient organizations in the cities. Rowe had predicted: "President Truman and the Democratic Party cannot win without the active support of organized Labor. It is dangerous to assume that Labor now has nowhere else to go in 1948. Labor can stay home."[392]

Truman had jeopardized the support of labor by breaking strikes that he thought were against the national interest. As a liberal Democrat, Truman praised the right of industrial workers to strike - in theory. As President, he exhibited a 19th century farmer's intolerance towards strikes that could harm the country.

Since 1920, a descendant of several generations of Welsh coal miners, John L. Lewis, had run the United Mineworkers (UMW). Truman and Lewis did not get along, but then Lewis did not get along with many people.

Sporting the bushiest eyebrows in America, his mane of hair, flair for drama, and the tact of a blackjack made Lewis the nation's most colorful and controversial labor leader. He was also one of the most effective. He singlehandedly pulled miners out of poverty between World Wars I and II, pioneering extensive welfare benefits and job security provisions.[393] His dictatorial control over the UMW let Lewis hold sway in national labor affairs and thus over the American economy.

He was powerful because the UMW was powerful. The UMW was powerful, because coal was powerful. After World War II, however, his power waned as the importance of coal declined. The increased availability of cheaper, cleaner, more efficient, and more reliable (because of Lewis' frequent strikes) energy sources imperiled coal mining jobs.

The UMW struck again on April 1, 1946. Lewis had defied Roosevelt who preferred compromise. Defying Harry Truman was a mistake.

Truman seized the mines. When the operators refused to accept a contract that had been negotiated by federal authorities, the government kept control over the industry. In November 1946, Lewis issued a second strike call and the government replied with injunction proceedings. When Lewis ignored the injunction, a federal judge fined him $10,000 and the United Mineworkers $3.5 million.

Unchastened, Lewis began to focus on pensions. For centuries, people had been expected to work until infirmity or death. In 1948, 47 percent of men over 65 worked, as did 90 percent of men between 55 and 64. The New Deal had created Social Security, but the unions saw that as a foundation on which to build. In 1948, nearly half of the country's workers were excluded from any federal retirement income, while inflation had cut purchasing power of old age beneficiaries to well below the payment levels of 1940.[394]

In February, 1948, Lewis demanded the mine operators pitch in $100 a month for each 60 year or older miner with 20 years of service. When the operators balked, on March 15, almost 360,000 of 400,000 UMW members working in soft coal mines stopped work.

On April 3rd, a federal judge issued a temporary restraining order against the strikers. When Lewis did not direct them back to work, on April 7th, the judge ordered Lewis and the UMW to show cause why they should not be held in contempt.

On April 19th, he fined Lewis $20,000 and the UMW over a million dollars. Lewis ordered the miners back to work "immediately." But by then the UMW and the mine owners tentatively agreed on the $100 a month pension upon retirement at the age of 62.

Not only the UMW had a beef with Truman. In 1946, he had crushed the strike of the Brotherhood of Railway Trainmen. As he was addressing Congress to formally seek the power to draft the strikers, he was handed a note that the strike was settled. Truman's sledgehammer threat of conscription had cost him much of his labor support.

Less than a month after breaking Lewis' 1948 strike, Truman broke another railroad strike. On May 10, 18 hours before the strike deadline, President Truman ordered the Army to operate the nation's railroads to prevent "a nationwide tragedy." Then he gave the three labor unions involved, the engineers, firemen, and switchmen, until 5:00 that afternoon to call off the strike. That and a federal judge ended the strike.

Truman's merciless response to strikes or threatened strikes scared Labor. The CIO called him the nation's number one strike breaker. Ironically, Truman's savior with labor was the Taft-Hartley Act he vetoed but used so effectively. Fearing Republican Dewey in the White House and Taft still dominating the Senate, Labor reluctantly supported Truman, but Labor's support was not unanimous. Lewis called Truman totally unfit to be President. Wallace would almost certainly make inroads here. So Truman's first trip strove to shore up labor support.

THE LABOR DAY TRIP

The Truman Special with about 80 reporters and photographers, Secret Service, Signal Corpsmen, a dozen White House aides and secretaries, chugged out of Washington's Union Station at 3:40 p.m. Sunday, September 5th.[395]

On Labor Day, he spoke first at Grand Rapids, Michigan, shortly before 7 a.m., next an extemporaneous talk at Lansing, Michigan, then to Hamtranck, Michigan, before rolling to Detroit.

Before 150,000 workers in Cadillac Square, he delivered a stinging, blunt and truculent attack. Roaring that only he and the Democrats cared for them, he lambasted the Taft-Hartley Act and the Congress that had passed it over his veto.

TIME noted: "Then candidate Truman let his campaign theme run away with his judgment: 'If you let the Republican reactionaries get complete control of the government...I would fear not only for the wages and living standards of the American working man, but even for our Democratic institutions of free labor and free enterprise...These are critical times for labor . . . there is great danger ahead,'" the President warned. Dewey's election would surely usher in a return of the vicious cycle of boom and bust, helping only those who sought to "totally enslave the workingman." He repeated that melody in every labor center he visited. Such an outburst was not going to be the exception over the next eight weeks but the rule.

The response was also to be the norm. Dewey said nothing. Instead, he sent Stassen a few days later to defend the Taft-Hartley Act before 3,000 Detroit business executives, who probably did not need convincing, in the 5000 seat Masonic Temple. Stassen stressed the hypocrisy of Truman's criticizing the Act yet often using it to break strikes. Labeling Truman's speech an extreme demagogic appeal and a call for class warfare, Stassen accused Truman of sowing "the seeds of disunity for the sake of fleeting political advantage."[396]

THE SEPTEMBER 17 TRIP

Truman's biggest whistle-stop trip began on the morning of September 17th and lasted for 15 days. Secretary of State Marshall and vice presidential candidate Barkley saw Truman off at Union Station. Barkley yelled out, "Mow 'em down, Harry." Dressed in a tan double-breasted suit, Truman hollered back, "I'll mow 'em down, Alben, and I'll give 'em hell."[397] Reporters described the exchange and by the time Truman reached the West Coast, people were shouting, "Give 'em hell, Harry."

That first day set the pattern for the strenuous ordeal that a campaigning President endures. The daily White House pouch arrived containing reports and documents for Truman's signature. At 10:15 p.m., he was mourning Bernadotte's assassination in a rear platform appearance at Crestline, Ohio. At 2:15 a.m. Central Standard Time Saturday, in the Englewood switching yards in Illinois, he met with local politicians while sitting in his bed. At 5:44 a.m., he blasted the special interests to 2500 at Rock Island, Illinois. At 6:10 a.m., at the Iowa border, he greeted Senate candidates. Then to farm country.

THE FARM VOTE

The Rowe memorandum targeted farmers as the number one priority because they were enjoying such prosperity under the Democrats. Parity payments and Marshall Plan purchases, both Democratic programs, would keep the farmer comfortable. Could their traditional Republican ties be cut?

As the Ferdinand Magellan readied to leave Washington on September 17th, Clifford received a memo from the Secretary of Agriculture suggesting that in farm country, Truman exploit the failure of Congress to provide storage bins.[398]

In June, the Commodity Credit Corporation (CCC) needed a new charter. As an economy measure, Congress had put in the bill a provision barring the CCC from buying more grain storage bins. Without such government bins, farmers who did not have their own storage would have to sell their surpluses immediately at prices that would be lower, the better the harvest.

The bill came up on June 18th, the day before the session adjourned. Remember the last minute flurry of activity before the adjournment for the Republican Convention. The House and Senate were still fighting over the Marshall Plan appropriations, the draft bill and other major legislation. So the leadership of both Houses had suspended the rules and prohibited amendments. No Democrat objected to the bill, nor did the National Grange and American Farm Bureau, although the National Council of Farm Cooperatives did. The bill slid through with no debate and the Senate accepted it without change in its closing minutes. On July 3rd, Truman signed the bill into law.

The Dayton Daily News ran a series of articles under headlines such as "Congress acts to force down farmers' price at behest of grain lobby," but with surprisingly little notice along the coasts. Then the weather gods smiled on Harry Truman.

On August 10th, the Agriculture Department forecast the greatest crop in the nation's history: the largest corn crop, 3,681,000,000 bushels, or a billion, 55%, greater than 1947; the second largest wheat crop; and crops of oats, barley, rice, beans, hay, sugar cane, and beet sugar all well above the 10 year averages.

Farmers needed storage, but with bins scarce, food prices collapsed. Corn slid from $2.46 a bushel in January to $1.78 by September 15th and to $1.26 by the end of October. Wheat fell from $2.81 a bushel in January to $1.97 a bushel by September.[399] Without bins to store the surplus, a bumper crop for the farmers would mean not prosperity but heavy losses.

To reap this vote bonanza, Truman went to Dexter, Iowa, 40 miles west of Des Moines,on September 18 to address 80,000 at the National Plowing Contest.

Since 1940, farmers purchasing power had risen by 70% versus just 50% for all groups. At least 60 farmers flew to Dexter in their personal planes. Farmers were comfortable and meant to stay that way.

Truman blistered the Republicans with some of his most acerbic condemnations yet and focused on the grain storage issue. Even though Truman had signed the bill that the Democrats had not opposed, he now labeled it as a purely Republican idea which "stuck a pitchfork in the farmers' back."[400] "These big business lobbyists and speculators persuaded the Congress not to provide storage bins for the farmer . . . They don't want the farmer to be prosperous. . . ."

He stridently labeled the GOP "cunning men [who] want a return of the Wall Street economic dictatorship," and prisoners of "that notorious do-nothing Eightieth Congress." What Congress had already stolen away from the farmer was "only an appetizer," said Truman. "First the little cuts, then all price supports would be thrown out."

After listing the litany of problems the farmers had suffered under Republicans, Truman asked, "I wonder how many times you have to be hit on the head before you find out who's hitting you?" His closer hit home. "I'm not asking you just to vote for me. Vote for yourselves! Vote for your farms! . . . Vote for your future!"[401]

As a Midwesterner talking to Midwesterners, a former farmer talking to farmers, Truman suction-cupped himself to the storage issue in the 13 farm states. He could talk about plowing an arrow straight field and never having a "skipped place" when he sowed wheat. One farmer remarked to a reporter: "Young fellow, I want to tell you something. We farmers here in the Midwest like President Truman. What he says and how he says it makes sense to us. We don't care for this smart aleck fellow from New York, who doesn't know anything about our problem."[402]

Although Dewey was born in a small town in Michigan, he had become thoroughly easternized after attending Columbia. He now seemed the suavely automated epitome of eastern patrician Republicanism. His idea of a campaign photograph that would appeal to farmers was to milk a cow in white shirt, tie, and vest.[403] Only a month before the election did he even establish a farm division, but he chose New York's Assistant Commissioner of Agriculture to run it. 60% of New York's agriculture was marginal dairying, as Dewey's farm was. Growing wheat, corn or soybeans was a foreign language.

HUAC's Karl Mundt, running for the Senate in South Dakota, warned: "The farmers are getting disenchanted with Dewey. He has to come out here and make a farm speech. He can't win without the farm vote, and the farmers think they have a problem." Others voiced their concern about the farm vote, but Dewey, swayed by the polls, did not make any major farm speeches. The man who said, "My farm is my roots" snubbed the farm vote.

RACE RELATIONS

1948 was a year of black and white in television and race relations. The war had lifted Negroes economically. Negro employment in industry increased sharply. In aircraft factories alone, it rose from 0 to 5,000 - and in government service from 60,000 to 200,000. Negro women especially benefited. Previously relegated to working as domestics, they joined the industrial ranks for the first time.[404]

But economic progress did not mean social progress. During the war, Negro soldiers had entered a lunch room in Salinas, Kansas. "You boys know we don't serve coloreds here," the manager announced, but the soldiers had not come to eat but to see. They stood "inside the door, staring at what we had come to see - German prisoners of war who were having lunch at the counter...it was no jive talk." Hitler's soldiers, interned at the local POW camp, were welcome but not America's Negro soldiers.[405] Pride at what Negroes had suffered and accomplished during the war translated into a refusal to recede into a second class mentality.

After his two executive orders on civil rights, Truman dared not campaign in the Deep South. Speeches to segregated crowds would hurt him among northern Negroes. Insistence upon mixed audiences would rank him with Henry Wallace in the minds of southern whites. The South became Barkley's territory.

Truman's efforts had won him the support of the most famous Negro. Joe Louis announced: "Harry S. Truman has done more for my people than Franklin D. Roosevelt ever did." Louis aimed to replace every dollar and every vote that the Dixiecrats cost the party with a Negro dollar and a Negro vote.[406]

THE COURTS BREACH THE SEGREGATED WALLS

On January 12, the Supreme Court had ruled that no state could discriminate against a law school applicant on the basis of race. In the first week of October, a federal court ruled unconstitutional a state law that barred Negroes from the University of Oklahoma's graduate school. The University then seated its first Negro in an anteroom where he could see and hear the professor, but was kept separate as Oklahoma's Jim Crow law demanded. Also, in October, the state Supreme Court declared California's ban on mixed marriages unconstitutional by a 4 to 3 vote.

For the first time in history, some 35,000 South Carolina Negroes voted freely in the Democratic primary. They owed it to Federal Judge J. Waties Waring. When he ordered the Democratic Party to open its enrollment books to Negroes and permit them "full participation in Party affairs," he became a pariah. When lightning struck a house next to his summer cottage, its owner put up a sign, "Dear God, he lives next door."

John Gunther wrote in his classic 1947 best seller Inside America: "That the United States is very nearly 10% a black nation is known to everybody and ignored by almost everybody--except maybe the 10%."[407] Gunther realized "the most gravid, cancerous, and pressing of all American problems is that of the Negro, insoluble under present political and social conditions though capable of great amelioration."[408] Despite the depth and breath of the problem, some rays of hope appeared. Victory on the military and civil service fronts were not the only successes. Gunther reported: "I watch

Negroes shopping in the best Atlanta department store (they could not, however, work as clerks there), and where as before World War II, it was almost unthinkable that a Negro girl could serve whites at a drug store or similar establishment, this is now fairly common."

Segregation was breaking down not only because it was unjust. Bigotry was staggeringly expensive and thrust the South into poverty. It meant two of everything, schools, insane asylums, penitentiaries, playgrounds had to be built and maintained.

THE TRAVELING MEDICINE SHOW

To reach all these disparate groups, Truman lived on the road. Campaigning is show business which, in 1948, did not mean television nor even radio. It meant an old time carnival, barnstorming from one small town to another, complete with shills, advance men, and props.

By the next cross country trip, Truman's campaign had settled into a frenetic routine. September 30 was typical. The President spoke at Mt. Vernon, West Frankfort, Herrin, Carbindale, Marian, El Borado and Carmi, all in Illinois; Mt. Vernon and Evansville in Indiana; and Henderson, Owensboro, Hawesville, Irvington, and Louisville, Kentucky. Between breakfast and midnight that day he had traveled 500 miles by train, 141 by automobile and bus, made 15 speeches in 15 different towns, changed his clothes 8 times and met 250 politicians, labor leaders and civic dignitaries. [409]

Often he made his first rear-platform talk before six a.m. Even after night rallies, the train would stop at a small town, and he would come out (often in a bathrobe) and talk to people waiting in the darkness. Bess had his bed kept made up so he could nap between shows.

TIME's October 11, 1948 issue announced that Truman's chronic cheerfulness and energy amazed newsmen. Despite a sore throat, this 64 year old leaped out of bed early every morning "apparently unable to wait for another exhausting day."

Trying to keep as much as possible to his White House schedule, Truman arose at 5 a.m. (Pundits jibed that he did it only to have more time to put both feet in his mouth.) Then, with the Secret Service, he took a vigorous one or two mile walk at the Army marching pace of 120 steps per minute.[410]

He kept himself in good shape. The 5 ft. 9 inch Truman weighed 170 - 175 with blood pressure 120 to 128 over 80. He ate heartily, preferring steaks and roast beef as did most American men, but not to excess. He boasted he could still wear suits bought during his first year as a senator.

He dressed with unusual care, preferring well cut, double-breasted suits, often gray or tan but always, like Alger Hiss, wearing a "display handkerchief," folded into four points in the breast pockets. People who saw him for the first time that campaign remarked that the supposedly homespun Truman was certainly a natty dresser. Then they were reminded that he was an ex-haberdashery store owner.

The campaign train became a fast moving, well-rehearsed masterpiece of corn and the common touch. First, the high school or other local band greeted Truman with "Hail to the Chief," "The Missouri Waltz," his campaign theme "I'm Just Wild About Harry" or the state anthem, depending on its repertoire. Next would appear a town beauty, a local union or fraternity man who would present him with a gift of the city's specialty, a bag of peaches, a bunch of celery, a miner's hat or just a key to the City. A local political leader would then say a few words to introduce the President.

Truman's staff sent a list of questions to each town, asking for local color, local history, the names of local officials, any mottos, and then, "What are the particular complaints that people have about high prices in your town? What is the housing situation in your town? How many veterans do you have?" So, Truman would warm the crowd with enough local tidbits to show he knew who they were. Then he would quip some pleasantries. For example, he hoped they would vote so that he would not have to go "hunting around in this housing shortage" but could stay in the White House.

Truman would next launch into his tirade about the Republicans, giving apocalyptic predictions of what would happen if the GOP won. His "shills," such as Clark Clifford, mingled in the audience to clap at the right time and to bellow out, "Give 'em hell, Harry," if necessary.

His diatribe over, "With a surer sense of timing than he shows in major addresses, he pauses a moment, looks quizzically at the crowd, smiles, and asks, very humbly, 'And now, how'd you like to meet my family?' He cocks his head slightly to catch the response; he has the appealing look of a man who wouldn't be surprised if your answer was no, but would be terribly hurt." [411]

First, "Mizz Truman", he would often refer to her as "the boss." The plump, motherly Bess Truman would then come through the dark green drapes which curtained the Pullman's rear door and stand on Harry's right beneath the striped canopy. Bess stuck to a slate blue suit, a basic black dress or other sober costumes, but women oohed and aahed over her enormous purple orchids. The normally dour first lady grinned happily. "And now I'd like to have you meet my daughter Margaret," who was called Miss Margaret in the border or southern states. Margaret would step forward. Wearing a gracious smile and a thin red wool suit, she got the best hand of all, a few wolfish whistles, and a dozen long stemmed roses."[412]

After the Truman womenfolk flanked Harry, a railroad official at a telephone in the car ahead of the President's, would call the locomotive engineer - fifteen cars or a quarter of a mile, down the track - and tell him to get slowly underway.[413] Thousands of American voters would always remember the tableau of a smiling, waving Harry Truman, the only President they had ever seen in person, standing beneath that canopy as his train pulled slowly away and faded from sight, surrounded by his wife and daughter who would often throw a rose to the crowd.[414]

On that cross country September train trip, Truman delivered at least 126 speeches with 140 stops. The Ferdinand Magellan wheezed back into Union Station, Sunday morning, October 2nd, with the presidential party exhausted, but not the candidate.

THE NAYSAYERS

Truman worked so hard on the campaign that his enemies touted it as proof of his irrelevance. Walter Lippman wrote, "But for Mr. Truman's campaign tour, it would never have been possible to prove to the country how small a part Mr. Truman actually plays in the great office which he holds. . . . Mr. Truman may get reports on what is happening . . . but there is not even an attempt to pretend that the President is directing affairs, is making the decisions, is forming or conducting policy."

Lippmann's statement had some truth. No one can campaign as hard as Truman did and remain a fully involved President. During the campaign, Truman delegated more than ever to the dutiful Marshall in whom he had absolute faith.

Day after day, newspapers that had favored Roosevelt over Dewey four years before, were endorsing Dewey, including in Missouri, the St. Louis Post Dispatch, the St. Louis Star Times and St. Joseph News Press. Most of the papers had switched reluctantly. They favored the Democratic Party and liked Truman personally, but they felt he lacked the leadership needed. The Baltimore Sun stated in a front page editorial, "However much affection we may feel for Mr. Truman and whatever sympathy we may have for him and his struggles and with his difficulties, to vote him into the presidency on November 2nd would be a tragedy for the country and for the world."[415]

CHAPTER SIXTEEN

THE MEN WHO WOULD BE KING - NOW OR LATER

DEWEY'S CAMPAIGN

In one of those odd coincidences in political life, at the end of August, Dewey attended the funeral of Charles Evans Hughes. As the Republican candidate in 1916, Hughes ran against incumbent Woodrow Wilson. On election night, he had gone to bed thinking he had won. He awoke to find his victory had evaporated in California by 3,777 votes. Hughes lost by 23 electoral votes. As if to ward off the curse of what had befallen Hughes in his quest to defeat an incumbent Democratic president, Dewey promised newsmen at the funeral that the campaign would be "rugged and extensive."

He lied. He had every advantage except spirit. The Dewey campaign suffered from the two deadly sins of politics. It was boring and it was lazy.

BORING - DEWEY'S RELUCTANCE TO FIGHT

Gone was the fire-breathing campaigner of Oregon who had attacked Truman for causing the inflation, mishandling domestic Communists, letting 200 million fall into Soviet clutches and rapidly abandoning 400 million Chinese. After the nomination, he preached prattle and refused to put on any Indian headdress or cowboy hat, saying he "just wouldn't look right." He became as exciting as moss.[416]

Fretting that the "precise nature" of most of 1948's issues were already too negative or "too complex for campaign oratory," he announced: "I will not get down into the gutter with that fellow." In 1944, Dewey had attacked Roosevelt for not preparing the country for war. While many Republicans loved the speech, Dewey concluded that it had cost him votes. He resolved not to repeat the mistake. He shelved his combative instincts and ran as a statesman, calling for national unity, never mentioning Truman, and avoiding issues that could split his own party. His campaign became a lecture tour.[417] Newsweek reported the obvious: "His speeches bristled with platitudes...His confident speechwriters took no chances by getting too concrete or offending anybody."

Jules Abels, a historian of the campaign, gave a perfect example: "What does this mean? It is from his speech at the Alfred E. Smith Memorial Dinner on October 21st. 'By a simple rediscovery of our devotion to human rights and the protection of others from the abuse of those rights, we can draw a line through every conflict and draw it straight and true. It can be drawn so that both civil liberty and social responsibility complement and fortify each other.'"[418] What does that mean?

Forty years later, Dewey's campaign manager, Herbert Brownell, listened to a recording of a major Dewey speech that he had helped write. At the end, he shook his head. "There's nothing there."[419]

As the Louisville Courier Journal mocked after the election: "No presidential candidate in the future will be so inept that four of his major speeches can be boiled down to these historic four sentences: Agriculture is important. Our rivers are full of fish. You cannot have freedom without liberty. The future lies ahead. (We might add a fifth...the TVA is a fine thing, and we must make certain that nothing like it ever happens again.)" [420]

Dewey's above the fray approach was premeditated. Attacking the Roosevelt/Truman administrations for appeasement and foreign policy blunders at Yalta and in China would erode the spirit of bipartisanship. Vandenberg warned that the next "Republican Secretary of State is going to need Democratic votes in the Senate just as badly as the present administration has needed Republican votes. . . . It is peculiarly our job--yours and mine--to see that bipartisan liaison of the next Congress does not become impossible. Otherwise November will represent a phyrric victory."[421] Dewey agreed.

So Dewey spoke in lofty generalities of America's destiny - his speeches more like an inaugural address than a candidate's compellingly persuasive oratory. The New York Times reported that Dewey was "acting like a man who has already been elected and is merely marking time, waiting to take office."

In its September 20th issue, TIME Magazine pointed out that the campaign would be notable for its irresponsible charges and ridiculous statements and picked some of Truman's and Wallace's comments, but noted: "Candidate Dewey had not yet said anything."

The man who had stared down Lucky Luciano and a horde of Murder Incorporated's killers came across as a wimp. Alistair Cooke captured Dewey's campaign: "He has gone after the Presidency with the humorless calculation of a certified public accountant in pursuit of a holy grail."

MISSED CHANCES

What was so maddening to Republicans then and so mystifying today is why Dewey, the skilled debater, failed to emphasize the following legitimate points.

Dewey never emphasized his career as the racket-busting prosecutor of organized crime or his extensive accomplishments as New York's governor. An honorable, efficient, and fiscally prudent, slightly liberal governor, Dewey had cut taxes, doubled state aid to education, raised salaries for state employees, reduced the state's overall indebtedness by over $100 million, and put through the first state law in the country prohibiting racial discrimination in employment.[422]

Dewey never attacked Truman for his hypocrisy. Despite all his harangues to Labor about the Taft-Hartley Act, six times Truman had crushed strikes using the Act's injunction. Dewey virtually snubbed the labor vote. His labor committee was headed not by a union man, but by a utilities and corporation lawyer. So, Labor solidly backed the Democrats, if not Truman.

The Rowe memo feared that Negroes would defect to Dewey, with good reason. On April 5th, 1948, Dewey signed a bill outlawing racial and religious discrimination in admitting students to colleges in New York. He described such practices as "obnoxious and undemocratic." The Republican platform was equally adamant on civil rights but, inexplicably, Dewey ceded civil rights to Truman.

Dewey could have vigorously defended Congress, especially in the field of foreign affairs. Instead, he offered only mild, isolated and low key remarks that he was proud of that Congress. He never pointed out that despite Truman's constant bluster about gluttons of privilege and Wall Street bloodsuckers, his administration buldged with Wall Street habitues. Even liberal columnist I.F. Stone labeled Truman's blasts at Wall Street as "transparent forays into a ludicrous demagogy."[423]

Inflation was still a problem. Truman had refused to increase the defense budget, because it would add to the inflation. Yet, he did not hesitate to urge greater spending on all his target voting blocs. Unashamedly, he complained to city crowds about high food prices and to rural audiences he clamored for high farm supports and more payments to farmers. H.L. Mencken wrote after the election: "If there were a formidable body of cannibals in the electorate last Tuesday, President Truman would have promised them American missionaries, fattened at the taxpayer's expense."

Nor did the GOP prove adept at appealing to Jewish voters. In late October, after Dewey disagreed with the Bernadotte plan and pointed out Truman's inconsistency, he kept silent on the issue while Truman did an abrupt about face, promising Israel both financial aid and de jure recognition.

The spy allegations, especially the brewing Hiss case, transfixed the nation more than any soap opera. Republicans urged Dewey to trumpet that lax security and imprudent appointments had damaged foreign policy and national security, and beat Truman over the head with it.

A big applause getter was Dewey's boast that Republicans would not appoint Communists to official posts in the first place. Yet he used the line surprisingly rarely. Dewey never ripped into Truman for his "I like old Joe" (Stalin) speech nor did he respond when Truman charged: "The Republicans have impeded and made more difficult our efforts to cope with Communism in this country."[424] As Senator Hugh Scott explained, Dewey "was no McCarthy. He thought it degrading to suspect Truman personally of being soft on Communism. He wasn't going around looking under beds."[425]

Any of America's millions of boxing fans could recognize and appreciate Dewey's strategy. He was way ahead on the scorecards of all the ringside experts. All he had to do was avoid a knockout by a lucky punch and the victory was his.

LAZY

Dewey kept a decidedly less frenetic pace. Dewey left the Philadelphia convention and went home to rest. He would not leave Albany to begin campaigning until September 19, six weeks before the election, which, as the New York Times noted, would make his campaign "the shortest undertaken in recent years by the presidential candidate of the major party out of power."[426] When Stassen suggested that Dewey answer Truman's Labor Day harangue himself, his staff replied, "The governor doesn't want to start his campaign for another two weeks." Dewey would deliver his first speech on September 20th.

Dewey's train campaign kept part time hours. On his first transcontinental trip, Dewey made fifty rear-platform appearances to Truman's 140. Dewey started his campaign day in retiree leisure at 10 a.m. Truman was haranguing at the crack of dawn. Even an eager crowd could not break Dewey's routine or disturb his sleep.

While Newsweek marveled at "the unprecedented grind Harry Truman had mapped for himself," it noted that Dewey "all but punched a time clock." In its election eve issue, Newsweek gasped: "If Thomas E. Dewey was indeed running for the presidency, he gave little outward sign of it last week." From Monday through Sunday, he remained strictly within the borders of his own state of New York. He did not give a single campaign address.

THE POP UP TOASTER

Whatever Dewey lacked in warmth, he made up for in a coldly efficient campaign machine. Dewey was a much more experienced campaigner than Truman. Truman had won two Senate campaigns in Missouri and had run for the Vice Presidency in 1944, but this was Dewey's third campaign for the Presidency. Just as at the convention, the experience showed. Fat cats seeking to ingratiate themselves with the next occupant of the Oval Office showered him with money. Much of that money ensured that the campaign train ran smoothly with plenty of food and drink for the reporters.

Everyone who boarded the Dewey train received badges and baggage checks with the inscription "Dewey Victory Special." The press received Dewey's speeches usually 12 to 24 hours before delivery. Correspondents on Truman's train often missed deadlines because his speeches were extemporaneous or in final script only a few minutes before delivery. Such helter skelter organization caused the newsmen on the train to file only

75,000 words a day, half the "copy drop" from Dewey's train.

One correspondent who traveled on both trains wrote that transferring from Truman's train to Dewey's was "like leaving a casual, free and easy theater stock company on tour to join up with a sleek New York musical." Richard Rovere called it "the difference between horse hair and foam rubber, between the coal-stove griddle and the pop up toaster. Dewey is the pop up toaster."[427]

THE PRESS SAW WHAT THEY WANTED TO SEE

Ignoring Dewey's vapid prose and leisurely pace, the press reported what the polls said they were seeing. Early in the campaign, reporters breathlessly portrayed Dewey's mesmerizing effect on the crowds and that people were eating up Dewey's talks, even about unity, while Truman was seen as oddly and pathetically flailing about. Newsweek's Lindley credited Dewey "not only with smart campaign tactics, but with the sound strategic preparations for the trials beyond November 2nd." James Reston of The New York Times sighed that Truman was not conveying "the one thing he wants to convey, a conviction that something really fundamental is at stake in his campaign."

Joseph Alsop's depiction was typical: "There was something rather sad about the contrast between the respective campaign debuts here in Iowa. The Truman show was threadbare and visibly unsuccessful--the Dewey show was opulent. It was organized down to the last noisemaking device. It exuded confidence. The contest was really too uneven. After it was all over, one felt a certain sympathy for the obstinately laboring President." Alsop did not mention and perhaps did not appreciate that Dewey had addressed a crowd of 8,000 in the Drake University fieldhouse, while Truman had spoken to 75,000.

WALLACE

In contrast to Dewey's relaxed pre-victory lap, Wallace also set a furious pace, traveling more than 55,000 miles, mostly by plane, and visiting nearly every state. Naturally shy and retiring, ill at ease in public places, rumpled, and completely incapable of small talk, Wallace was a political oxymoron.[428]

Truman had said in 1945, that despite four years of presiding over the Senate, Wallace hardly knew any senators.[429] Yet, he steeled himself to campaign strenuously for his principles and desire for world peace.[430]

Unfortunately, the more he campaigned, the more he barbecued himself. His statements grew more inflammatory, shrill and apocalyptic. He accused both Truman and Dewey of manufacturing the Berlin crisis to fuel a war economy. Wallace blamed Bernadotte's murder on "British and American imperialism." Not to be outdone, Glen Taylor announced: "Nazis are running the U.S. government. So why should Russia make peace with them?"[431] H.L. Mencken announced that Wallace had lost "what little sense he had formerly, if indeed, he ever had any at all."

Stalin crumbled Wallace's keystone appeal. As Cabell Phillips wrote in the New York Times, Wallace's movement had "lost much of its zealous appeal, chiefly because of the paradox of Mr. Wallace's pro-Russian policy in the face of the realities of Russian conduct in Europe and the United Nations.[432] Even the crowds at his meetings had become uneasy at some of his speeches and often would literally sit on their hands at obvious applause lines. Sensing the dissatisfaction, in a September 23rd speech, Truman played his trump card to wavering Wallacites: "Think again. Don't waste your vote."

Many idealistic youngsters, leftist educators and intellectuals supported Wallace, but that took courage. Merely appearing at a Wallace rally could taint them as Communists. One Wallace supporter was stabbed to death in Charleston, South Carolina when someone cut "the Communist nigger-lover's" jugular vein with a ten-inch knife.[433] Another key supporter was stoned in Illinois; four women supporters were kidnapped and beaten in Georgia; a campaigner was kidnapped, beaten and head-shaved with a pen knife in Pontiac, Michigan.[434] At numerous colleges, especially public universities where the conservative state legislatures could cut funding, professors who openly campaigned for Wallace often suffered reprisal, including dismissal.

Wallace matched the courage of his supporters, as even his critics had to admit, braving insult and injury. In September, he toured the South to challenge the racists on their home turf.[435]

In Durham, North Carolina, 25 noisy anti-Wallace firebrands threw eggs and set off firecrackers and stink bombs. In the resulting riot, one Wallace supporter was stabbed twice in the arm and six times in the back. When order was finally restored, Wallace demanded a police escort. While the half Negro audience of 1500 eyed the main entrance, a seldom used door on the opposite side opened. A uniformed National Guardsman, pistol in hand, entered followed by Wallace, surrounded by four plainclothes officers. He began his speech by acknowledging that this was "the most unique introduction I ever experienced." His speech was frequently interrupted and constantly heckled.[436]

Next day, on Main Street in Burlington, North Carolina, he was pelted with eggs and tomatoes. Turning to a man in the crowd, Wallace asked plaintively, "Am I in America?" In Greensborough, demonstrators greeted Wallace with another shower of eggs and tomatoes. Some struck his head and shoulders and splotched his white shirt. An 8 yr. old boy sat on his father's shoulders, busily heaving tomatoes at Wallace, while other members of the crowd booed and pitched eggs.

For the rest of his tour in North Carolina, people pelted this basically very good man with everything from eggs and tomatoes to peach stones. President Truman and the governors of North Carolina and Mississippi denounced such mob violence, but local officials did little to quell the disturbances.[437] In Houston, John J. Staskiel, a seaman from Pennsylvania, had let loose just as Wallace began to address an unsegregated crowd of 4,000. Throwing eggs and tomatoes, he hit the microphone and rostrum and only splattered Wallace's suit. Said an apologetic policeman who hustled Staskiel out, "I gave the guy three chances and he still couldn't hit Wallace, so I threw him out."

Wallace went South to prove a point, but also for the publicity. He addressed only unsegregated audiences; refused to stay in hotels enforcing discrimination; dined only in unsegregated restaurants and, if that were impossible, ate a box lunch on a train. He slept in the homes of Negroes. In Little Rock, Arkansas, he could have spoken in ten different places, but he chose four where he knew that he would be prohibited. On leaving the South, he fired his most provocative shot, that Dixie's laws should be changed to permit intermarriage.[438]

One commentator wrote of Wallace's southern campaigning, "His journey may well turn out to have been the redeeming feature of an otherwise ill advised candidacy."[439]

THURMOND

Meanwhile, James Strom Thurmond was campaigning at an 18-hour a day clip, covering 25,795 miles, making 107 speeches and earning a place on the October 11 cover of TIME. With his forefinger chopping at the microphone, Thurmond would harangue the crowd about a new police state with all power centered in Washington. Thurmond labeled Truman's fair employment practices committee "Communistic" and racial integration of the Armed Services "un-American."

Considered a moderate among southern politicians, Thurmond had sought to repeal the poll tax, punish lynchers, and enlarge educational facilities for Negroes. It was impossible to distinguish Thurmond from the Dixiecrat movement, however. H.L. Mencken called him, "An intelligent and honest man and probably the best of all candidates, [but] he is handicapped by the fact that all the worst morons in the South are for him."

OTHER FUTURE PRESIDENTS ON THE HUSTINGS

A new generation of political leaders came on the national scene. Men who had recently returned from the War were entering politics and would shape the post war world.

Five present or future U.S. presidents were campaigning that year. John Kennedy and Richard Nixon sought re-election to the House. Gerald Ford campaigned to get to the House. Lyndon Johnson was fighting to win the Senate seat that had eluded him in 1940. This was the race of Johnson's life. If he won, he would be a United States Senator. If he lost, he would just be another Texan.

Johnson's opponent, former Governor Coke Stevenson, was a Texas Dewey. He did not campaign as hard or as long as Johnson and was much less flamboyant. Reserved and quiet, he stumped Texas in his dusty Plymouth, unadorned with any campaign banners, let alone loudspeakers.

Copying the Truman method, Johnson rarely gave set speeches, but personal extemporaneous talks repeating constant themes and getting to know his audience. Only the mode of travel differed. To spread his name and to attract crowds, Johnson became the first politician to campaign by helicopter - an essential prop not only to cover Texas but a masterful crowd builder. Most people had never seen a helicopter. So, after advance men announced his coming, Johnson had the pilot circle and descend slowly so curious crowds could gather.

The August 23rd Newsweek highlighted Johnson's campaign and called him the "man from the skies," and a "seasoned and ambitious man." Campaigning "with the fervor of a thirsty desert wanderer heading for a water hole, he had leapfrogged across the state in a helicopter, had done his best to get siren-tooting motorcycle escorts when campaigning by automobile."

So tireless was Johnson, covering 4500 miles and 178 towns in 3 weeks, that his helicopter needed a factory overhaul. Without slackening his own pace, Johnson merely switched to a smaller "windmill" and kept flying. He also used radio and advertising extensively.

Normally, the Texas senate race would have been decided already. In Texas, the real election came not in November but in the Democratic primary. There, Stevenson had defeated Johnson and the other candidates but had not won a majority. In the runoff, Stevenson again won but Johnson demanded a recount, alleging irregularities. On the recount, Johnson won by 87 votes out of 1 million. The margin earned Johnson the nickname "Landslide Lyndon" and permanently sullied his reputation because of the allegations of lost ballots, phony ballots, dead voters and a cover up in counties controlled by Johnson's backers. But Johnson went on the ballot, became a senator, majority leader, then Vice President and President.

∾

CHAPTER SEVENTEEN

THE FINAL STRETCH

TRUMAN'S LARGE CROWDS

Autumn sparkled almost everywhere. The bright blue October sky oversaw already scarlet New England sumac. TIME reported "Last week, north, south, east and west, the U.S. was a fat and prosperous land." Mississippi and Arkansas had the biggest cotton crop in a decade. In Illinois, Iowa, and Indiana, the greatest corn crop in history awaited picking. "There was a new confidence in the U.S., born of the harvest and nurtured with the sweat of work that matched the weather and the scene."

Americans had a saying in 1948 that people did not get interested in the election until after the World Series. So once the Cleveland Indians beat the Boston Braves on October 11, America's attention could shift from the national pastime to politics. As the fall got chillier and the nights longer, Truman's crowds grew larger, friendlier and louder.[440]

In October, in St. Paul, Minnesota, 21,000 people, (15,000 inside the auditorium, 6,000 outside) interrupted Truman 42 times for applause. Dewey appeared in St. Paul two days later and drew only 7,000.[441] In Montgomery, West Virginia, Truman was so stunned by the turnout at 10:45 p.m. that he asked the photographers to turn around and take a picture of the people. That was the real news to show the country, he said.[442]

Newsweek noted: "Crowds, far bigger crowds than were being drawn by Thomas E. Dewey, were flocking to see and hear him." TIME reported: "Politicians and columnists seem puzzled by the phenomenon" that Truman was drawing such large crowds even though the polls said he could not win. It tried to explain it by sympathy for the underdog, admiration for spunkiness, or just plain curiosity about his speeches, which it called frantic and just a little ludicrous.

But sharp-eyed observers realized that they came for more than a glimpse at a living snapshot. Charles T. Lucey of the Scripps-Howard chain wrote on October 15: "The polls and the pundits say Harry Truman hasn't a chance to be returned to the White House, but you'd never guess it from the way people come out to see him. . . ."

SIGNS OF DEWEY'S WEAKNESS

Not only crowd size signaled an undercurrent. In October, the Baltimore Sun, the New York Times, and TIME Magazine all noted that Dewey's campaign was sagging while Truman's was ascending. Farm state representatives wrote to Dewey expressing some concern, but nothing changed.

Using his celebrity from the Hiss case, Nixon toured nine states on behalf of the Dewey/Warren ticket. On one of his trips, he complained, "We're losing this thing--we're throwing it away. I didn't find any Republican enthusiasm anywhere and I was in some pretty conservative places. The party leaders and workers are rolling in complacency; they think it's in the bag. Well it isn't..."[443]

On October 18, a new Gallup poll showed Dewey's lead cut to six points. Two Republican fund-raisers in Massachusetts warned Dewey's campaign, "We can't find that there is any interest at all in Dewey. . . He's not stirring the people with the kind of campaign you're running." The warning was ignored.

Contrary data was disbelieved. When Denver pollsters found that Truman would carry Colorado by 3%, they assumed they had made a mistake and predicted that Dewey would win the state.[444]

Carl McCardle, national correspondent for the Philadelphia Bulletin, had spent much of the fall traveling with Dewey and Truman switching from one train to the other. After viewing the crowd response, he told his editor Truman was going to win. "Don't write that!" the editor exploded, "Don't talk to me about it. Don't even think about it. You're wrong!"[445]

POLLS AND PUNDITS CONTINUE THEIR UNANIMITY

Despite Truman's large crowds and the other signs, the polls and pundits unfailingly supported each other.

Clark Clifford stepped off the train to buy the October 11 Newsweek with a poll of 50 leading journalists. Truman was sitting reading a newspaper as Clifford tried to slip by on his return. Not wanting to share the bad news with his boss, Clifford had hidden the magazine, but Truman asked, "What does it say, Clark?" After Clifford feigned a lack of understanding, Truman put it more directly. "What have you got under your coat, Clark?" "Nothing, Mr. President." "Clark, I saw you get off the train just now, and I think that you went in there to see if they had a newsstand with a copy of Newsweek. I think maybe you have it under your coat." Clifford reluctantly handed it over.

Newsweek's fifty top political writers, all gave victory to Dewey, with an average of 366 electoral votes, a flat hundred more than he needed. Truman's verdict: "Don't worry about that poll, Clark. I know every one of those 50 fellows, and not one of them has enough sense to pound sand into a rathole."[446]

The next week's TIME predicted Dewey would win 29 states with 350 electoral votes, Truman would earn only 9 with 83 electoral votes, Thurmond would take 4 with 38 electoral votes, and 6 states with 60 electoral votes were still doubtful. When 51 members of the National Press Club in Washington were polled, 50 selected Dewey, 1 selected Truman. The dissenting vote was cast by Truman who as President was a lifetime member of the club.

FOREIGN AFFAIRS

The world was a dangerous place in 1948 as fighting and violence flickered menacingly. Besides the Arab-Israeli War, Communists would soon win the civil war in China, a series of military coups and attempted coups ran like a fever through Latin America.

In the Spring of 1948, the Gallup Poll found that 65% of the people sensed foreign problems as the most important issue in the campaign. As 1948 went on, Truman's foreign policy won increasingly strong popular bipartisan support, especially his actions on Berlin and Israel.

While Dewey believed that the Berlin crisis stemmed from the Democrats' failure to negotiate specific corridor rights, he decided not to make this a political issue. On July 24th, Dewey declared, "The present duty of Americans is not to be divided by past lapses but to unite to surmount present dangers. We shall not allow a domestic partisan irritation to divert us from this indispensable unity."[447]

Truman did not politicize the Berlin Airlift. When reporters asked him about it, he referred them to General Marshall. He did not have to politicize it. News of the airlift filled the papers and Americans strongly supported this refusal to knuckle under to Stalin. With Dewey silent on the issue, every plane flying into Berlin might just as well be fluttering a "Vote For Truman" banner!

So despite its importance, foreign policy never became a major issue in the campaign.

THE CAMPAIGN'S LAST TWO WEEKS - DEWEY COASTS, HARRY GOES ALL OUT

The October 25th TIME declared: "Few people outside of Harry Truman give him even an outside chance of getting the electoral vote necessary for election." TIME opined that the sure loser Truman and the clear winner Dewey campaigned in the last half of October only because control of the 81st Congress remained in doubt. During the last swing through the Great Plains, the confident Dewey appealed more for GOP senators than for himself.

Actually, Dewey's combative juices had started to flow. Tired of being a punching bag, the ex-prosecutor wanted to strike back at Truman. He did let loose in a few speeches, but his press secretary polled the newsmen and reported that all of them believed a slugfest would be a mistake. To be sure, Dewey conferred with ninety of the ninety-six Republican State committeemen and committeewomen. All but one urged him to stay on the high road. The election was won, and Harry's rhetoric would only stain his already blotched reputation. Dewey resumed his high road campaign [448] and lost his last chance at victory.

HARRY COURTS OHIO - DEWEY IGNORES IT

Truman campaigned furiously in Ohio, especially rural Ohio. On October 11th, he whistlestopped Lima, Ottawa, Deshler, Fostoria, Willard and Rittman, all small towns in Ohio. Columnists thought he was wasting time speaking to a few hundred people in such a Republican stronghold. But Ohio proved crucial and this single, supposedly unsophisticated trip may have made the difference.[449]

At the end of October, Dewey made his only trip to Ohio. Taft boarded the train in Toledo but had virtually no exchange with Dewey. He appeared with Dewey in Cleveland where he praised Dewey and the Ohio ticket. Dewey ignored Taft's praise and the Ohio ticket. Instead, he focused on aid to Europe. As a liberal/moderate Republican, he viewed many Congressional leaders, such as Taft, as not merely conservative but reactionaries. Dewey relied more on Stassen and drove a permanent wedge between the liberal/moderate and conservative wings of the Republican party.

The Dewey campaign proceeded with leisurely assurance, as it heard "Hail to the Chief" many times in the closing weeks. Dewey took the Midwest for granted, much like the Democrats had taken the South for granted.

Dewey refused to make whistle stop talks when his train passed through Ohio and Indiana, even though crowds could be easily assembled. When the Dewey campaign train rolled into Terre Haute, Indiana, at 7 a.m., a crowd had gathered, expecting him to say a few words, as Truman had done earlier. When word circulated that he would not come out, they pelted his car with tomatoes and cabbages.[450] For a man who said, "The heart of this nation is the rural small town," he certainly didn't show it.[451]

Dewey's arrogance stunned political reporter Thomas F. Reynolds, who rode with Dewey in the final days. "When Dewey's organization calculates an area is in the bag, it wastes neither action nor words." Dewey was to lose Ohio--and its 25 electoral votes--by 7,107 votes.[452]

The responsibilities of power already weighed on him so heavily that newsmen joked: "How long is Dewey going to tolerate Truman's interference in the government?" That pomposity flabbergasted correspondent Edwin

A. Lahey of the Chicago *Daily New*. In an off-the-record chat with reporters, Dewey proclaimed his hope that "Harry Truman would just keep his hands off things for another few weeks! Particularly if he will just keep his hands off foreign policy, about which he knows considerably less than nothing!"

"Jesus, my eyes began to pop out. Here was this man saying that the President of the United States should keep his hands off foreign policy until this bum was elected, [so] the world would be safe."[453]

TRUMAN'S FINAL WHISTLESTOP TOUR

On Sunday evening, October 24th, the Ferdinand Magellan rumbled out of Washington for the final whistlestop campaign to Chicago, Cleveland, Boston, New York, and then home to St. Louis and Independence. Few people came to see Truman off, mostly White House staffers. Washington, D.C. had decided that he was a loser. A friend told Mrs. Truman, "All everybody talks about is who's going to be in Dewey's cabinet."[454] Republicans had already heavily booked Washington hotels for the inauguration.[455]

Desperate to provoke Dewey into a response, early on October 25, at Gary, Indiana, Truman charged that the GOP were "special privilege boys" who wanted to move the capital to Wall Street, and that "if anybody in this country is friendly to the Communists, it is the Republicans." Then, he went further, charging that Dewey's party paid only "lip service" to democracy itself. That tough speech was merely a warmup for later that day in Chicago. A monster rally greeted him where Boss Jake Arvey's minions kindled flames and fireworks. Truman supplied heat of his own.[456]

Truman charged that Dewey was the front man for special interests: "When a few men get control of the economy of a nation, they find a front man to run the country for them." He then cited Hitler, Mussolini, and Tojo as prime examples, thus insinuating that Dewey was in their class,[457] a tool of reactionary big business interests;[458] that a GOP victory might lead to fascism in America. His vituperation in Chicago was disgraceful. The New York Times accurately headlined the speech "President likens Dewey to Hitler as Fascists' tool." Robert Donovan delicately called it "a rather nasty speech." Irwin Ross, the chronicler of the campaign, branded it Truman's "most intemperate of the campaign. It was a liberal version of McCarthyism."[459]

On October 26, speaking in Chicago Stadium twenty-four hours after Truman's appearance there, Dewey said, "Faced with failure, with their party split in all directions, his candidates have spread fantastic fears among our people. . . They have attempted to promote antagonism and prejudice. They have scattered reckless abuse along the entire right of way from coast to coast and have now, I am sorry to say, reached a new low in mudslinging."[460]

Undeterred, Truman went to New York City for two days. A Truman aide had to pull Democratic Bronx boss, Ed Flynn, a former Democratic national chairman, from his car to have him appear on the platform with Truman. Flynn did not want to be seen with a sure loser. The Liberal Party sponsored a Madison Square Garden rally when the New York Democrats refused to pick up the tab in a losing cause.[461]

Truman used that rally to firm up Jewish support. He made his strongest commitment to Israel by renouncing the Bernadotte partition plan and strongly hinting at economic and military aid to Israel.[462]

On Friday, October 29, in his only civil rights speech of the campaign, Truman addressed the biggest open air rally in Harlem's history. The speech graphically showed the profound geographic and social shift within the Democratic Party. For the first time, a Democratic candidate had gone into the ghettos to solicit votes.[463]

For 48 hours before that, Dewey presented the spectacle of a candidate not campaigning at the climax of the race. His only public appearances were Friday evening and early Saturday - shaking hands at the Women's National Republican Club and a hike around the Central Park reservoir. "I thought I would take a little time off," he explained.

On October 31, Truman's train chugged into the Missouri Pacific Railroad depot in Independence. "It's grand to be home," Truman told the welcoming crowd. Since his June thinly disguised cross country trip, he had traveled 31,700 miles, made 356 speeches, and been seen by between twelve and fifteen million people.[464]

Reporters began to resemble vultures awaiting the end, not only of the Truman administration, but of the New Deal. The Washington Star wrote: "The campaign now closed marks the passing of the strange political alliance which served to elect the late President Franklin D. Roosevelt four times."[465]

The St. Louis *Post-Dispatch* wrote Truman lacked the "stature, the vision, the social and economic grasp, the sense of history required to lead the nation in a time of crisis." The St. Louis Star Times also endorsed Dewey, giving him a clean sweep of the major papers in Truman's home state.

Alistair Cooke, the correspondent for the Manchester Guardian, titled his dispatch for November 1st, "Harry S. Truman, A Study of a Failure." Cooke concluded it was not a failure of philosophy or party but of the candidate. "There is enough evidence in the fight for Senate seats, and in the good showing of unrepentant New Dealers, even in states where Dewey will be chosen, to show that if an impressive man is spouting New Deal doctrine he will be heeded. But Mr. Truman is by now worse than unimpressive."

THE LAST PREDICTIONS

The New York *Times* published a state-by-state survey giving Dewey 345 electoral votes, 78 more than he needed to win. Newsweek was even more generous, forecasting 366 electors and a popular margin of 4 million.

Life captioned a full-page photograph of Dewey, "The next President travels by ferryboat over the broad waters of San Francisco Bay." *Changing Times* magazine proclaimed on its cover "What Dewey Will Do," and gave a full issue of predictions.

In their last published tallies, the three major pollsters proclaimed:

	Dewey	*Truman*	*Wallace*	*Thurmond*	*and other*
Roper	52.2	37.1	3.2	1.7	5.8
Gallup	49.5	44.5	4	2	--
Crossley	49.9	44.8	3.3	1.6	4

Gallup, Crossley, and Roper, who had not bothered to interview a voter since September 9, believed not only that the race was over; they felt it never really started. [466] Even in the farm belt, both the Gallup and Des Moines Register polls indicated a Republican landslide. [467]

The pollsters dismissed the clear improvement in Truman's standing in the first weeks of October as too little too late. They failed to investigate whether it would continue through election day. The last Gallup Poll, conducted October 15th to the 25th, showed Dewey ahead 49.5% to 44.5% but, with the 4 point plus or minus error margin, Truman could have been leading with 48.5% to 45.5% even then.[468] The same was true with Crossley but Republicans had no fear - whatever the popular vote, they owned the electoral college because Truman would lose New York and the deep South.

In his column, Ed Sullivan posted odds on Dewey's election of 1 to 3.[469] He was being conservative. Bookies quoted odds of 1-15 on a Dewey win. (even in 1936, FDR had only been a 1-3 favorite.)[470] The editor of *Who's Who* sent Dewey an advance copy of the 1949 edition, listing his address as 1600 Pennsylvania Avenue.[471]

ELECTION EVE

Mencken wrote, "Neither candidate made a speech on the stump that will survive in the schoolbooks, but those of Truman at least had some human warmth in them." Truman had infused the campaign with some real energy, and given the fractured, whining Democratic Party more spirited leadership than it deserved. He had bolstered a Democratic drive that threatened to capture or deadlock the Senate.

Dewey campaigned six weeks to Truman's eight. Dewey covered sixteen thousand miles; Truman, twenty-two thousand. Dewey made 170 speeches; Truman 271.

The dilemma among traditional Democrats over Truman split two New York Post columnists. Dorothy Schiff Thackrey was a liberal but voted for Dewey. "I cannot vote for candidate Truman because he has proved himself to be the weakest, worst informed, most opportunistic President ever to hold the highest office in the land." She stated that he had used the Taft-Hartley law often although he had vetoed it, state delegations under his thumb had voted against the strong civil rights plank at the Democratic Convention, and characterized his record on Israel as disgraceful.[472]

Gerald W. Johnson opted for Truman. "Stacked up against the Arkangel Gabriel, Truman doesn't look so good, but stacked up against the array opposing him, he begins to look like the Arkangel Gabriel. After all, Gabriel is not a candidate."[473]

Elmo Roper had stopped regular polling early in September, but he did take a final sample of voter expectations. In July, just after the conventions, by a margin of 64 to 27 percent, American voters, regardless of personal choice, expected Dewey to win. At the end of October, Roper found that after all the speeches, three times as many voters believed that Dewey would win as expected a Truman victory. Although as much as two weeks old, the data was compellingly persuasive. With such favorable portents, Tom Dewey drifted off to sleep on the night of November 1.[474]

Some Democrats, however, smelled victory. McGrath polled the Democratic leaders of the 48 states who said with surprising frequency, "We've got a good chance for the [Senate/Governorship/House] but it looks bad for Truman." McGrath concluded: "You can't win all the things they say we're going to win and not elect a President, too. Either we are going to lose everything or we'll elect a President. I think we'll elect a President."[475]

On election eve, Lowell Mellett wrote: "It has been a strange campaign. To take it all in all, we shall not look upon its like again."[476]

It was now up to the people.

~

CHAPTER EIGHTEEN

THE PEOPLE - A SNAPSHOT

Two World Wars, a Great Depression and post war economic, political, and technological upheavals had molded and recast the nation's spirit and outlook.

FAMILY LIFE

The cries of so many infants thundered in the land that the Gerber Products Company sold 2 million cans and jars of baby food per week. As of October 1st, there were 147,280,000 Americans, up 15,500,000 since 1940, and up 1,800,000 since January 1st. Every month, the nation's population rose 200,000.

Babies did not guarantee a happy family, however. Divorce ended one of every two marriages in America's 30 largest cities and one in every three throughout the nation – the world's highest average. Chattanooga, Tennessee averaged 3.5 divorces for every one marriage. On June 28th, actress Jane Wyman divorced Ronald Reagan, president of the Screen Actors Guild, a liberal Democrat who publicly endorsed Truman at a rally in Hollywood.

Officially, divorces were difficult to obtain and required one spouse to prove "fault" of the other. But there were ways around that. In New York, the only ground for divorce was adultery. Manhattan's district attorney officially discovered what many common citizens had long known. "Divorce rings" faked evidence of adultery. His chief witness was a 20-yr-old mother of 3 whose fee for being "discovered" in a hotel room with a divorce-seeking husband was $10.

One thing that society did not wink at was abortion. For selling $5 tubes of "abortion paste" commonly known as a uterine salve, enough for 3 abortions, Charles A. Famin earned 2 years in prison.

SEX AND THE KINSEY REPORT

With all the new babies, you'd think Americans were experts on sex. Not exactly.

On January 5, a mild-mannered zoologist and world authority on the taxonomy of gall wasps, whose previous texts included Edible Wild Plants of Eastern North America, published a tome devoted to sex. It both shocked and titillated the public.[477]

In 1938, Indiana University asked its staid, uncontroversial Professor Alfred Charles Kinsey to teach a marriage course. The course became popular with students, but a passion with Kinsey. So little data existed about human sexual activity that he could offer only guesses to his students. Kinsey subjected humans to the same methodical scrutiny he had applied to the sex life of wasps. In 1942, Kinsey founded the Institute for Sex Research to produce a more realistic understanding of sexual behavior. The subject was so taboo that one faculty wife had refused a secretarial job with Kinsey, because she did not want to be associated with sex behavior research. William Manchester writes that Americans, now long jaded by literature on sex, "may find it hard to recapture the innocence of sex before Kinsey." One Kinsey investigator found one thousand virgins and their husbands with no clue why their marriages had been childless.[478]

Kinsey planned to announce the findings of his thousands of sexual histories. The University president begged him not to publish the report while the state legislature met or immediately before it convened, fearing it might cut the University's funding. As a further precaution against overreaction, he asked Kinsey to use a medical publisher, not a commercial one, who might sensationalize the topic with a prurient dust cover and lurid advertising copy. Kinsey agreed and selected W.B. Saunders Company, a dignified Philadelphia medical publisher.

Saunders did not sense a blockbuster. Such phenomena are rare in medical publishing, especially for a book weighing nearly three pounds with 804 pages of pedantic text, technical jargon and statistical charts. Besides, it cost $6.50, expensive for 1948 when the minimum wage was $.40. Saunders had commissioned a public opinion poll to forecast sales. The pollsters' "considered scientific opinion" confirmed that it would not sell very well.

The plain, modest Kinsey disagreed and predicted a big sale. Badgering journalists had been hounding him for a sneak preview. Working from proof copies, Look, Life, Reader's Digest, Science Illustrated and other newspapers and magazines seized upon Kinsey's raw data--especially the high incidence of extramarital sex--and in their December issues billed the book as a sensational expose of sexual mores.

Sexual Behavior in the Human Male was formally published on January 5, 1948. Kinsey's findings exploded America's Victorian conception of the seldom-mentioned subject of sex.

Sexual activity begins early; occurs both in and out of marriage (fifty percent of American husbands had committed adultery and 85 percent had had premarital intercourse); not necessarily with a loved partner (nearly 90 percent had had relations with prostitutes by their 35th birthday); a human partner (one out of six farm boys had copulated with farm animals) a female partner, or any partner at all.[479]

The shock produced a cultural phenomenon. Kinsey's name had become a byword overnight. The book hit the best seller nonfiction list within three weeks and stayed there for 27 continuous weeks. By mid-February, it had climbed to first place. Saunders rushed into a 6th printing, totaling an amazing 185,000 copies. By the first week of March, 200,000 copies had been sold, and Saunders had two printing companies working around the clock to stay ahead of demand.

Newsweek stated: "Not since the Darwinian theory split the world wide open has there been such a scientific shocker." As the book's far-reaching influence became clear, the initial reviews which had cheered Kinsey's pioneering efforts gave way to critics, both individual and institutional, who cursed its controversial subject matter and methods.

One newspaper editorialized: "Instead of admitting that they are compiling pornographic literature for the money they make out of it, these depraved characters offer it as scientific research."[480] LIFE Magazine condemned Kinsey's Report as an "assault on the family as a basic unit of society, a negation of moral law, and a celebration of licentiousness." Ministers, psychiatrists, anthropologists, statisticians, and educators charged Kinsey with everything from personal bias to important omissions to unrepresentative sampling. A Delaware woman wrote that Kinsey should "be imprisoned for life" since he was doing all he could to "push this civilization down the hill."[481]

The criticism stung the happily married father of four who had married the first woman he ever dated. In defense, Kinsey emphasized that his report showed what males do, not what they should do. His explanations and protestations did not stop the debate. A cottage industry of competing and counter studies developed. In late April, five New York editors almost simultaneously hatched the idea of a report on the Kinsey Report. Authors and publishers rushed out volumes - such as "About the Kinsey Report," "Sex Habits of American Men," "American Sexual Behavior and the Kinsey Report," "The Sexual Conduct of Men and Women" - which appraised Kinsey's statistics, argued with his conclusions or just correlated and corroborated his statements. Free lance "researchers" also were at work. On December 31, 1948, the New York Times reported that telephone calls from spurious Kinsey interviewers were harassing respectable matrons.[482]

Sex fascinated Americans, but they viewed it as a private matter. The Atlanta Police Department ordered department stores to draw their window shades when putting new costumes on dress dummies. As TIME reported, the extremely popular historical novels seemed the only public expression of the libido. Such novels normally boasted dust jackets, depicting a red lipped siren, with a low-cut dress and an incredibly pneumatic bust. Any deviations from natural heterosexual marital sex were intolerable, however. When TIME reviewed 23-year-old Truman Capote's first novel, "Other Voices Other Rooms," it squirmed with displeasure at the homosexual theme that "overhangs like Spanish moss."

A WOMAN'S CHANGING ROLE

Females had long been relegated to women's work - typists, phone operators, waitresses. Hitler had done more for women's liberation than all the suffragettes combined. Millions of men had left such jobs as shipbuilder or steelworker for the occupation of soldier or sailor. These manly industrial jobs still had to be done - now more than ever - but men were scarce. So necessity ordained that women, single, married, middle aged, and even elderly, be introduced to much higher paid industrial life. The difference was staggering. A woman shipbuilder in Mobile earned $37 a week, a saleswoman $21 and a waitress a lowly $14. Over half the women employed in Mobile in 1940 had changed jobs by 1944.[483] Mobile was a microcosm of America.

By 1942, one of every three workers was female. By 1944, 1.25 million or about one-half of all employees in the aircraft industry were women.[484] Even more surprising was that for all their gripes at the long hours and lousy conditions and their announced yearning for "when the boys come home," most women decided they liked working those jobs and wanted to keep them or move onto something better. [485]

These higher paid jobs, however, were viewed as temporary expedients. A wartime government pamphlet explained: "A woman is a substitute - like plastic instead of metal. She has special characteristics that lend themselves to new and sometimes superior uses"[486] but a substitute nonetheless. Women were laid off in droves when the war ended.

A 1946 Fortune poll had asked women whether they would prefer to be born again as women or men. A startling 25% declared they would rather be born men, while only 3.3% of men said they would prefer to be born women.[487] The reason was clear. Many jobs, activities, and life styles were simply off limits to women. But that attitude was changing as women never fully retreated from their wartime gains.[488]

The April 19th Newsweek reported that a million more women were employed than in 1947. Economists said that high prices were forcing women to work to make ends meet. In fact, women accounted for virtually all of the increase in the labor force since 1947. Their new status was matched by their new numerical dominance. 1945 was the last year in which men outnumbered women.[489]

LIGHTNING ON THE GROUND

Contrast the average American home of 1948 with a modern home. It is night and day. What Americans took for granted by the 1960's barely existed in 1948.[490] Many areas still lacked electricity. Even in New York, the most modern state, one third of the farm houses had no electricity.

The electronics industry, fattened by wartime research and expenditures,

225

offered a cornucopia. The war had made electronics America's fifth largest industry and the fruits of that industry were now crowding into homes.

In 1948, appliance makers turned out 4,710,000 washing machines, 4,500,000 refrigerators, 27,300,000 radios, toasters and irons. 76.6% of Americans owned refrigerators (still considered a modern marvel) and gutted the ice-making industry; 4.3% owned freezers, 51.6% owned vacuum cleaners, 67.4% owned electric washers.[491] Garbage disposals appeared. GE's advertisement ran "Garbage? What's Garbage?"

CITIES

Only 0.4% of the people owned a dryer, but that scarcity created a diorama outside as clotheslines of billowing sheets and unmentionables dotted neighborhoods. Wash and wear clothing had not yet appeared so dry cleaners and the stereotypical Chinese laundries were common. Women took the family wash and their gossip to "launderettes" which became a modern urban equivalent to the village well.

Downtowns still pulsed with vitality but not for long. Central city population peaked in absolute numbers and as a percentage of the American population in 1947 and 1948. Suburbia was booming!

Besides educating the veterans, the GI Bill bought them houses, securing mortgages so they could buy mass produced houses. Before the war, 2/3 of Americans were renters. Because of the GI Bill, 2/3 soon owned their own homes. Home ownership rose sharply [492] and those homes were not being built in the inner city. They also were not being built for Negroes. Developers refused to sell to Negro veterans with ready cash. As Builder Levitt admitted: "We can solve a housing problem, or we can try to solve a racial problem. But we cannot combine the two."[493] Denied suburbia, Negroes turned the inner cities into black enclaves ringed by white suburbs.

Technology changed the urban skyline. Before, companies could build skyscrapers, but how to get people up to their offices and down again quickly and efficiently? Wartime advances in electronic systems, especially computing equipment, solved such scheduling problems as morning and evening peak loads and traffic balance and eliminated operators. Elevators became completely automatic and common.

COMMON LIFE

Cash was king with the first credit card, Diner's Club, still a year away. Without ATMs, people stood in line for bank tellers to dispense cash.

With no suburban malls and relatively few catalogs other than the Sears goliath, people shopped in downtown local stores that emphasized personal-by-name service. There were no K-Marts or Wal-Marts but plenty of Woolworths. Ubitquitious door to door salesman hawked vacuum cleaners, encyclopedia, or brushes.

People spent days on their front porches conversing with passers-by. When air conditioning came, modern houses dropped the front porch. Telephones were common but had rotary dials and often on a party line.

Americans were taken with frozen foods, and chlorophyll candies, toothpaste, and gum. Nestles Quik, the Franklin 50-cent piece, color newsreels, the new board game Scrabble (originally called CrissCrosswords), and the Nikon 35mm all rolled out in 1948.

The use of plastics had become commonplace during the war, and now spread in the civilian, especially the baby boom, market. Children's toys were plain and uncomplicated: yo-yos, Mr. Potato-head kits, simple board games. Bikes had only one speed. "Fancy toys were anything that required a battery."[494]

Without television, many mid size cities boasted morning and afternoon papers, often more than one of each. Most Americans got their news from newspapers. So columnists like Drew Pearson, Walter Winchell, Walter Lippmann, and Stewart and Joe Alsop wafted an influence that is unknown today.

With no Saturday morning TV cartoons, the comics reigned. To America's kids, the most familiar face in public life was Dick Tracy, identified by 97% of the children interviewed by the Ladies Home Journal. Bing Crosby was spotted by 95%, while 93% recognized Harry Truman. Blondie ran in more papers, 846 in 34 countries, than any other comic.

FASHION

Americans dressed more formally in 1948 - suits and ties for men, dresses for women and, of course, a hat for both sexes. They wore hats to the movies, dinner, church and to baseball games - America's national religion. The one big assault on such formality hit the beaches that year - the bikini, named after the site of atomic testing.

Clothes came from natural fibers that needed ironing and wrinkled badly in the heat,[495] but new fibers and products appeared. Nylon dresses were popular and DuPont introduced a new synthetic textile, "the best we know of for outdoor use." Called "Orlon," it was described as warm as silk, as wrinkle resistant as wool, and resistant to moths, mold and mildew. Adidas in Germany developed sneakers, made from war-surplus canvas and fuel-tank rubber.

EDUCATION - THE GI BILL TRANSFORMS AMERICA

Schools bulged with students. The U.S. Office of Education estimated that a record 32 million students (more than 1 out of every 5 Americans) would attend school in the fall: 23 million in elementary schools, over 6 million to high schools, and 2-1/2 million to colleges and universities.

They could afford it because the GI Bill of Rights in 1944 had offered, to every able and honorably discharged member of the Armed Forces, scholarships in colleges or trade schools with subsidence for up to 4 years. In 1948, Congress raised the benefits to $75 per month for a bachelor; $105 for a couple; and $120 for a couple with child. By 1947 to 1948, the Veterans Administration was paying the bills for almost 50 percent of the male college students, paying for 2.3 million veterans between 1945 and 1950.[496]

The GI Bill transformed America while the Marshall Plan saved Europe. Before the GI Bill, leaving one's station in life was rare. A son was free to follow his father into the steel mills or farming but not to become a lawyer or a doctor. Despite the American Revolution, the old English tradition of "gentlemen" and common folks still continued. The dividing gate was college through which few common folk could send their children to the upper class. A high school diploma was the mark of an educated person.

If the GI Bill had a sound, it was the noise of class barriers crumbling as the children of recent immigrants invaded the exclusive clubs of Mayflower descendants. These graduates, 60% of whom majored in engineering and sciences, entered white-collar jobs and grew a vibrant middle class society as a new managerial class. Salaried middle class workers rose 61% between 1947 and 1957. The GI Bill became the most successful domestic program ever.

College life was not for everyone as many veterans had no taste for school; but that was fine. The industries that would be rusting by the 1970's were still vibrant and required only a strong back and a repetitive nature.

ECONOMY

Materially, the U.S. was rich--richer than any nation ever. No depression, recession, unemployment, or starving veterans blackened the landscape. Almost no one expected growth after World War II, but 1947's GNP of $231 billion rose to $258 billion in 1948.

Money was plentiful! The money supply surged from $68 billion in 1939 to $173 billion by 1948, spurred by higher wages, farm price supports, and an easy money policy. Installment buying accounted for 62% or $5,200,000 of the $8.5 billion rise in total consumer credit in the three years after V.J. Day.

Personal income in August was running at an annual rate of $215 billion, a record. Between early 1946 and the middle of 1948, income after taxes had jumped 26%. The average weekly income rose some 6% during the year to about $54.65.

Even more startling was the increase in dollars available for nonessential spending. After paying for food, clothing, shelter, and taxes plus laying aside essential savings, consumers in 1940 had only $22.8 billion left over. In 1948, they had about $90 billion.

Despite inflation and record retail buying ($10 billion a month), citizens who well remembered the Depression would put $12 billion in the bank in 1948 as compared with $8.8 billion in 1947 and $2.7 billion in 1939.

To put that amount in perspective, a postage stamp cost $.03; a loaf of bread was $.14; a quart of milk $.21; a six-pack of Budweiser $.56; a gallon of gas ranged from $.16 to $.28; the average car cost $2055 with a Cadillac at $3,657 while a Chevrolet cost $1,587. A tube of Ipana toothpaste cost $.41 and a suit at Sears cost $36.50. The minimum wage was $.40 per hour and the median family income was $3187.

Not only the people were fiscally sound. In July, Secretary of the Treasury John Snyder announced the biggest surplus in U.S. history. Receipts of $44 billion versus expenditures of $36 million meant a surplus of approximately $8.5 billion. Except for 1948, the rise in federal spending led to unbalanced budgets in the post war period.[497]

BUSINESS

All that money produced a banner year for business. U.S. builders started 45% more houses than any other year. Automakers rolled out more than 5,200,000 vehicles, about 8% more than 1947, and more than 80 million auto tires. Textile industries spun out 13,621 billion yards of cloth, enough to reach 311 times around the world. Factories spewed 540 million pairs of nylons (10 pairs for every U.S. woman).[498] Before the war, the U.S. had turned out 35% of the world's goods, with only 6.8% of the population. In 1948, it made over 50% of the world's goods.

Most industries had re-converted easily and rapidly to civilian work. But such a fast paced economy could be fickle. While traditional manufacturing, transportation, and mining jobs continued to dominate the economy, jobs in those fields increased only marginally after the war. Most new job opportunities came in wholesale and retail work, in state and local government (where employment in twenty-five years more than tripled) and in construction, in finance, and in insurance.[499]

Some businesses would thrive; others would become dinosaurs, unable to adapt. For example, many of the 100,000 beauty shops saw business drop 20% to 40% from 2 years before. The decline stemmed mainly from the home permanent wave kits sold by the Toni Company that had begun on a shoestring in 1944. Toni had sold 20 million home sets in 1947, and was clearly selling more in 1948.

The Berlin Airlift succeeded because of the assembly line approach in which people scrutinized operations from start to finish, eliminating wasted motions, designing more efficient equipment, and substituting material. It worked well for airplanes. Why not on hamburgers?

In San Bernadino, California, Richard and Maurice McDonald surveyed their small hamburger operation and decided that success depended on speed (fast food), consistency - not great food but dependably good food, and low prices. They replaced their small 3 ft. cast iron grill with two custom designed, easier to clean and more efficient, stainless steel 6 footers. Paper bags, wrappers, and paper cups replaced the plates and silverware that tended to disappear anyway; so out went the dishwasher. The menu shrank from 25 items to 9, featuring hamburgers and cheeseburgers. A newly devised patty making machine made the same smaller size every time - 10 hamburgers from one pound of meat instead of 8. They preselected their condiments and gave no options on the burgers since choices meant delays and higher costs. The result - "Buy 'em by the bag," invited McDonald's sign. Hamburgers cost $.15; cheeseburgers $.19; french fries $.10 and milkshakes $.25.[500]

To show the business landscape had room, another company triumphed with a totally opposite method. The Baskin-Robbins chain began with the philosophy of giving customers higher quality ice cream and more choices that no other company could match.

EMPLOYMENT

Employment averaged over 59 million workers throughout 1948, a record, with an all time peak in July with 61,600,000 Americans at work. Not only were there more workers but more efficient workers.

Frenzied wartime schedules had forced the development of tools and techniques that enabled industry to reach levels of mass production once thought impossible. Industry applied these same methods to the mass consumer production after the war.

Productivity had increased from 1% to 28% over 1947 with an average increase of 7-1/2%. With 4% more in the industrial labor force, the nation turned out 9% more goods. All these jobs and productivity meant boom times for labor.

LABOR

Relations between labor and management were particularly mellow with fewer and less violent strikes.

During the war, labor unions had taken a voluntary no-strike pledge for the duration. On the whole, they lived up to their agreement despite a thirty percent rise in prices. Once the war ended, however, unions struck repeatedly to regain parity; but once pre war parity was achieved, labor was relatively content.

Unionized workers had increased more than five-fold since 1933 to more than 14 million - about 30% of all workers, but labor had fallen victim to its own successes. The standard of living of workers had increased tremendously in the past thirty years. Hard won battles coupled with progressive legislation had landed many workers comfortably in middle class ranks. With the booming economy plus plentiful employment and overtime, labor management relations, while still adversarial, were not the life and death struggles of decades before.

Most industrialists looked at soaring sales and decided it was smarter to raise wages and then prices than to risk strikes. Unions had developed a healthy respect for the hated Taft Hartley Act, especially after seeing the fines levied on Lewis and the UMW. Efforts now focused on increasing the benefits already won, keeping pace with inflation, and avoiding strikes that hurt all sides and risked the enmity of the public. Man-days lost from strikes dropped to 34 million, lowest in 3 years.

The epitome of this mutual recognition came in the Spring of 1948. Seeking to make peace with the union rather than suffer crippling strikes in such a booming and competitive market, General Motors decided it could easily administer the higher prices in an orderly but radical fashion. At 6:30 a.m. May 25th, bleary eyed women locked in a room on the 11th floor of the General Motors Building in Detroit finished a secret typing job. Six floors below, four haggard men, exhausted by 17 hours of negotiating, grabbed the copies, called in reporters and announced sensational news. To avoid a strike, the world's largest automobile manufacturer and one of the world's largest unions had agreed on an unprecedented formula for hitching wages to living costs.

General Motors would hike the pay of 225,000 UAW members by 11 cents an hour to $1.61. Next September 1st and each quarter thereafter, workers' wages would rise or fall in relation to the movement of the Bureau of Labor Statistics and Consumer Price Index. Soon, other companies followed suit so as not to hamstring production profits.

AUTOMOBILES - THE AMERICAN DREAM ON WHEELS

When gasoline and car rationing ended,[501] the automobile seized the high ground in America. The move to suburbia and the abundance of cash had so increased the demand that more than 9 million Americans, one of every seven workers, made, sold, serviced or used automobiles, but that was just the start of the car's influence.

The automobile shifted wealth and power from the downtown retail districts and hotels. Fewer people rode busses and ridership of urban mass transit topped out in 1948, almost killing the already feeble railroad industry. The big winners were the oil business, gasoline stations, roadside hotels and restaurants, and highway departments.[502]

People took their cars seriously. Glendale, California voted to recall its mayor and 3 councilmen because they had installed parking meters. In 1948, 54% of families owned an automobile. A lot more wanted one. Ford had a backlog of 2 million unfilled orders. The other companies had similar backlogs.

People eagerly awaited the new models. Truman motorcaded into Dexter from Des Moines in a fleet of 35 brand new convertibles with the top down. Richard Rovere could not figure out why the crowds were still gazing adoringly at him and the other newsmen in car No. 30, until he realized that people weren't looking at the occupants, but at the Packards.[503]

At the present rate of output, Detroit would build the second hundred million cars in half the time it took to produce the first, not only due to demand but also techniques. The first transfer machines for building engine blocks could perform 550 tooling operations in 15 minutes. Machines became a competitive threat to workers and presented the next major dispute with management - job security.

And though car prices rose, the comparative cost of a car dropped. The average U.S. factory employee took fewer hours than ever to pay for a new car, but cars were expensive to maintain. In 1939, the cost of repairing, greasing, parking, storing and washing the private car totaled $462 million. By 1947, it had risen to $995 million and soared over a billion dollars in 1948. Many car owners complained that the post war models seemed to have been designed to "damage easy and repair hard."

Motorists traveled 395 billion miles in their 41 million cars in 1948 - pretty amazing since the national highway system did not yet exist. With all that driving came 30,000 deaths and 36,772 arrests for drunken driving. Several states did not even make driving licenses compulsory;[504] so enforcement was difficult.

Changing the dating ritual, the nation's youth now necked at drive-in movies, called "passion pits," rather than shady lanes. The 480 drive-ins in the country in 1948 zoomed to 4,000 by 1958.[505] The San Jose, California, High School Herald printed seven rules for social success. "One--have a car, two--be pleasant conversationalists; three--have a car; four--be congenial; five--have a car; six--be a good listener; seven--have a car . . . (numbers two, four and six can be omitted if the car is a red convertible)."

Cars became bigger, more powerful, resembling truncated locomotives with gaping mouths filled with ill fitted chromium teeth.[506] New makes, models and options appeared - the Land Rover, Porsche sports car, and the Honda motorcycle. (The first Honda car would not appear for another 15 years.) The first automobile air conditioner went on the market, a crude affair installed under the dashboard, as did nonglare headlights and heat-conducting windshields. Michelin introduced the world's first radial tires. The Ford Motor Company switched from the rounded body to the square back rear end.[507] General Motors' Cadillac automobile introduced tail fins, copying some World War II planes, starting a trend that lasted throughout most of the 1950s.

SCIENCE AND TECHNOLOGY

A development of small physical size but enormous consequence occurred. The new transistor would permit miniaturization of radios, television sets and computers.

Speaking of computers, two of the first computer, Eniac's, builders issued a catalog for a machine called the Univac. Much smaller and more versatile than the Eniac, and no larger than an office desk, it could switch from higher mathematics to simple bookkeeping. To make computers more efficient, developers introduced the magnetic drum for data storage. It consisted of a rapidly spinning drum covered with a magnetic film on which the data was encoded as tiny magnetic domains.

On October 22nd in Detroit, inventory Chester F. Carlson displayed to the Optical Society of America the results of a decade's development- -photography without chemicals and printing without ink. The new process was named xerography, the xero (pronounced zero) derived from the Greek word for dry. Newsweek quoted that "the electrostatic printing feature is also being applied to a new kind of office duplicating machine." The name would soon be shortened to "Xerox."

Not to be outdone for office efficiency, Dictaphone introduced a portable electronic dictating machine weighing less than 20 lbs. Five "memo-belts," each holding 15 minutes dictation, could be mailed for 3 cents in a standard envelope.

New gadgets and techniques abounded. After a walk in the woods with his dog, Swiss engineer George deMestral copied the cockleburs in his socks and the dog's coat and invented the fastener "Velcro." An ad for Plexiglas announced "the amazing acrylic plastic that puts new come-over-and-see-me into both merchandise and merchandising."

Two Swiss dentists reported their impressions of Los Angeles. "Everything here is automatic. Automatic machines toast your bread, pour your soft drinks, change your phonograph records, even shave your face." The other responded, "Your beer is nearly frozen. Your beefsteak, vegetables, milk are frozen nearly hard. Everything is refrigerated, even your young ladies."[508] Not everyone could adapt to these new fangled gadgets. In Tupelo, Mississippi, when shiny new garbage containers were installed downtown, garbage collectors spent a hard day sorting the rubbish from the outgoing mail.

BASEBALL - THE NATION'S PASSION

In 1954, Jacques Barzun wrote "whoever wants to know the heart and mind of America had better learn baseball." It was just as true in 1948. People followed baseball in a way that is incomprehensible today. Where else but America would headline: "War With Japan Perils World Series?"[509] Baseball dominated.

Why did they love a sport that today people ridicule as too slow? - for reasons that teach us much about 1948. First, a baseball stadium was an oasis of tradition and constancy - a cathedral. While the world and their everyday life swirled and changed, people could sit in the same stands as they had with their fathers and as their fathers had sat with their fathers, watching the same teams play by the same rules. Their fathers and grandfathers had grown up watching and loving baseball, when professional football and basketball were literally unknown.

Second, it was a slower time. Without faxes, computers, microwaves, TV dinners, or instant anything, people tolerated a slower pace and had greater patience. Today, we have conquered time and space and can do in nanoseconds what took weeks in 1948. Besides, baseball did not dawdle then. In 1947, Bob Feller took an hour and 42 minutes to pitch one game, and another game took an hour and 34 minutes. Games routinely lasted less than 2 hours.

Baseball was still played predominantly in the afternoon in an open air stadium in the heart of the city, on real grass and by franchises that had not changed cities in almost 50 years. It was primarily a northeast sport. The westernmost city with a baseball team was St. Louis. The southernmost was Washington D.C. Boston had two teams as did Philadelphia, Chicago and St.Louis. New York City had three. So most of the major league teams were centered from Boston to New York to Philadelphia. A trip out west meant to Chicago or St Louis with teams going on trains or busses.

Good players stayed with their teams throughout their careers, not out of loyalty but the chain of the contract clause. Free agents did not exist. With no multi year contracts, every year, players began spring training fearing that someone else could take their job. Some superstars received phenomenal salaries. Bob Feller was the highest paid player - $80,000 a year while Ted Williams and Joe Dimaggio made $75,000 and $65,000 respectively. Normal players and even lesser stars had to work in the off season to make ends meet.

After the First World War, the Chicago Black Sox scandal had almost killed baseball. It survived by the legendary, almost Homeric, exploits of George Herman Ruth. No one ever dominated a sport like he did nor did so much for it.

One of the best left-handed pitchers the game has ever known, Ruth pitched in 163 games, winning 92 and losing 44, a .676 percentage. But his enduring fame rests on his home runs. Ruth led the league in home runs in twelve seasons. In one season he hit more home runs than any other team except one! In 1927 he hit 60 home runs in 154 games, a major league record that still stood. He retired with the assumed unbreakable lifetime record of 714 home runs in regular-seasons plus a lifetime batting average of .342. Ruth was among the first constellation elected to the Baseball Hall of Fame in 1936, one of the most phenomenally gifted and popular players in baseball history and a symbol of America. No one was even close to his records, 13 years after he retired.

Babe Ruth Day was April 27 in all major league stadiums. At Yankee Stadium, leaning on Bob Feller's bat for support, The Babe addressed the crowd in a gravelly voice ravaged by the cancer that was stealing his life. His last public appearance was in late July at the premier of "The Babe Ruth Story" starring William Bendix.

In August, he checked into the Memorial Hospital that was soon awash in letters wishing him well. Newspapers were swamped with calls asking how he was doing. Ballpark crowds stood in silent prayer for his recovery.

For days, the headlines had read: "The count is 3 and 2 on The Babe." When he died at 8:01 p.m. on August 16, newspaper switchboards lit up within minutes after the radio bulletin and stayed jammed for hours. Memorial

Hospital put five extra operators on to repeat over and over that Ruth had died. No death since Franklin Roosevelt's had so moved the people.

As part of American folklore, even today his name and face are immediately recognized by people who never open the sports section. Such giants can not pass quietly. They require a national requiem.

He lay in-state appropriately at the House that Ruth Built, Yankee Stadium, in the main lobby behind the lowest tier of grandstand seats, only 150 feet from the home plate that he trotted on so many times. Long before dawn, the crowd started gathering and when the gates finally opened at 10, the line wound around the stadium six blocks long. Like the opening day of the World Series when the fans swarmed to see The Babe, they filed in at a rate of 100 a minute, five abreast, past his candle-lit mahogany casket to see him for the last time. On Tuesday, August 17th, well into the night and all the next day, the fans paid him a final tribute. When the gates closed at 7:30 Wednesday night, 115,000 had said goodbye and thousands still crammed the streets outside the stadium.

On Thursday, 75,000 more surrounded the entrance to St. Patrick's Cathedral where 6,000 mourners attended a requiem mass with Governor Dewey, plus the mayors of New York and Boston, as pallbearers. 100,000 lined the streets and 10,000 watched from windows. Even in death, The Babe packed them in.[510]

But what about professional football and basketball? In 1948, the vast majority of Americans simply ignored these sports. While college ball had a substantial following, people slighted the pros. A reader would be hard pressed to find a single article on these sports in TIME and Newsweek in 1948.

On October 3, 1948, the National Football League became the first professional sports organization to allow regular weekly network television coverage. As with radio, the Sunday afternoon NFL contests were on ABC because both NBC and CBS did not consider pro football worth covering.[511]

Only two National League teams, the Chicago Bears and the Washington Redskins, and one team from the upstart All America Football Conference seemed likely to show a profit. Some sports executives blamed television for 1948 attendance drops in both football's major leagues and some of

238

minor league baseball's important spots. They asserted college football might compete against the comforts of a television set on a cold or rainy day, but pro football could not.

BOOKS

As December began, some 8,671 books had been published, 599 more than during the first eleven months of 1947. 135 million paperback books were sold. The quantity also reflected a higher quality. 1948 was the best year American letters had experienced since the war.[512]

Eisenhower's "Crusade in Europe" was released in November to great acclaim. Newsweek called it "as nearly a great book as any soldier has written in our time." Besides Eisenhower, other generals and statesmen created some of the year's best nonfiction. Churchill wrote "The Gathering Storm," the first of his six volume history of World War II. Having helped win the two world wars, Churchill had become the leading historian of both.

A new crop of talented young novelists appeared, plus a fair showing from the old hands. Few new writers burst on the scene as Norman Mailer did with his first novel "Naked and the Dead." Calling his grimly moving story of a platoon in the Pacific "perhaps the best novel yet about World War II," Newsweek labeled the 25-year-old Mailer "a writer of unmistakable importance." He had produced in this huge, brutally realistic, cynical best seller a war story that "not only stands far above anything which has yet been written about the recent war, but also one which ranks with the best fiction that came out of the First World War." The book's graphic portrayal had one lapse. The publisher demanded that "Fug" substitute for more explicit obscenities.

John Steinbeck came out with "The Pearl." Graham Green wrote "The Heart of the Matter" and Thomas Merton wrote "The Seven Storey Mountain." Evelyn Waugh skewered the American funeral industry in "The Loved One." William Faulkner published his "Intruder in the Dust." Alan Paton's "Cry The Beloved Country" savaged apartheid. The cream of the novel from the continent was Albert Camus' "The Plague," the first genuinely important work from Europe since the war's end.

W.H. Auden won the Pulitzer for poetry; James Michener's "Tales From the South Pacific" won the pulitzer for fiction; and T.S. Eliot won the Nobel Prize for Literature.

MUSIC

The biggest sounds in music in 1948 came not from musicians but from scientists. Columbia Records, Inc., had discussed a project in hushed tones, referring to it only as "LP," and had cloaked it in secrecy worthy of Oak Ridge. In New York on June 18th, they unveiled the first successful long playing (LP) 12" multigroove phonograph. The first records were made of vinylite plastic, with 250 "microgrooves" to the inch, and played at 33-1/3 revolutions per minute instead of the usual 78. LP meant that the two sides of a 12 inch record allowed the listener to hear 45 minutes of music -- a whole symphony, an entire concerto or any given combination of music lasting that long. A catalog of 101 LP records at $4.85 each went on the market, offering a selection from Bach to Harry James. LPs would replace the old five minute per side recordings and revolutionize the record industry, music tastes and listening habits.

RCA soon responded with the 45 which also gave good sound but not as long. RCA and Columbia battled until they compromised that the 45 would be used for single songs while the album would be the province of the 33.

Both adults and "teenagers" (a brand new word) normally bought the same records. With the music gap between the ages several years away, the entire nation listened to *Once in Love with Amy*, from the hit play, *Charley's Aunt*, sung by Ray Bolger; *Buttons and Bows* from Bob Hope's new movie, *The Paleface; Easter Parade* from the movie of the same name; *Red Roses For a Blue Lady*, and, the new Christmas song, *All I Want for Christmas is my Two Front Teeth*.

MOVIES

The movies were a major diversion. People did not go to see "a movie." They "went to the movies" - out of habit and to see the genre itself rather than any one product. Some eighty million tickets were sold each week, sixty-five percent of the population. (In the 1980s, each week about twenty million tickets were sold, about ten percent of the population. [513])

Americans went so often for two interrelated reasons. Without TV, they had no visual home entertainment vehicle. Also, without TV's and therefore without VCR's, or DVD's if they missed a film, they really missed it. It would not be coming out on video in a few months or on TV in a few years. It vanished into the nether world.

To meet that demand, the country boasted approximately 20,000 theaters, although "theaters" is an understatement. Many were palaces, with fountains in the lobby, box seats like those in opera houses, and enough seats (spread over three levels) to host a convention.[514]

Bing Crosby remained the nation's number one box office draw for the fifth straight year, runner up was Betty Grable, and Abbott & Costello moved into 3rd place. Gary Cooper stayed in 4th, followed by Bob Hope, Humphrey Bogart, Clark Gable, Cary Grant, Spencer Tracy and Ingrid Bergman. Just missing the top 10 were Esther Williams, Gregory Peck and Lana Turner. Roy Rogers finished 1st in the Western Division and topped that success by marrying another western star, Dale Evans. Wannabee stars had a tough time. In September 1948, Columbia Pictures fired Marilyn Monroe after playing her first part. "The studio comments included "Can not act," "Voice like a tiny squeak," "Utterly unsure of herself," and "Unable even to take refuge in her own insignificance."[515]

People adored their movie stars and sometimes the badder the better. Robert Mitchum, the $3,000 a week screen actor, was scheduled as the principal speaker on juvenile delinquency at a Los Angeles youth rally on September 1st. He could not make it; the night before he had been arrested for possessing and using marijuana. Mitchum feared his career was over. Far from it, his latest film, 'Rachel and the Stranger,' was rushed into release to take advantage of the publicity.

WESTERNS

To understand the American of 1948, you must understand the Western. Westerns - morality plays that celebrated the individual striving alone against adversity - turned not on plot (which could be mind numbingly similar) but on character development. They always ended the same way - one or two simple men of dignity walking down a dusty street to meet the forces of evil and shoot the stuffings out of them! Americans immediately recognized the Berlin Blockade and Airlift as the villain trying to take over the town, while the good guys round up the posse to stop him.

Hollywood produced 75 westerns in 1948, including classics such as 'Red River' with John Wayne and Montgomery Clift, and 'Fort Apache,' John Ford's last of his trilogy about the U.S. cavalry, starring John Wayne and Henry Fonda. Westerns were so predominant and popular that TIME described 'Fury at Furnace Creek' starring Victor Mature as "a better than average western and thus a considerably better than average movie." The preference for westerns showed a simplicity of values.

 In one of the first examples of brilliant planning involving television, actor William Boyd had bought the rights to his old cowboy series, 'Hopalong Cassidy,' and could now license them directly to TV. TV stations leaped at the opportunity to have relatively new films and agreed to have Boyd host many of the shows. So, in November, 1948, television presented its first western series, initially on a local station and then on a network in 1949.

CONCLUSION

So that is a snapshot of the people who would go to the polls on November 2, 1948.

CHAPTER NINETEEN

ELECTION DAY

THE DAY

Some 78 percent of the nation's newspaper readers received a pro-Dewey gazette this day of the 41st presidential election. Only 15 percent received a pro-Truman paper. Outside of the farm belt few noticed that corn was selling for $1 a bushel, down from $1.78 in September.

Manhattan experienced a warm, almost spring-like day. In his overcoat, as Dewey entered the voting booth, he asked the clustered photographers, "You fellows all set?" Moments later, he emerged from behind the curtain, smiling. After Mrs. Dewey voted, he announced, "Well, that's two votes we've got anyway." He then returned to The Roosevelt Hotel, named for Theodore, not Franklin. After a light lunch (V8 vegetable juice which the Campbell Soup Company had introduced in 1948, salad, milk), he relaxed confidently on a couch in the green-walled living room in Suite 1527-29, brimming with complimentary and congratulatory flowers. The Republican faithful were already gathering in The Roosevelt's ballroom, where a big scoreboard awaited the victory tallies. Dewey's staff mimeographed hundreds of copies of the victory statement, stressing (What else!) national unity.[516]

Joining the Republicans at the hotel were 150 city police and six Secret Service agents, including the head of the Secret Service, James J. Maloney. Sure that Dewey would triumph, he had forsaken the incumbent in Missouri. [517]

Also at the hotel was Merriman Smith, the Associated Press's senior White House correspondent, who chose to cover Dewey instead of Truman, his normal quarry. In an elevator, he overheard two young Republicans. "Wouldn't it be awful," one said to the other, "if something were to go wrong?" Smith shuddered. "Jesus," he told a fellow reporter, "if Truman wins, you know what'll happen to me? I'll wind up as rewrite man in our Tahiti bureau."[518]

TRUMAN'S DAY

Truman and his family voted at 10 a.m., in Independence's Memorial Hall. He ate lunch at a local country club with 30 old friends who were in on a disappearing trick Truman had devised, but they did not know the details.

After lunch, Truman said, 'Now, fellows, don't worry. I'm going to get elected. You can depend on it. But you'd better go out in the precincts and do a little work, see that the vote gets out."[519]

A short time later, Truman excused himself, ostensibly to use the restroom. Instead, he and two Secret Service agents snuck out a back door and off to the Elms Hotel in Excelsior Springs, some 30 miles from Kansas City. To fool reporters, he had departed without baggage, so he borrowed a bathrobe and slippers from the hotel manager. After a Turkish bath, a rubdown, a ham sandwich, and a glass of buttermilk, he walked to a room in the third floor rear and went to sleep. A silent radio sat on a table beside his bed. To celebrate victory or numb defeat, the management had left a bottle of scotch and a bottle of bourbon on the dresser.

RADIO AND TV PREPARE

ABC boasted that for the first time in history, networks would televise a presidential election and Americans in eight major cities could see it.

Viewers on the Boston to Richmond hookup would get the best show, with cameras in the New York Republican and Democratic headquarters. If Dewey won, his victorious visage would be aired live. If Truman won, no live TV interviews would be possible. The networks viewed 1948 as a dress rehearsal for the 1952 election when they expected television to be coast to coast.

Regular programming had been pre-empted for the evening, except, of course, for the untouchable Milton Berle show. Television and radio had assembled some stellar commentators. ABC listed George Gallup, Walter Winchell and Drew Pearson among its pundits. Roper was working for CBS. Armed with George Gallup's reference book on political statistics, H.V. Kaltenborn, NBC's 70 year old dean of commentators, expected a short evening. For those along the East Coast coaxial cable, NBC planned a visual treat - an enormous cardboard model of the White House, complete with a treadmill to carry miniature elephants inside as soon as Dewey was elected. No one had bothered to prepare miniature donkeys.[520] Within a few hours it became a useless paperweight, shoved against the wall.

THE EVENING

People of that generation would always remember where they were when Pearl Harbor was bombed, President Roosevelt died, and Harry Truman beat the invincible Tom Dewey.

Sure of defeat, the Democratic National Committee had not even reserved the ballroom at its headquarters, the Mayflower Hotel in Washington DC, to get an early start on a war chest for '52. The downcast Committeemen retired to their office suite, took the phone off the hook, and began to ease their despondency with a couple of bottles of whisky, without even so much as a radio to interrupt their drinking. [521]

The initial returns surprised Dewey at dinner. The first New Hampshire towns to report were not as good as one might expect.[522] The early tallies from the Eastern Seaboard similarly unsettled the Republicans, but did not terrify them. Although the radio blared Truman leads, the traditionally Democratic big city votes came in first. Dewey was running somewhat better than in 1944; but this was 1948 - "somewhat" was not what they expected! At 8 o'clock, Gallup turned to his staff and said "Boys, I think we're in trouble."[523]

At the Ritz Carlton, one of campaign manager Herbert Brownell's dinner guests received a call from her father. He asked what she was wearing and her favorite restaurant. When she answered, he replied that she should get her favorite young man to take her there because "You may have just lost yourself an election." When she returned to the table, she stunned her companions with the news. They raced to The Roosevelt for reassurance.[524]

Although Truman was not doing as well as Roosevelt, he was running much stronger than anticipated. By 10 p.m. EST, Truman had carried the first major city to complete its returns, Philadelphia, by only 6,000 votes against FDR's 150,000 in 1944. However, astute observers remembered that, in July, Dewey had led in the city by 27 percentage points!   A half hour later, Baltimore reported Truman 134,000, Dewey 111,000.   FDR had carried the city 4 years earlier by 51,000, so Truman had not done quite half as well but still far better than projected. New York City hurled the most personal and first major dejection.   It looked like Truman would carry the city by over half a million.

Also disconcerting was the surprisingly strong vote for local and state Democrats, but the first consistent trend graphed the collapse of Henry Wallace.   The polls and pundits had expected such a heavily credentialed candidate, wrapped in the mantle of the New Deal, to steal hundreds of thousands of votes, virtually all from Truman. Very early, it was clear that he was not drawing anywhere near that, in areas that he should have. One of the major underpinnings of the polls crumbled.

As the Midwest vote started to come in at 10:30 EST, Hugh Scott proclaimed: "Now we come to the Republican half of the evening."   His statement made sense.   The Northeast with its large urban centers was Democratic, populated by the Irish and other minorities, often Catholic and union, and controlled by bosses like Frank Hague of Jersey City.   Once those returns finished, the Republican heartland began.

Scott could not have been more wrong! The Republican high water mark had already been reached.   As the vote rolled westward, Truman's lead grew. He was winning not only in the South (except the four Dixiecrat states) but was making a strong run in the Republican Midwest.   When Scott made his statement, New York Democratic headquarters, a few blocks from the Roosevelt, had been gloomy and deserted, but it soon percolated to life.

While amazement, jubilation, and agony engulfed the nation, the Chief Executive snoozed. Truman awoke at midnight and snapped on the radio. Kaltenborn reported that Truman led by 1,200,000 votes, but that he could not win because the rural vote would soon be coming in. In fact, the rural vote had been pouring in for quite some time and was either just narrowly for Dewey or solidly for Truman. An astute politician, Truman chuckled, clicked off the radio, turned over and went back to sleep.

Journalist Cabell Phillips, who had ridden the campaign train with Truman, sat out the returns, opting for a Broadway play with Alfred Lunt and Lynn Fontaine. Nestled in his seat, he managed to lose himself in the play, oblivious to the maelstrom outside. He stayed in his seat for the first two intermissions, then, before the third act, he went to a nearby bar for a drink. From the saloon's radio, Phillips heard some isolated returns but had not pieced them together; then the announcer reported: "Truman's lead appears unassailable..." Phillips nearly choked on "a swallow of scotch just on its way past the windpipe." He raced from the bar toward his office abandoning his brand new topcoat at the theater.[525]

At CBS, Roper was disconsolate, while at ABC, George Gallup sat shattered. He could only sigh, keep shaking his head and repeating to his audience: "I just do not know what happened."[526]

Truman's sleep kept being interrupted. Secret Service agent, Henry Nicholson, awoke him when he had won Massachusetts. The agent noticed that about an inch of bourbon was gone from the bottle. Truman said: "Nick, stop worrying, it's all over. You all go to sleep, and we'll get up early in the morning."[527]

At 1:30 a.m., New York definitely went to Dewey, and Brownell tried to rally the troops with a bravado announcement. Standing on a chair, he proclaimed, "We now know that Governor Dewey will carry New York State by at least 50,000 votes and is the next President of the United States." The Republicans cheered and reporters raced to the telephones, but the distressing returns kept spewing from the news tickers. While individual states were close, Truman's steady lead kept growing even in Ohio and Iowa. Richard Rovere wrote that "Republican matrons were eating their corsages, Republican gentlemen were wilting their collars with nervous perspiration."[528] Weary, the GOP faithful began leaving, realizing the promised farm vote had long since come and gone.

An elevator operator at the Roosevelt asked if the rumors were true that nets were being spread beneath Suite 1527, where Dewey chain smoked Marlboro cigarettes in his aluminum holder. When he and his wife finally went to bed,[529] the Secret Service agents whispered among themselves; then, one by one, began slipping, as unobtrusively as possible, out of the suite.

By 5:00 a.m. EST, agent Jim Rowe woke Truman to hear Kaltenborn (whom Truman would gleefully mimic for the rest of his life)[530] say that Truman was still ahead by almost 2 million votes, but that the election would be decided in the House. Squinting without his glasses, Truman pronounced, "That's it." Newsweek had reached the same conclusion about the same time.

At exactly 4:46 EST on the morning of November 3rd, Newsweek flashed: "Hold everything" to its production office in Dayton, Ohio. Scrapping photos for a tentative 16 page layout on a Dewey victory, the staff went to work on the greatest political upset in American history.

At 9:30 a.m. EST, radio announcers in near hysteria cried "Ohio has gone Democratic! This puts Truman over the top . . . Ladies and gentlemen, President Truman has won the election."[531]

At 10:30 a.m. EST, Truman won Illinois and California. So, two hours after Dewey had gone to sleep, Brownell woke him with the bitter news. Dewey had lost the unloseable election. At 11:14 a.m. EST, he wired Truman: "My heartiest congratulations to you on your election. . . I urge all Americans to unite behind you in support of every effort to keep our nation strong and free."

Dewey's gentlemanly telegram contrasted sharply with Wallace's shrill and unyielding screed. Stomping on the virtually unbroken American custom of congratulating the winner, Wallace sent a 300 word telegram berating Truman and telling him how to run the government.

In his room, after pouring the first celebratory drinks for the Secret Service,[532] Truman decided to go to Kansas City where he feasted on ham and eggs, while Charlie Ross showed him the returns. Truman called in a barber, had a shave and a trim, then changed into a fresh white shirt, blue polka dot tie, and double breasted blue suit. Nattily dressed, the "accident of democracy," Harry Truman walked slowly into the lobby, past the haggard reporters who had come expecting to record his political eclipse.[533]

RADIO AND TV'S PERFORMANCE

While perhaps not as good as its wonderful coverage of the conventions, some of TV's grainy images were unforgettable, especially seeing pollsters George Gallup and Elmo Roper squirm as their predictions evaporated; the smug expression on the face of Republican campaign manager Brownell as he twice claimed a Dewey victory, and the camera's slow pan around GOP headquarters after dawn, showing the empty, gaily decorated Hotel Roosevelt ballroom, but missing the planned victory speech.

Television viewers witnessed stark reality as cameras basically photographed the radio men at work. In the early evening, the commentators were fresh shaven, ties straight, collars crisp. By the end of the night and early morning, their beards poked through the pancake makeup. ABC's Winchell and Drew Pearson, old-fashioned working reporters, kept their hats on despite the pleas of cameramen. The objective had become information, not appearance.

Not since the war had a night so frazzled reporters. CBS radio's Bob Trout had sat down in a straight-backed chair on the reporter's rostrum at 8 p.m. EST Tuesday. At noon Wednesday, he signed off the network's coverage. Except for one moment at 10 a.m. on Wednesday, when Trout stood up, stretched and sat down again, he had not left his chair for any reason for 16 hours.

Television had survived its baptism by fire - the biggest single event it had handled.

THE REACTION

Groucho Marx quipped, "The only way a Republican will get into the White House is to marry Margaret Truman."[534] Bob Hope sent Truman a telegram "Unpack." Truman enjoyed it so much that he put it on his desk under the glass top.[535]

Wall Street trembled. On Wednesday, November 3rd, Truman's victory triggered a selling avalanche at the New York Stock Exchange of 2,670,000 shares in the first four hours. For the day, the Dow Jones Industrial Average, which had been rising steadily for a month anticipating a Dewey victory, dropped 8.33 points on sales of 3,230,000 shares. On Friday, investors unloaded another 2,530,000 shares. In three days, the value of all stocks on the exchange dropped approximately $5 billion. The market fell 10.82 points in a week, the worst break since the spring of 1940, when France fell.

Despite the stock exchange, the aftermath contained surprisingly little bitterness. Even the Republicans joined in the cheers once they got over the shock. Vandenberg said to his staff: "You've got to give the little man credit. There he was flat on his back. Everyone had counted him out, but he came up fighting and won the battle. That's the kind of courage the American people admire."[536]

THE DAY AFTER

The next day's newspapers were especially embarrassing. Not only did the front page proclaim how wrong they had been, but many of the columns had been filed before the election. They announced that Dewey was President-elect, pontificated on why Truman had lost and what President-elect Dewey should do. The Detroit Free Press praised Truman as "a game little fellow who never sought the presidency and was lost in it but who went down fighting with all he had." The Alsop Brothers column began: "The first post election question is how the government can get through the next 10 weeks . . . Events will not wait patiently until Thomas E. Dewey officially replaces Harry S. Truman."

Drew Pearson's column the day before the voting said a Truman victory was "impossible"; the day after the election his column began, "I surveyed the closely knit group around Tom Dewey who will take over the White House eighty-six days from now." He profiled them. Pearson called the Dewey campaign "one of the most astute and skillful campaigns in recent memory."[537] The Hanford California Sentinel on November 3rd had black borders surrounded the gaping white space which should have been the syndicated column. It substituted one droll line--"In memory of Drew Pearson's column on Dewey."

Many reporters blamed the pollsters, but The New York Times' James Reston blamed himself and the other reporters, pointing out that they spent their time interviewing each other, rather than the people, assuming that someone who they spoke to had interviewed the people.[538] TIME agreed, the press had "delegated its journalism to the polls."[539]

When Truman left for Washington, 10,000 people crammed St. Louis's cavernous Union Station to see him, but many could not get past the concourse's gates. From the Ferdinand Magellan, Truman shouted through a microphone, "Let the people behind those bars get in if they want in. Open the gates! Open the gates!" As the crowd rolled around the train, someone handed him a copy of the early election night edition of the Chicago Tribune with a banner line, "Dewey Defeats Truman." He held up the paper with an ear to ear grin that became the most remembered photograph of 1948.

Wherever the train stopped, enroute to Washington, the Ferdinand Magellan was stormed by people eager to get on the bandwagon they had abandoned earlier. Party leaders, and government officials, including Senator Johnston of South Carolina, who had snubbed Truman at the Jackson Day Dinner months before, now elbowed their way onto the train to announce that they had supported Truman all along.[540] Businessmen who had sat on their hands or checkbooks now let loose a blizzard of back-dated checks, about $750,000 worth, that blanketed finance chair Louis Johnson. The Trumans labeled all of them "Wednesday Democrats."[541]

In the last month of the campaign, Truman's arrivals and departures from Washington drew sparse crowds of no more than 5,000 morose Democrats. The others had left Harry Truman to mourn alone what they thought would be his own wake; but on Friday, November 5th, Truman drew the greatest D.C. throng ever to greet a President. 750,000 welcomers, including government workers and school children dismissed for the day, crammed every square foot of sidewalk. Hawkers sold new blue buttons reading "I Told You So." His motorcade passed the Washington *Post* building, festooned with a sign: MR. PRESIDENT, WE ARE READY TO EAT CROW WHENEVER YOU ARE READY TO SERVE IT.

No other election in history so proves and exalts the individuality and independence of Americans - and they revelled in it! Only nineteen percent of Americans had expected a Truman win.[542] Despite the unanimous chants of pollsters and experts that they were voting for a loser, they voted for him anyway. Whatever their politics, the nation bathed in a great emotional satisfaction from Truman's election. He had humbled the press, bewildered the pollsters, and proven the old fashioned virtues of work and determination.

CHAPTER TWENTY

WHAT HAPPENED AND WHY

The November 8th Newsweek, with Truman on the cover under the caption "Miracle Man," editorialized:

> "Facing repudiation by his own party only six short months ago, he literally forced himself upon the Democratic Party, splitting it wide open and thoroughly demoralizing it. Instead of attempting to heal the wounds which his stubbornness had opened, he angrily rubbed salt in them. Almost everyone believed that he had committed political suicide when he vetoed the income tax reduction bill which the 80th Congress had passed. No politician had ever dared to shoot Santa Claus before. He not only shot Santa Claus, he boasted upon it."

Truman said: "You not only have to be good, but be lucky." He was the luckiest candidate, the accidental beneficiary of circumstances. Wallace, Stalin, Hiss, Dewey, the 80th Congress, Thurmond, and even the weather all helped him. But he played the accidents well.

His victory has now assumed legendary proportions. Three myths predominate: that Truman won by a landslide; that his campaign so excited the people that they flooded the polls; and that Truman outpaced the Democrats. All are hogwash.

THE PAPER THIN LANDSLIDE

The election was the tightest presidential election, both in popular and electoral votes, since Wilson's victory in 1916 over Charles Evans Hughes. Truman had won twenty-eight states with 304 electoral votes; Dewey sixteen states with 189 votes, Thurmond his four Dixiecrat states with 39 votes. Truman polled 24,179,345 popular votes to Dewey's 21,991,291, Thurmond's 1,176,126 votes, and Wallace's 1,157,326. For the first time since 1916, more people had voted against the winner than for him.

He had won key states by tissue thin margins: California by 17,865 of 4 million votes; Ohio by 7,107 votes of 3 million. A switch of 12,000 votes in those two states would have thrown the election into the House to decide. Truman won Illinois by 33,612 of nearly 4 million ballots cast. Out of nearly 50 million votes, a shift of 29,000 selected votes, just over .05 percent of the total, would have elected Dewey by 267 electoral votes to 225[543] despite Truman's wide popular vote lead.

Had Wallace done just a little better in California, and not been kept off the Illinois ballot, Truman would have lost both states to Dewey and the election would have been decided in the House of Representatives.

A BORED ELECTORATE STAYED HOME

People were content and a contented people feel no need to flood the polls. Only 53 percent of those eligible voted - the lowest since 48.9% had turned out in 1924. The percentage was even lower for presidential voters as 683,382 persons who went to the polls left the presidential line of their ballots blank. The November 1st Issue of TIME noted how surprisingly little election fervor there was. "The most energetic efforts of two major and three minor candidates had apparently either soothed, dulled or completely anesthetized the electorate." Both sides in the closing days had trouble raising funds. The Democrats because they were sure they would lose, the Republicans because they were sure they would win.

The people did not pay much attention to the election, discussed it comparatively infrequently, and argued about it even less. 1948 might have been unique because people picked a president with less enthusiasm than they displayed in contests for alderman. Only the followers of Wallace and Thurmond had whipped up any fervor at all.

Some argued that the extremely low turnout had hurt the GOP. Overconfidence may very well have kept 2 to 3 million Republican votes at home. The Republican turnout was 21.9 million compared with 22 million in 1944 and 33.9 million who voted for Eisenhower in 1952. Thirteen percent of Dewey's supporters did not bother to vote. Thousands of farmers decided either to vote Democratic or to stay home. In the normally Republican counties of rural Illinois, the vote was 150,000 less than in 1944, and 400,000 below 1940.

Others argued equally convincingly that most of the stay-at-homes had been apathetic or gloomy Democrats, especially in the East. Because the Democrats were the larger party and better organized at local levels, their best hope lay in a large turnout. "Far from costing Dewey the election, the [Democratic] stay at homes may have saved him from almost as crushing a defeat as Landon suffered in 1936.[544]

THE PARTY VICTORY AND REVERSE COATTAILS

Far from leading his party to victory, Truman ran 4 percent behind the Democrat congressional tickets; Dewey ran 5 percent ahead of the GOP's[545] Truman admitted, "It was not my victory, but a victory of the Democratic Party for the people."

The election showed that the Democratic coalition did not depend on Roosevelt alone. Besides eight more Democratic governors, the Democrats had the best showing in Congressional races between the Roosevelt landslide in 1936 and the Eisenhower recession of 1958. They did especially well in the Senate races, winning 56% of the vote nationally, to control the new Senate 54 to 42, a 9 seat gain over 1946. In the House, Democrats led by a 52 to 46% margin, and won 263 seats, a 75 seat gain over 1946. Truman had gotten the house cleaning he wanted.[546]

In nineteen states, Democrat candidates polled far ahead of Truman and may have drawn just enough Democratic voters to the booths to enable him to win.[547] Truman almost surely would have lost Illinois but for Paul Douglas' race for the Senate and Adlai Stevenson's for governor. Both won by large margins, providing him with a reverse coattail effect.

THE POLLS MADE TRUMAN A LEGEND

What made the election so memorable was not the people, but the polls. Without the pollsters' arrogant predictions of the opposite result the day after headlines, would have read "Incumbent President of Majority Party Wins Election Amid Booming Economy" - hardly stunning stuff!

Why were the polls so wrong? Three reasons spring to the front. The pollsters' middle and higher income groups that preferred Dewey were over-weighted. Gallup had combined each poll with those that preceded it. So once Truman began behind, he never quite caught up. But worst of all, the polls and pundits were so convinced they were right, that they stopped watching, weeks or, in Roper's case, months before the election.

Thus they missed two last-minute trends: the decision of the undecideds to vote for Truman and the shift to the Democrats among groups that had previously planned to vote for someone else.

Millions of votes changed hands. Many Thurmond and Wallace supporters voted instead for the man they perceived as the lesser of two evils. Protest votes seem righteous in the spring, but wasted self-indulgences in November. Some 14 percent of Dewey's own supporters changed their minds.

Nowhere did more votes shift than in the farm belt. Wisconsin, Ohio, Illinois, and Iowa all switched to Truman. "I kept reading about that Dewey fellow," said Charles Crenshaw of New Lebanon, Ohio, "and the more I read the more he reminded me of one of those slick ads trying to get money out of my pocket. Now Harry Truman, running around and yipping and falling all over his feet--I had the feeling he could understand the kind of fixes I get into."[548]

On September 24th, Gallup foresaw 46.5 percent for Dewey to 38 percent for Truman. His last column, appearing two days before the election, showed Truman had surged to 44 percent -- and that based on interviews conducted two weeks earlier! Votes were shifting daily, almost hourly and the preeminent pollster blithely ignored it.[549]

The pollsters believed that people decided early in the campaign and did not change afterwards. That might have been true for Roosevelt but not for Truman. Dewey led until the last two weeks of the campaign, when one voter in every seven (6,927,000) made up his mind. Of these, seventy-five percent (5,195,000) picked Truman; twenty-five percent (1,732,000) chose Dewey, a difference of 3,463,000. Truman outpolled Dewey on November 2 by 2,135,000. Dewey lost in the last days when he wanted to slug it out with Truman but did not, because all the experts told him he should not.[550] 1948 showed the campaign was vitally important.

Polling was disgraced. Alistair Cooke wrote: "Your correspondent will now sell his telephone and subscription to Mr. Roper's poll and get back to the use of his legs and other humble sense." So many people did as Cooke did, that polls would have ended. Only the great commercial uses of polling for marketing research kept the polls alive.[551]

REVOLT AGAINST THE 80TH CONGRESS

While criticizing Dewey for the loss, Republicans glumly realized that the people had rejected the 80th Congress even more. "The luckiest thing that ever happened to me was the Eightieth Congress," Truman later said.[552]

The Republicans had misinterpreted the 1946 election, believing it signaled a conservative rejection of the New Deal. Not at all - the electorate liked the New Deal. Roosevelt's radical solution to the depression had given the national government an active social and economic role. After 15 years, it had become the status quo that meant guaranteed security for the farmer, the worker, the old, and the sick. In 1948, Americans wanted a man who believed in that doctrine and rejected the party that it suspected of wanting to change it. The 1946 election had helped Truman win in 1948 by giving him a target. Truman had excoriated Congress and Dewey had not responded. Voters assumed that the liberal/moderate Dewey agreed with the conservative Congress.

The New Republic stated "nothing less than an era of reform has been demanded by America and nothing less will Americans accept."[553] Perhaps James Reston said it best when he castigated his own performance and the performance of all the press, polls and pundits: "We were wrong not only on the election, but what's worse, on the whole political direction of our time."[554]

THE STATES

Dewey swept the traditionally Democratic industrial Northeast, from Maryland through Maine, except for Massachusetts and Rhode Island. Dewey fared better than he had in 1944 in industrial areas, beating Truman in four of the largest industrial states, New York--47 electoral votes,

Pennsylvania--35, Michigan--19, and New Jersey--16. Roosevelt had won Pennsylvania and New Jersey in all of his four elections.

The Dixiecrats took South Carolina, Alabama, Mississippi and Louisiana, but the Democrats held Arkansas, Florida, North Carolina and Virginia, with Texas giving Truman his biggest majority. The South contributed almost 70 electoral votes, even without the 39 votes of Thurmond.

Truman carried the four border states of West Virginia, Kentucky, Oklahoma and Missouri. By winning the farm states of Iowa, (the bedrock of Republicanism), Wisconsin, Ohio, Wyoming and Colorado, Truman took five states that had been lost by FDR in the two previous elections. Of the 11 Great Plains states of which Dewey had carried 7 in 1944, he carried only 5--Indiana, North and South Dakota, Nebraska and Kansas.

In the traditionally Democratic West, the Republicans had expected to make important gains. At the start, only Arizona had looked safe for the Democrats, but Truman swept the whole tier of 11 states except Oregon that remembered Dewey's whirlwind primary campaign. Warren had been expected to lend strength to the ticket in California and Minnesota. He failed in both.

Truman had won without the Solid South and without New York, which a Democrat supposedly could not do. His biggest loss, New York, would have been a landslide if Wallace had not pulled 500,000 votes. As it was, Dewey, the state's governor, only won by 61,000 out of more than 6 million ballots.

NEGRO

Truman's civil rights program while forfeiting the Deep South may well have won the election. Truman won more than two thirds of the Negro vote. One Negro editor wrote: "Negroes felt that if they did not support Truman after that, no other politician would ever take such a stand."[555] In Illinois, Ohio and California, his majorities in the Negro districts exceeded the margin by which he carried the state.[556]

LABOR

1948 marked labor's first formal entry into a presidential election, but the last time that labor voted as a block in a presidential election. In eight years, white collar workers would outnumber blue collars workers.[557] With the decline of blue collar industries, the rise of technology and the entrance into the middle class of many workers, the labor vote disintegrated. Union members felt that Democrats got them into the middle class, but Republicans would keep them there.

Nevertheless, in 1948, organized labor did a masterful job of pulling out voters for the rest of the Democratic ticket, devastating Republican congressional majorities and tugging Truman to victory in several states, especially via wins in all 13 American cities with populations of more than 500,000.

FARM

Corn decided the election. Of the eight largest corn producing states, Truman carried six. "I talked about voting for Dewey all summer," one farmer put it, "but when voting time came, I just couldn't do it. I remembered . . . all the good things that have come to me under the Democrats."[558] Farmers saw no reason to believe that the GOP cared about them. One farmer said, "I wasn't voting for a man or a party. I was voting for the price of wheat."

Dewey had swept the industrial Northeast, pared Democratic margins in the big cities by a third, run better than any Republican since Hoover in the South--and still lost.[559]

Dewey admitted: "The farm votes switched in the last ten days, and you can analyze the figures from now to kingdom come and all they will show is that we lost the farm vote, which we had in 1944, and that lost the election." [560] He concluded that when the GOP carries New York, New Jersey and Pennsylvania, and then loses the election in the farm belt, the world is upside down.

As with Labor, 1948 may have been the farmers' last hurrah. The migration from the farm to the city made the small family farm less able to compete against the huge agri-business conglomerates. They were soon gobbled up. Farmers' importance in American politics dwindled.

WALLACE

Wallace cost Truman victory in New York, Maryland and Michigan, but nowhere else, even in narrow losses in Pennsylvania and New Jersey.[561] But the impact could have been greater.

The Progressives were kept off the ballot in Illinois, primarily because the state Republicans felt Dewey would safely carry the state. They did not want to establish a precedent for future third parties. That proved problematic. Truman carried the state by only 33,612 out of nearly 4 million votes. Because the Progressive candidate had garnered some 313,000 votes in 1947, Wallace should easily have taken enough votes from Truman to shift Illinois into the Dewey column.[562]

A series of court and administrative maneuvering put the Progressives on the ballot in Ohio, but only in a convoluted way. The Progressive electors were listed without party designation, so a citizen wishing to vote for Wallace had to make 25 separate x's, one before each name. That was significant, because Truman carried the state by only 7,000 votes.[563]

Oddly, the Dixiecrat revolt hurt Wallace. Truman could then promote a more liberal agenda without fear of antagonizing the southern conservatives. Equally important was that the Dixiecrat revolt proved to Negroes that Truman was serious about civil rights. Wallace's campaign had hurt Dewey more than Truman, because it showed Truman to be the more moderate Democrat.

Third parties influence elections but rarely win them. Wallace forced Truman to adopt more liberal positions, but the Progressives did not even run second in any state. Leo Isacson, whose victory in the special election in February had so scared Democrats, was trounced by a coalition candidate. Wallace lost strength as the weeks went by, and Thurmond and Dewey did not increase theirs.

FOREIGN AFFAIRS

Rowe had noted in his prescient memorandum that: "There is considerable political advantage to the administration in its battle with the Kremlin. In times of crisis, the American citizen tends to back up his President."[564] 1948 had provided more than its share of crises.

In his decisions on Berlin and Israel, Truman enjoyed strong public and Congressional support even though he had not formally consulted Congress in either instance. The Republicans simply could not convince people that Harry Truman was soft on Communism, when he was staring Stalin down in the Berlin Airlift and in the Truman Doctrine.

The election ended isolationism. The senators elected in 1942 and up for re-election in 1948 were the most isolationist in the Senate. Of the 10 senators in the group who voted against the Marshall Plan authorization, only 1 survived the 1948 election. Four chose not to run again. The internationalist trend swept Republican Gerald Ford into Congress. As Arthur Vandenberg's protégé, he beat an incumbent isolationist in the primary.[565]

IT WAS THE ECONOMY, STUPID

People vote their pocketbooks and their pocketbooks were bulging, despite such irritants as inflation, some continuing consumer shortages and credit controls. Well over 61 million people were employed; production soared, profits levitated, and national income hit $210 billion. Taft griped, "It is almost impossible to put an administration out of office at the very peak of a boom."

The booming economy torpedoed Wallace. Bad times allow third parties to build a considerable core of support among the unemployed and downtrodden. Contentment, especially economic, proves a barren field for third party movements.

Columnist Raymond Moley wrote: "Prosperous farmers, overconfident Republicans, labor concentration on Congressional candidates, better candidates on state tickets, and a light vote were too much even for as good a ticket as Dewey and Warren."

DEWEY'S UNSCALABLE OBSTACLE

Truman declared that his biggest asset was Tom Dewey. People were convinced that Dewey would be an efficient captain of the Ship of State, but no one had any clear idea of where he would steer. Truman on the other hand would have plenty of stops and starts, but people knew and liked where he was headed.

Fundamentally, people could not warm up to Dewey. The issues were secondary. Dewey realized that too late. After his defeat, Dewey went to the El Conquistador Hotel, near Tucson, Arizona, where one evening his sons asked to be excused from dinner to pitch pennies outside. Dewey agreed. A few minutes later, he removed his coat, rolled up his sleeves, and squatted down next to the boys. Frances fretted that a photographer might capture her husband in such a pose. Dewey straightened himself, stared off blankly into space for a moment, then said introspectively, "Maybe if I had done this during the campaign, I would have won."[566]

WINNERS AND LOSERS

In terms of winners and losers, Truman won a lot more than an election. His gutsy refusal to quit earned him a special place in the affections of America and made him an inspiration to underdog candidates ever since.

The others lost in more ways than one. Dewey became the quintessential loser. His decades of honorable and heroic public service are mere footnotes to his humiliating defeat, that is inevitably attributed to his cold personality and vacuous speeches.

Perhaps the biggest losers were the Dixiecrats. Like many political entities, their power rested on their assumed strength and the threat of losing it. When Truman won without them, their influence within the Democratic party vanished. Since 1948, the South shifted toward the Republican party.

The political bosses also lost. Truman had won without them; but even if he had not, their influence was waning. Four ingredients combined to destroy them. Suburbia robbed them of voters, especially the ones with growing money and influence. Television ended their monopoly on the eyes and ears of their constituents. A Republican speechmaker would have fared poorly in Frank Hague's baliwick: the cops would have hustled him away and, equally important, locals would not want to be seen listening to his speeches or reading his handbills. But not even Hague could monitor TV ads. Soon, in the privacy of their homes, voters could see and hear other candidates than the boss' slate and make up their own minds.

Armed with that new knowledge, voters could exercise that fundamental right so anathema to the bosses - *ticket splitting*! The new educated and informed electorate also demanded something else that cut the legs from under the bosses - *open primaries*.

In all the hoopla and congratulations that Truman earned in his loneliest campaign, it is easy to forget that he engaged in a negative, mudslinging crusade that often sank to unabashed class warfare.[567] His language, intemperate and salty in the best of times, worsened during the heat of the campaign - made starker because Dewey was not responding in kind but was spouting banalities. Truman's fire breathing screed stained a noble effort.

Eric Golden said Truman spat the roughest English used by a presidential candidate since the frontier days.[568] William Manchester labeled it demeaning, in ghastly taste, an ugly precedent for future campaigns, and it was unfair to Republicans like Vandenberg, without whom there would be no Truman Doctrine, no Marshall Plan, no Berlin Airlift.[569]

Fortunately, for Truman, his victory, so unexpected and against such odds, overshadowed his tactics and language.

CHAPTER TWENTY-ONE

A RETURN TO NORMALCY

HARRY IS EJECTED FROM THE WHITE HOUSE

When Truman returned to 1600 Pennsylvania Avenue on November 5, 1948, the building's architect and engineer overruled the voters. They ordered him out of the White House!

The old house was falling apart. An inspection had revealed that the second floor stayed up more "by force of habit" than any architectural support. The marble grand staircase could collapse. The heavy frescoed ceiling in the east room had a 6 inch sag and had to be shored up with timbers to prevent its caving in. Only a few rusty nails supported it. Horrified engineers reported that Truman's bathroom could fall into the Red Room, and, fearing for the stability of his bedroom, too, moved him into Lincoln's bedroom.[570]

So, on Sunday, November 7th, Truman flew to Key West Submarine Base for a two week vacation at the white cottage which had housed him on four previous visits. The next morning, he caught up on some lost sleep and stayed in bed until 8 a.m. For the rest of his stay, he would sleep until 7:30 a.m., far longer than normal; then he would walk over to the secluded enlisted man's beach, don some swimming trunks, and swim in the cold green waters using the head-out-of-water technique he called the "Missouri side stroke." Later, he would put on a pith helmet and read newspapers on the beach. In the afternoon, he would roam around the base dressed in a tan slack suit with rayon trousers which bore a conspicuous patch.

Within a week, though, he had summoned his aides to work on the new budget and the next State of the Union Address. Truman saw his narrow victory as a mandate for an ambitious legislative program, which he called the Fair Deal. He also planned the inauguration that would be especially lavish. The Republican Congress, assuming a Dewey victory, had appropriated $100,000, a record![571]

He would begin his second term in historic Blair House, a 124-year-old four-story yellow stucco house at 1648 Pennsylvania Avenue. He had begun his days as President there, while Mrs. Roosevelt moved out of the White House.

THE NATION GIVES THANKS

On Thanksgiving Day, as Truman sliced into a 16-1/2 pound prize turkey, the U.S. had reason to be thankful. In the midst of hunger and want, it knew unequalled prosperity – the biggest harvest in history and, with few exceptions, everyone who wanted a job had one. Employment at 60.1 million was almost 1 million above the end of 1947. Prices inched upward and everyone complained about them, but the U.S. citizen had more actual buying power than ever before. He also managed to save some money. (Personal savings were up $4.9 billion over 1947). A new entertainment vehicle, television, became an accepted part of U.S. life. With only six percent of the world's area and seven percent of its population, the United States had 46 percent of the world's electric power, 48 percent of its radios, 54 percent of its telephones and 92 percent of its modern bathtubs.[572]

THE OLD SOLDIER TRIES TO FADE AWAY

At his first news conference in the White House since the election, Truman said that all the cabinet members were willing to stay and he planned no change in the administration. That was not to be.

In the summer of '48, after discovering that he tired easily, Marshall submitted to his first thorough physical since Pearl Harbor. The doctors found cysts in one kidney. He postponed the surgery, afraid that it might affect the election.

Marshall was in Paris when he delightedly learned of Truman's re-election. He decided to return home and schedule the surgery, especially after a painful attack in his hotel suite. On Monday, November 22, Truman stood in the pouring rain to National Airport to greet an ailing Secretary Marshall. The mutual respect and admiration between the two was well known.

A few months earlier at a private dinner, the taciturn, straight-laced Marshall stood, looked straight at Harry Truman, and waited for silence. Then he said with deep seriousness, perhaps to atone for his biting criticism over the recognition of Israel, "The full stature of this man will only be proved by history. But I want to say here and now that there has never been a decision made under this man's administration, affecting policies beyond our shores, that has not been in the best interest of this country. It is not the courage of these decisions that will live, but the integrity of them." Truman was so deeply moved by the tribute from the man he most deeply respected that he grappled for words, and finally could just gasp, as he gestured toward Marshall, "He won the war."

Truman urged Marshall to stay, as did others. In December, Vandenberg wrote to the New York Times, "While men are never permanently indispensable, Secretary Marshall and Undersecretary Lovett come close to it for the time being . . . whether we agree with them in all things or not."

But soon after his return, in early December, Marshall collapsed with a sudden terrible pain and was taken to Walter Reed hospital. The operation to remove his terribly diseased kidney went well, but it ended his tenure as Secretary of State. He sent his resignation on January 3, 1949. Truman chose Dean Acheson to succeed him.

CHINA'S LAST GASP FOR HELP

After World War II, the Communists led by Mao Tse Tung, operating from bases in northern China and Manchuria, had resumed battling the Nationalist regime. The Communists repeatedly whipped the Nationalist Army in battle after humiliating battle.

Although Chiang Kai Chek and his charismatic American educated wife were often portrayed as freedom fighters against the Japanese and the Communists, the truth was much less heroic. If Chiang and his generals were as competent as they were crooked, the Communists would not have stood a chance. But, as the American ambassador said, Chiang was the best asset the Communists had; compared to him, Czar Nicholas "was far sighted and daring." [573]

Chiang was not only losing the support of the people, he was losing control of his soldiers. By early 1948, nearly half of Chiang's troops, including whole divisions, with all their American equipment, had defected. As much as 80% of his American equipment had either fallen into Communist hands or been sold on the black market. The Chinese nationalists had surrendered 236,000 rifles, 14,000 machine guns and 26,000 tommy guns in recent battles to the Communists without a fight.

The well supplied Nationalist army had all that it needed except one thing--the will to fight. As China specialist John K. Fairbank put it, "The United States government has done practically everything possible to save Chiang Kai Chek except actually shoot Chinese for him."[574]

By the fall of 1948, the situation was beyond hope. Control of all China, together with the areas already held, would place 40% of the world's population in Stalin's grasp. Chiang sent Truman a frantic appeal for help, but Truman ignored it. General David Barr, who commanded the U.S. Military Advisory Group in China, reported to the White House: "I am convinced that the military situation has deteriorated to the point where only the active participation of United States troops could effect a remedy. No battle has been lost since my arrival for lack of ammunition or equipment. Their military debacles, in my opinion, can all be attributed to the world's worst leadership and many other morale destroying factors that led to a complete loss of will to fight."[575] Chiang's days on mainland China were numbered.

CHRISTMAS AND THE BOOM SUBSIDES

For Christmas Day 1948, merchants were hawking a Santa-graph in which children were photographed in a department store on Santa's lap. Three Chicago department stores began the idea in 1946. In 1947, the business expanded to 8 stores in 7 cities. They snapped 250,000 photos and sold 120,000. In 1948, photographers were snapping children at 25 stores from Minneapolis to Houston to Miami to Philadelphia.

At Truman's prompting, Air Force Secretary Stuart Symington asked Bob Hope to take a show to the GIs involved in the Berlin Airlift. Hope agreed as long as he could do his regular Tuesday night show on December 25.

He brought over Irving Berlin, the composer of God Bless America, Easter Parade, and White Christmas, vice president-elect Alben Barkley, General Jimmy Doolittle and the Radio City Music Hall Rockettes. They did an impromptu show in England, put on shows at three bases in Germany and then flew to Berlin. Because of bad weather they had to forego their larger Constellation and flew in a smaller cargo plane. Its flight into Templehof was made rougher for reasons other than the weather. The plane had to fly low because of the Airlift and Soviet anti-aircraft "practice."

The toy industry looked forward to a boom Christmas, with 24 million new customers born since 1940, and expected to ring up record sales of $300 to $400 million, at least 20% above 1947. But the economy was cooling down, finally. The Federal Reserve Board announced that inflationary pressures might be subsiding as the long awaited post-war recession began.

Consumer prices had accelerated during the World War II era, rising at an annual average rate of 7.0 percent from 1940 to 1948, when the U.S. had its first $1 a pound round steak. By autumn, prices started to fall. The Bureau of Labor Statistics cost of living index that peaked at 174.5 in August had shrunk to about 172. What brought it down chiefly was the greatest crop in U.S. history. By mid-December, crop prices stood 13% below the all time high of January 1948. In two months, wholesale food prices had tumbled 10%.

A drop in retail sales had scared department stores into slashing pre-Christmas prices. Prices of electrical appliances slipped 25% from their peak. Even then, stores barely managed to sell as much as in 1947, because demand had finally ebbed.

One of the best ways to fight inflation is to boost production. Americans had done that - and not only on the farm. The Taft-Hartley Act and smart business meant fewer strikes. That plus increased productivity had finally sated the pentup demand from World War II and lowered inflation.

Retail stores found themselves overstocked. For the first time in a long while, consumers could walk into an auto showroom and buy a Lincoln, Packard, Hudson Kaiser, Fraser or Chrysler right off the floor. Even major appliances, the bellwether of the post war boom, were selling more slowly. The Hoover Vacuum Company let 400 workers go.

All this finally signaled a return to a new normalcy with TV, global police responsibilities, and a new economy. But before the U.S. could free itself of its World War II mentality, it needed the catharsis of settling some debts.

EXORCISING THE LAST GHOSTS OF THE WAR

Thirty seconds after midnight December 23rd, four Japanese warlords, including Hideki Tojo, who had ruled an empire greater than Alexander's, Caesar's or Napoleon's stood erect in GI olive drab fatigues, while three others waited in a Buddhist chapel.

The four then mounted the traditional 13 steps to the gallows. They stood under the glaring lights while nooses and black hoods were fitted. The executioner saluted. One minute after they entered the chambers, four traps were sprung at once. At 12:10:30, Tojo was pronounced dead. Soon, the three other condemned men followed the first group. By 12:35, the verdict of the International Military Tribunal for the Far East had been executed. After the seven hangings, MacArthur asked for a day of prayer throughout Japan. The book on World War II, while not closed, could now move from center stage.

EPILOGUE

Some of the events of 1948 are seared into our memory. Other events of transcending importance were not noticed at all until long afterward.

What was clear to all was America's new place in the world. The U.S. had become that necessary and hopeful "island of order" in a chaotic, war-littered and dangerous world.

The British historian Robert Payne wrote, after an extensive visit in 1948-49: America "bestrides the world like a Colossus: no other power at any time in the world's history has possessed so varied or so great an influence on other nations. . . . [I]t is already an axiom that the decisions of the American government affect the lives and the livelihood of the remotest people."[576]

The January 3, 1949 issue of TIME, with Harry Truman on the cover as Man of the Year, proclaimed that 1948 was a fitful year in a nervous century.

> "Historians could recall that a mass of U.S. intentions, promises and pledges had hardened into resolve and action. In 1948, the world's greatest nation of free men finally resolved to meet communism's deadly challenge with every weapon of peace that it possessed; and if the struggle against communism required war, the U.S. would fight.

Communism had enjoyed one minor and one major victory in Czechoslovakia and in China, but elsewhere Stalin did little more than hold his own. The Communists suffered electoral defeats in France, South Korea, Germany and Italy; Yugoslavia's strong-willed Tito brashly challenged Stalin's absolute authority.

The U.S. had taken a long step toward creating a more stable world and had achieved most of its foreign policy goals in 1948. The economic and political security of Western Europe was improving Europe. Israel seemed to be satisfactorily established albeit amidst sworn enemies. The Soviet bluff had been called in Berlin.[577] The German currency reform revitalized post war Europe. It brought an explosion of industrial expansion and economic prosperity for West Germany, and bound that country to the West. A revitalized America had also shown that it had the tools to stabilize its boom and form the keystone of a new world economic arch.

The Founding Fathers' advice was ignored about overseas entanglements, and large standing armies and the Bill of Rights took a beating in some of the witch hunts for Communists. But Truman's July Executive Orders and court decisions elevated the phrase "Equal Protection Under the Law" in the nation's consciousness. On balance, 1948 did the Constitution proud.

In a modern management self-assessment, individuals select their most important goals and then are judged after a year as to how well they met those criteria. By that standard, Americans in 1948 had done well. In December 1947, Roper had done a poll:

Suppose only two of these things could really be attempted during 1948, which two would you like most to see the Government try to do?[578] The two digit answers:

Lower the cost of living	52%
Strengthen our Army, Navy, and Air Force	23%
Fight Communism here and abroad	23%
Keep peace between labor and capital	22%
Strengthen the United Nations	21%
See that more houses are built	19%
Protect the rights of minorities	15%
Help European countries to recover	13%

For all their griping, alleged apathy, and distractions, an entire nation had kept its New Year's Resolutions to improve itself and the world around it.

The biggest impact would not be felt until later. Children born that year and that era have changed the nation more than any other generation, becoming the richest, biggest and best educated generation ever produced.[579]

Raised in a land and time of unequaled opportunity, they were twice as likely as their parents to go to college and three times as likely as their grandparents. Their affluence reformed the economy that contorted to sate and shape their voracious market.[580] What was revolutionary to the adults of 1948 was second nature to their children. They cannot remember a time without televison. Where their parents had known haunting poverty and all enveloping pessimism, they have known plenty and optimism.

The last day of 1948 marked the last day of the Republican 80th Congress. The 80 minute session was devoted mostly to eulogies of deceased and retiring members. Then Charles A. Halleck of Indiana in his final action as GOP Majority Leader announced that the President had passed the word that as far as he was concerned, the 80th Congress could adjourn immediately. After the laughter died away, the House did just that at 1:20 p.m. In the Senate, the eulogies lasted only eight minutes longer.

The experts had proclaimed that Republicans would control the next Congress. But, just as they had with the weather forecast at the start of 1948, the projected sales of the Kinsey Report, the viability of the Berlin Airlift, the Israelis' chances against the Arabs, and Harry Truman's prospects against Dewey, the experts got that one wrong, too!

~

BIBLIOGRAPHY

PERIODICALS

In preparing this book I have relied heavily on the issues of TIME and Newsweek from 1948 and the first few weeks of 1949. Such publications were excellent sources for three reasons. First, they gave a truly national perspective. Second, they were contemporary without being instantaneous. The vast majority of the articles were written 2-9 days after the event occurred. So, the staff had the chance to reflect, gather facts, and discard many of the erroneous "facts" that often arise after a sudden event. Third, they were also able to rely upon and cite the most incisive writings of the newspapers of the day.

ALMANACS, TIMETABLES AND CHRONOLOGIES

TIME and Newsweek suffer from two problems. Being contemporary, they often do not notice matters of tremendous concern such as the invention of the transistor. Second, because they wrote their articles 2-9 days after an event, it is impossible to get exact dates from the magazine. One oft repeated phrase was "in Washington last week..." with no statement as to the precise date. To fill the gaps, other volumes are outstanding.

The 1949 and 1950 World Almanacs were indispensable for their detailed chronologies of 1948 which give not only a list of important and less important events but the dates. In addition, they provided some critical statistics on the year.

But the World Almanacs were published too close to 1948 to recognize some vital events. For that, other chronologies, sometimes specialized, are invaluable.

David Brownstone and Irene Franck, Timelines of the Arts and Literature, Harper Collins, New York 1994

David Brownstone and Irene Franck, Timelines of War: A Chronology of Warfare from 100,000 BC to the Present, Little Brown, Boston 1994

Thomas Dale Cowan and Jack Maguire, Timelines of African-American History - Four Hundred Years of Black Achievement, Berkley Publishing Group, New York 1994

David Brownstone and Irene Franck, Timelines of the Twentieth Century: A Chronology of 7,500 Key Events, Discoveries and People That Shaped Our Century, Little Brown, Boston 1996

Sue Heinemann, Timelines of American Women's History, Berkley Publishing Group, New York 1996

Judah Gribetz, Edward L. Greenstein and Regina Stein, Timetable of Jewish History: Chronology of The Most Important People and Events in Jewish History, Simon and Schuster, New York 1993

Bryan Bunch and Alexander Hellemans, The Timetables of Technology: A Chronology of the Most Important People and Events in the History of Technology, Simon and Schuster, New York 1993

James Trager, The Peoples Chronology: A Year by Year Record of Human Events from Pre-History to the Present; Henry Holt & Co., New York 1994.

Grun, The Timetables of History, Simon and Schuster, New York 1991

Arthur Scheslinger, The Almanac of American History, General Editor, G.P. Putnam's Sons, New York 1983

GENERAL HISTORIES

In studying 1948, it is necessary to put that year in perspective, both within the period (five, ten or fifteen years) and longer histories. The following volumes place 1948 in context within the stream of the nation's history.

Carman, Syrett, Wishy, A History of the American People: Volume II, Since 1865, Alfred A. Knopf, N.Y., 1961;

Samuel Elliott Morrison, The Oxford History of the American People, N.Y., Oxford University Press 1965;

Geoffrey Perret, A County Made by War: From the Revolution to Viet Nam--The Story of America's Rise to Power, Random House, N.Y., 1989;

Frank P. Chambers, This Age of Conflict: The Western World--1914 to the Present, Harcourt, Brace & World Inc., New York, 3d ed., 1962,

Quigley, Tragedy and Hope, A History of the World In Our Time, MacMillan Company, New York 1966

Daniel Boorstin, The Americans: The Democratic Experience, Random House, New York, 1973 - an excellent study especially of the Kinsey Report at pages 239-244.

PERIOD HISTORIES

Period histories allow a greater focus on the events of 1948 which lap over into other years.

Barone, Our Country: The Shaping of America from Roosevelt to Reagan, Free Press, N.Y. 1990

Alonzo L. Hamby, Liberalism and Its Challengers: FDR to Reagan, Oxford University Press 1985.

Elmo Roper, You and Your Leaders: Their Actions and Your Reactions - 1936 to 1956, William Morrow & Company, New York, 1957.

James Reston, Deadline - A Memoir, Random House, New York, 1991 Written by one of the great journalists of the century, the book provides some fascinating glimpses of the major personalities of the day

Frederick F. Siegel, Troubled Journey: From Pearl Harbor to Ronald Reagan, Hill and Wang, N.Y. 1984.

William L. O'Neill, American High: The Age of Confidence 1945 to 1960, The Free Press, N.Y. 1986.

John Patrick Diggins, The Proud Decades: America in War and Peace, 1941 to 1960; W.W. Norton & Co., N.Y. 1988.

James Gilbert, Another Chance: Postwar America, 1945-1968, Temple University Press, Philadelphia, 1981.

William Chafe, The Unfinished Journey: America Since World War II (New York 1991).

D. Duane Cummins, William Gee White, Combat and Consensus: The 1940s and 1950s, Glencoe Publishing Company, Inc., Encino, California 1980.

William E. Leuchtenburg, In The Shadow of FDR: From Harry Truman to Ronald Reagan, Cornell University Press, Ithaca 1983

William E. Leuchtenburg and the Editors of TIME-Life Books, The Life History of the United States: Volume 12 The Age of Change - From 1945, Alexandria, Vrginia 1964 (TIME Life)

Jeffrey Hart, From this Moment On: America in 1940, Crown Publishers Inc., New York, 1987.

Marty Jezer, The Dark Ages: Life in the United States, 1945 to 1960 (Boston 1982).

Mooney, The Politicians: 1945 to 1960; J.B. Lippincott Co., Philadelphia, 1970.

Robert D. Marcus, A Brief History of the United States Since 1945, St. Martin's Press, New York, 1975.

Steve Fraser and Gary Gerstle, The Rise and Fall of the New Deal Order, 1930 to 1980, Princeton University Press, Princeton, NJ 1989.

Landon Y. Jones, Great Expectations: America and the Baby Boom Generation, Coward, McCann & Geoghean, New York, 1980.

John Gunther, Bernard Quint, Days To Remember: America 1945-1955, Harper & Brothers, New York 1956

Cabell Phillips, Decade of Triumph and Trouble, The Forties, MacMillan New York 1975 (Phillips, Forties)

Halberstam, The Fifties, Villard Books, New York, 1993.

Eric F. Goldman, The Crucial Decade - America: 1945-1955, Alfred A. Knopf, Inc., New York 1956

Joseph C. Goulden, The Best Years: 1945-1950, Atheneum, New York 1976.

William Manchester, The Glory and the Dream, A Narrative History of America: 1932-1972, Little Brown and Company, Boston, 1973

Richard M. Freeland, The Truman Doctrine and the Origins of McCarthyism: Foreign Policy, Domestic Politics, and Internal Security 1946-1948, Alfred A. Knopf, New York, 1972.

Richard F. Haynes, The Awesome Power: Harry S. Truman As Commander-In-Chief, Louisiana State University Press, Baton Rouge, 1973

Barton J. Bernstein, editor, Policies and Procedures of The Truman Administration, Quadrangle Press, Chicago, 1970

Howard Jones, A New Kind of War: America's Global Strategy and The Truman Doctrine in Greece, Oxford University Press, New York 1969

Paul Boyer, By the Bomb's Early Light: American Thought and Culture at the Dawn of the Atomic Age, Pantheon Books New York, 1985

Robert B. Luce, Editor, The Faces of Five Decades: Selections From Fifty Years of The New Republic 1914 to 1964, Simon & Schuster, New York, 1964

Mary Sperling McAuliffe, Crisis on the Left: Cold War Politics and American Liberals, 1947-1954, 1978, University of Massachusetts Press, Amherst, 1978.
J. Robert Moskin, Mr. Truman's War: The Final Victories of World War II and The Birth of the Postwar World, Random House, New York 1996

James T. Patterson, Grand Expectations: The United States, 1945 to 1974, Oxford University Press, New York 1996

Godfrey Hodgson, America In Our Time, Doubleday & Company, Garden City, New York 1976

Cedric Belfrage, The American Inquisition: 1945-1960, The Bobbs-Merrill Company, Inc., Indianapolis, New York, 1973

Carl Degler, Affluence and Anxiety: 1945 to the Present, Scott Foresman and Company, 1968

Kenneth T. Jackson, Crabgrass Frontier: The Suburbanization of the United States, Oxford University Press, New York, 1985

Especially valuable were collections of essays from distinguished contemporary columnists.

Richard H. Rovere, The American Establishment and Other Reports, Opinions, and Speculations, Harcourt, Brace and World, Inc., 1956, New York.

I.F. Stone, A Nonconformist History of Our Times, The Truman Era 1945-1952, Little Brown and Company, 1953

Alistair Cooke, America Observed: From the 1940s to the 1980s, Alfred A. Knopf, New York, 1988, especially A Study of a Failure, page 27.

BIOGRAPHIES

History is a study of biographies and 1948 is no exception. Some of the people spotlighted in this book cross over chapter headings - the most obvious is the President.

TRUMAN

His daughter, Margaret Truman has written two loving biographies of her parents which give glimpses into their private lives, Harry S. Truman, William Morrow and Company, New York 1972; Bess W. Truman, MacMillan Company, New York, 1976.

Harry Truman himself has given his version of the events in Harry S. Truman [hereinafter "Harry Memoirs"], Memoirs: Years of Trial and Hope, 1946 to 1952, Doubleday and Company, Garden City, New York 1956. Almost a memoir is Plain Speaking, an Oral Biography of Harry S. Truman by Merle Miller, Berkley Publishing, New York 1973

Professor Alonzo L.Hamby has produced two masterful studies of the Truman presidency. Man of the People: The Life of Harry S. Truman, Oxford University Press, New York (1995); Beyond the New Deal: Harry S. Truman and American Liberalism, Columbia University Press, N.Y. and London 1973.

Two reporters who covered the White House have written outstanding histories of the Truman Presidency. Cabell Phillips, The Truman Presidency: The History of a Triumphant Succession, The MacMillan Company, N.Y. 1966 (Phillips Presidency). Robert J. Donovan, Conflict and Crisis: The Presidency of Harry S. Truman, 1945 to 1948; W.W. Norton & Co., Inc., New York 1977.

The Truman Presidency, edited by Michael J. Lacey, Woodrow Wilson International Center for Scholars and Cambridge University Press, N.Y. 1989, contains some excellent studies which focus on specialized areas: Bruce R. Kuniholm, U.S. Policy in the Near East: The Triumphs and Tribulations of the Truman Administration; Nelson Lichtenstein, "Labor in the Truman Era: Origins of the "Private Welfare State";" Bruce R. Kuniholm,

U.S. Policy in the Near East: The Triumphs and Tribulations of the Truman Administration; William H. Chafe, Post-War American Society; Robert A. Pollard, "The National Security State Reconsidered: Truman and Economic Containment, 1945 to 1950."

Bert Cochran, Harry Truman and the Crisis Presidency, Funk & Wagnalls, NY 1973.

Donald R. McCoy, The Presidency of Harry S. Truman, The University Press of Kansas, 1984.
Robert H. Ferrell, Harry S. Truman: A Life, University of Missouri Press, Columbia, Missouri 65201

Harold F. Gosnell, Truman's Crises: A Political Biography of Harry S. Truman, Greenwood Press, Westport, CT 1980.

David McCullough, Truman, Simon & Schuster 1992

Roy Jenkins, Truman, Harper & Row Publishers, N.Y., 1986.

Robert Underhill, The Truman Persuasions, The Iowa State University Press, Ames, 1981.

Not a biography of Truman, but an eyewitness view of his presidency is Clifford, Counsel to the President: A Memoir, Random House, New York, 1991. Clark Clifford devotes a major portion of his autobiography to his years at Truman's side.

MARSHALL

George C. Marshall has been the subject of numerous biographies. The leading work is Forrest Pogue's treatise, George C. Marshall: Statesman; Viking Press, 1987. Other excellent works include Leonard Mosley, Marshall: Hero For Our Times, Hearst Books, New York 1982; Ed Cray, General of The Army: George C. Marshall, Soldier and Statesman, W.W. Norton and Company, New York 1990

WALLACE

Norman D. Markowitz, The Rise and Fall of the People's Century: Henry A. Wallace and American Liberalism, 1941-1948, The Free Press, New York 1973

Richard J. Walton: Henry Wallace, Harry Truman & the Cold War, Viking Press, N.Y. 1976

Karl M. Schmidt, Henry A. Wallace: Quixotic Crusade 1948, Syracuse University Press 1960.

LYNDON JOHNSON

Robert Caro, The Years of Lyndon Johnson: Means of Ascent, Alfred A. Knopf, New York, 1990 devotes pages 145-384 to Johnson's 1948 Senate race in a portrait extremely uncomplimentary to Johnson,

Robert Dallek, Lone Star Rising: Lyndon Johnson and his Times, 1908 to 1960; Oxford University Press 1991.

OTHER BIOGRAPHIES

Alan Bullock, Ernest Bevin, Foreign Secretary, Heinemans, London 1983

Ronald W. Prussen, John Foster Dulles, The Road to Power, Free Press New York, 1982.

George F. Kennan, Memoirs: 1925-1950, Atlantic, Little, Brown, Boston 1976,

Geoffrey Perret, Old Soldiers Never Die, The Life of Douglas MacArthur, Adams Masters Company, 1996

Arnold A. Rogow, James Forrestal: A Study of Personality, Politics and Policy, The Macmillan Company, New York 1963

Kinsey: A Biography by Cornelia V. Christenson, published by Indiana

University Press, Bloomington, 1971.

Anthony Holden, Prince Charles, Atheneun, New York 1979

Jonathan Dimbleby, The Prince of Wales, William Morrow and Company, New York 1994

Joseph Persico, Edward R. Murrow: An American Original, McGraw Hill, New York 1988

Richard Norton Smith, Thomas E. Dewey and His Times, Simon & Schuster, New York 1982

James T. Patterson, Mr. Republican: A Biography of Robert A. Taft, Houghton Mifflin Company, Boston 1972

D.B. Hardeman, Donald C. Bacon, Rayburn: A Biography, Texas Monthly Press, 1987

Joseph P. Lash, Eleanor: The Years Alone, W.W. Norton & Company, New York, 1972

THE ELECTION

Jules Abels, Out of the Jaws of Victory; Henry Holt & Co., N.Y. 1959.

Irwin Ross, The Loneliest Campaign: The Truman Victory of 1948, The New American Library, New York, 1968.

Allen Yarnell, Democrats and Progressives: The 1948 Presidential Election as a Test of Post War Liberalism; University of California Press 1974.

Robert A. Garson, The Democratic Party and the Politics of Sectionalism, 1941 to 1948; Louisiana State University Press, 1974.

Mencken's Last Campaign: H.L. Mencken on the 1948 Election, edited and with an introduction by Joseph C. Goulden; The New Republic Book Company, Inc.; Washington, D.C. 1976.

FOREIGN POLICY

Walter LaFeber, America, Russia, and the Cold War, 1945 to 1971; John Wiley & Sons, 1967.

Norman A. Graebner, Cold War Diplomacy 1945 to 1960, D. Van Nostrand Co., Inc., Princeton, New Jersey, 1962.

Richard W. Leopold, The Growth of American Foreign Policy, Alfred A. Knopf, New York, 1962.

Ulam, Expansion and Coexistence: The History of Soviet Foreign Policy 1917 to 1967; Praeger, New York, 1968.

Spence, The Search for Modern China, W.W. Norton & Co., New York, 1990.

Triska, Finley, Soviet Foreign Policy, The MacMillan Company, London 1968

Sterling, The Masaryk Case, Harper & Row, New York 1968

BERLIN

Jean Edward Smith, Lucius D. Clay: An American Life, H. Holt, New York 1990

John H. Backer, Winds of History: The German Years of Lucius DuBignon Clay, Van Nostrand Reinhold Company, New York 1983

Omar Bradley, Clay Blair in Bradley's autobiography, A General's Life, New York 1983.

Raymond, Power at the Pentagon, Harper & Row, New York 1964.

Richard Collier, Bridge Across The Sky, McGraw-Hill, New York 1978

Donavan, Bridge in the Sky, David McKay Company, Inc., New York 1968

Ann & John Tusa, The Berlin Airlift, Athenaeum, New York, 1988.

Robert Jackson, The Berlin Airlift, Patrick Stephens, Wellingborough, Northamptonshire 1988

ISRAEL

Memoirs: David Ben Gurion, The World Publishing Co., New York 1970.

Thomas E. Hachey, The Problem with Partition: Peril to World Peace, Rand McNally & Company, Chicago, 1972.

O'Ballance, The Arab Israeli War 1948, Praeger, New York 1957.

Frank Gervasi, The Life and Times of Menachem Begin: Rebel to Statesman, G.P. Putnam's Sons, New York 1979.

Gertrude Hirschler, Lester S. Eckman: From Freedom Fighter to Statesman: Menachem Begin, Shengold Publishers, Inc., New York 1979.

Warren I. Cohen, Dean Rusk in "The American Secretaries of State and Their Diplomacy" Series, Cooper Square Publishers, Totowa, N.J. 1980.

Thomas J. Schoenbaum, Waging Peace and War: Dean Rusk and the Truman, Kennedy and Johnson Years, Simon and Schuster, N.Y. 1988.

HISS

The Hiss case has received enormous attention not only for its importance but also because it launched the career of Richard Nixon.

Walter Goodman, The Committee, Farrar, Straus, Giroux 1968 studies HUAC.

John Chabot Smith's, Alger Hiss, The True Story, Holt, Rinehart & Winston, New York 1976

Two of the major participants wrote best sellers on the events. In Richard Nixon's, Six Crises, Doubleday, New York 1962, the Hiss case is the first crisis. One extra problem that Hiss had to overcome was that Chambers brilliantly wrote of the case in Whitaker Chambers, Witness, H. Wolff, New York 1952

Nixon: The Education of a Politician 1913-1962, Simon and Schuster 1987 by Stephen Ambrose.

Fawn M. Brodie, Richard Nixon: The Shaping of His Character, W.W. Norton & Co., 1981.

Richard Milhous Nixon: The Rise of an American Politician, Roger Morris, Henry Holt & Co., New York 1990.

RADIO-TELEVISION

Jerry Bowles, A Thousand Sundays: The Story of the Ed Sullivan Show, G.P. Putnam's Sons, New York 1980.

Milton Berle: An Autobiography, with Haskel Frankel, Delacorte Press New York, 1974.

Tim Brooks, Earle Marsh, The Complete Directory To Prime Time Network TV Shows 1946 - Present (1988).

Sally Bedell Smith, In All His Glory: The Life of William S. Paley, Simon & Schuster New York 1990

Harry Castleman and Walter J. Podrazik, Watching TV: Four Decades of American Television, McGraw Hill Book Co., 1982.

Stephen Davis, Say Kids! What Time is It? Notes From the Peanut Gallery. Little Brown & Company, Boston, 1987. A delightfully and lovingly written book by the son of one of the people who worked on the Howdy Doody Show.

Arthur Marx, The Secret Life of Bob Hope, Barricade Books, Inc. New York, 1993

Milt Josefsberg, The Jack Benny Show, Arlington House Publishers, New York 1977

Mary Livingstone Benny and Hilliard Marks and Marcia Borie, Jack Benny, Doubleday, Garden City 1978

SPORTS

John Kieran, and Arthur Daley, The Story of the Olympic Games: 776 B.C. to 1972 J.B. Lippincott Co., Philadelphia, New York 1973.

Chronicle of the Olympics, 1896 to 1996; D.K. Publishing, 1996.

Gilbert, Now Pitching Bob Feller, Birch Lane Press, 1990.
Eskenazi, The Lip: A Biography of Leo Durocher, William Morrow & Co., Inc., New York, 1993.

Sherman, 365 Amazing Days in Sports: A Day by Day Look at Sports History, Sports Illustrated, 1990.

Lou Boudreau, Russell Schneider, Lou Boudreau: Covering All The Bases, Sagamore Publishing, Champaign, illinois 1993

Dave Anderson, Pennant Races: Baseball At Its Best, Doubleday, NY (1994)

Halberstam, Summer of '49, William Morrow & Company, New York, 1989.

Holway, Josh and Satch: The Life and Times of Josh Gibson and Satchel Paige; Carroll & Graf Publishers, New York 1991.

Seaver & Appel, Great Moments in Baseball: From the World Series of 1903 to the Modern Records of Nolan Ryan; Carrol Publishing Group, 1995.

Stan the Man Musial: Born to be a Ballplayer, by Jerry Lansche; Taylor Publishing Company, Dallas, TX 1994.

Danny Peary, We Played The Game: 65 Players Remember Baseball's Greatest Era, Hyperion, New York 1994

ENDNOTES

1. Jones 7 quoting Dr. Bergen Evans.

2. Chafe 117

3. Gilbert 3

4. Throughout this book, the author, as Clark Clifford did in Counsel to the President and other authors, will use the term "Negro" rather than "black" or "Afro-American" because "Negro" was the term used in 1948. Robert Underhill, one of Truman's biographers, has stated that throughout most of Mr. Truman's active life, Negro was an acceptable term. The term black did not come into popular usage until later. "Truman would have felt that 'black' was pejorative." Underhill, 249

5. Patterson 16

6. Patterson 63

7. Jackson 282

8. Ferrell 264

9. Newsweek, August 9, 1948

10. Patterson 70

11. Goulden 140-1

12. Patterson 73; Jackson 235

13. Jackson 233

14. Jones 39

15. Degler 10

16. Clifford 187

17. Goulden 346

18. See Goulden 350   .

19. Walton 4

20. Goulden 348

21. Goulden 363-6

22. Many books discuss the memorandum. See Clifford 189-194 for the most personal view.

23. Liberalism 210

24. Walton 299, Clifford 193

25. Walton 304

26. Manchester 549

27. Hamby, Man of the People, 432

28. Newsweek, January 1948

29. Smith 479

30. Goulden 360

31. Leuchtenburg 25

32. Liberalism 214

33. Goulden 356

34. See Goulden 357

35. Goulden 357

36. See Manchester 546

37. Diggins 102

38. Schmidt 69-70

39. Mencken 19

40. Walton 113-4

41. Goulden 217-8

42. Liberalism 222

43. Newsweek extensively covered the Guru issue in its March 22, 1948 issue. See also Goulden 388-390; Walton 299; Ross 158 - 159. Both TIME and Newsweek in their August 2, 1948 issues covered the newsconference.

44. McCoy 154

45. Abels 113

46. Smith 27-8

47. See Goulden 372

48. Smith

49. Smith 482-3

50. O'Neil 93-4; Goulden 375

51. Halberstam 208

52. Degler 19

53. Ross 36.

54. Ross 36

55. Goulden 375

56. Manchester 547

57. Barone 221; Quigley 887-889

58. Phillips (Presidency) 168

59. Marcus 55

60. Manchester 535

61. Leopold 650-1

62. Manchester 534

63. Pogue 398

64. See Perret 443; Manchester 536

65. Goulden 273-4

66. Roper 171.

67. Roper 185

68. Manchester 537-539 discusses the inception and execution of the Plan as does Clifford 143-145.

69. Pogue 212

70. Patterson 129

71. Phillips (Presidency) 182

72. Ferrell 255

73. Pogue 236

74. Clifford 195

75. Reston 164

76. Reston 167-8

77. Rovere 186-187.

78. Degler 30-31.

79. Reston 164; see also Goldman 76.

80. Prussen 353

81. Goldman 77

82. Freeland 269

83. Siegel 66

84. TIME and Newsweek covered the speech in their March 15, 1948 issues as did Goldman 79-80.

85. Rovere 182

86. Freeland 275-276

87. Harry Truman 393-4

88. Ulam 437

89. LaFeber 67

90. Phillips (Presidency) 193

91. McCoy 128

92. O'Neil 73

93. Raymond 57

94. Goulden 266

95. Tusa 61-62

96. Raymond 103

97. Raymond 103; Donovan (Bridge) 9

98. Walton 96

99. Jackson 30

100. Tusa 96-100

101. Manchester 540

102. Tusa 100-104

103. Tusa 99 105

104. Tusa 109-110

105. Jackson 41; Collier 25-7

106. Jackson 41

107. TIME, June 21, 1948

108. Jackson 41, Donovan 74

109. Ulam 453

110. Donovan (Bridge) 35

111. Ferrell 257

112. Ferrell 258

113. LaFeber 71

114. Manchester 540

115. Manchester 540

116. Davison 105

117. Newsweek, July 12, 1948

118. Donovan (Bridge) 51

119. Donovan (Bridge) 77-78

120. Phillips 3

121. Morrison 1051

122. Hamby, Man of the People, 409-410.

123. Lacey 324

124. Miller 234-5

125. McCullough 591

126. Hamby, Man of the People, 414

127. Pogue 358

128. Abels 18

129. Hamby, Man of the People, 411.

130. Liberalism 215

131. Cohen 19-20

132. Lacey 322

133. Lacey 322

134. Schoenbaum 169

135. Lacey 324

136. McCullough 604

137. Schoenbaum 163

138. Jenkins 119

139. Hamby, Man of the People, 412-413

140. Cohen 23

141. Lacey 321

142. This confrontation is discussed by many authors - none more authoritatively then Clifford, 9-14

143. Pogue 237

144. Reston 185-6

145. Mosley 418-419

146. Clifford 19-20

147. Hamby, Man of the People, 417

148. Newsweek May 24

149. McCullough 618

150. Hamby, Man of the People, 435

151. Hamby, Man of the People, 435

152. Phillips (Presidency) 218

153. Smith 484

154. Manchester 548-9

155. Liberalism 227

156. Cochran 220

157. Cochran 95

158. Harry "Truman Memoirs," 26-27

159. The April 17 speech was such a surprising hit that TIME and Newsweek wrote of it. Also see Manchester 549-550.

160. Goulden 368-370; Phillips (Presidency) 212-3; Manchester 550-1

161. Underhill 256

162. Hamby, Man of the People, 441

163. McCullough 642

164. Manchester 551

165. Liberalism 238

166. Manchester 551-2

167. Manchester 553

168. Manchester 551

169. Hamby, Man of the People, 443; Manchester 552

170. Abels 45

171. Smith 486

172. See Goulden 376

173. Goulden 376

174. Manchester 554

175. Smith 487

176. Manchester 554

177. Smith 488

178. Abels 52

179. Smith 488-489

180. Patterson 406-7

181. Smith 486; Goulden 377-8

182. Smith 491; Newsweek May 31

183. Underhill 261. Abels 57

184. Smith 491

185. Smith 491

186. Smith 490; Goulden 377.

187. Manchester 554

188. Smith 493; Goulden 377-8; Ross 51-53.

189. Smith 492-4

190. Manchester 554-5

191. Manchester 555

192. Patterson 392

193. Newsweek June 21

194. Ray 362; Goulden 379

195. McCullough, 637; Hamby, Man of the People, 439

196. Manchester 553

197. Goulden 379

198. Gosnell 386

199. Smith 494

200. Smith 498

201. Smith 497-8

202. Roper 109.

203. Smith 499-500; Goulden 379

204. TIME June 21

205. Manchester 555

206. Donovan 402

207. Cochran 234

208. Liberalism 242

209. Garson 264

210. Harry Truman 7; Goulden 381-3

211. Harry Truman 8; Goulden 381; Ross 113.

212. Goldman Page 83

213. Goldman 83

214. Manchester 555

215. Goulden 381-4

216. Ray 334

217. Ray 334

218. Goulden 382

219. Goulden 385

220. See Goulden 386 for one of many depictions of the scene.

221. McCullough 637-642

222. See Goulden 386

223. Ray 337-338

224. Phillips (Forties) 333

225. Manchester 556

226. Manchester 557

227. Underhill 267

228. Manchester 557

229. McCoy 156; Clifford 214

230. Manchester 538-9

231. Harry, "Truman Memoirs," 15

232. See Goulden 174

233. Goulden 174

234. Goulden 388

235. Phillips (Presidency) 207

236. Abels 98

237. Goulden 402-4; Manchester 559

238. Abels 22

239. Goulden 348

240. Walton 283

241. Smith 509

242. Liberalism 223

243. Patterson 54

244. The incident was widely reported in newspapers and magazines. See Ross 156.

245. Walton 199

246. Manchester 559-560

247. Liberalism 246

248. Siegel 66

249. See Donovan 391

250. Liberalism 233

251. Bernstein 87

252. McCoy 109

253. Patterson 422; Manchester 561-2

254. Phillips (Forties) 334

255. Liberalism 247

256. Liberalism 248

257. Goulden 306

258. Degler 38

259. Abels 116

260. McAuliffe 27.

261. For example, Richard Rovere of the New Yorker admitted that he was one of the American intellectuals who succumbed to Stalinism "for a brief

but inexcusably long period in the late thirties." Rovere 286.

262. Goulden 314

263. See Freeland 359-360

264. Morris 397-8

265. Brodie 198; see also Goulden 322-334; Manchester 616-626; and the first chapter of Nixon's Six Crises

266. McCullough 652

267. Brodie 212

268. Goulden 324

269. Morris 398

270. Chambers 556

271. Ambrose 174

272. Chambers discusses the interview at 559-573

273. Morris 408; Goulden 326

274. Chambers 593

275. Goulden 327

276. Nixon 32; Goulden 328; Chambers 602-15 describes the confrontation.

277. Goulden 328-9; Nixon 31

278. See Nixon 31-37

279. Chambers 674-5

280. Chambers 695

281. Morris 447; Nixon 45; Goulden 333

282. Liberalism 251

283. Chambers 734-736

284. Goulden 332

285. Morris 457

286. Brodie 226; Morris 456

287. Nixon 47-51; Chambers 749-754

288. Goulden 333

289. Chambers 783

290. Goulden 340

291. Marx 239-240

292. Marx 239-240, 242

293. Goulden 176-178

294. Newsweek September 27, 1948

295. This is also discussed at Goulden 172-4.

296. Newsweek July 12, 1948

297. Gorgeous George's antics were described in numerous magazines and newspapers and in Manchester 593.

298. For the often quoted remark, see TIME May 24, 1948; Goulden 172-4

299. Castleman 35-36

300. Halberstam, The Fifties, 185

301. Berle 271

302. Berle 278

303. Castleman 36

304. Smith 270-1

305. Directory 615

306. Brooks, Marsh 754

307. Davis 31

308. Directory 720

309. See Goulden 176-7

310. Berle 278

311. Siegel 93

312. Gunther, Quint 40

313. Manchester 525.

314. Newsweek December 20, 1948

315. LaFeber 69

316. LaFeber 69-70

317. Davison 116-7

318. Jackson 41-67

319. Collier 76

320. Donovan (Bridge) 69; Davison 168-9

321. Dovoan (Bridge) 83

322. Donovan (Bridge) 77

323. TIME, July 19, 1948 and also in Collier 83

324. August 2, 1948 Newsweek

325. Davison 189

326. Newsweek September 20, 1948

327. Donovan (Bridge) 52-53

328. Donovan (Bridge) 153

329. The training was described in numerous magazine accounts, especially Newsweek, December 20, 1948, and in Manchester 541.

330. Jackson 92

331. Donovan (Bridge) 117; Collier

332. Donovan (Bridge) 65

333. Collier 125

334. Donovan 126-7; Newsweek October 18, 1948

335. Jackson 91

336. Davison 167

337. Donovan (Bridge) 129

338. Donovan (Bridge) 130-1

339. Manchester 541-2

340. Donovan (Bridge) 134-7

341. Donovan (Bridge) 132-3

342. Collier 146

343. Donovan (Bridge) 167-8

344. Goulden 276-7

345. Donovan (Bridge) 9; TIME July 12, 1948

346. O'Ballance 75

347. O'Ballance 76

348. Newsweek May 24, 1948

349. O'Ballance 162-164

350. Hachey 207-208

351. Both TIME and Newsweek of September 27, 1948 recounted the murder.

352. Liberalism 256

353. Donovan 428

354. Lash 128-9

355. Hachey 207

356. Rovere 82

357. Donovan 413

358. Cooke 27

359. McCoy 144

360. Donovan 400

361. Donovan 412

362. Gunther 533

363. Guenther 539

364. O'Neill 98

365. Gosnell 396

366. McCullough 653

367. Chambers 705

368. See Goulden 392-3

369. Smith 505-6

370. Abels 44

371. Abels 139

372. Abels 128-129

373. Abels 132

374. Abels 130

375. Goulden 393

376. Ferrell 277

377. McCoy 144

378. Manchester 564.

379. Liberalism 251

380. Gosnell 400

381. Gosnell 399

382. Miller 279-280

383. Phillips (Presidency) 233; Phillips (Forties) 335; Harry Truman 22-3

384. Donovan 419

385. Harry Truman 23

386. Harry Truman 23

387. Abels 252

388. Donovan 416

389. Goulden 398

390. Smith 524

391. Abels 150

392. Yarnell 34

393. Siegel 94

394. Lacey 151

395. See Manchester 563-4

396. Abels 170; Phillips 336

397. Numerous authors have described the various versions of the exchange. See Goulden 392-3

398. Phillips (Presidency) 235

399. Hamby, Man of the People, 459; Ross 184-186

400. Underhill 277; Ross 183

401. Clifford 227-228

402. Ferrell 278

403. Hart 49.

404. Chafe 18

405. Chafe 20

406. Harry Truman Memoirs 34

407. Gunther 679

408. Gunther 916.

409. Clifford 187-8 and TIME October 11, 1948

410. Hamby, Man of the People, 467

411. Rovere 68-69.

412. Newsweek November 8, 1948

413. Rovere 69.

414. Underhill 274; Newsweek October 4, 1948

415. McCullough 698

416. Chafe 104

417. Smith 515

418. Abels 189

419. Hamby, Man of the People, 458

420. Patterson 425

421. Prussen 361-3.

422. O'Neil 98

423. Liberalism 259

424. Underhill 284; Smith 507

425. Smith 507

426. Ross 191

427. Rovere 76; Underhill 287

428. See Goulden 217-8

429. Goulden 217-8

430. Gosnell 390

431. Abels 212

432. Schmidt 223

433. Belfrage 85-86

434. Belfrage 86

435. Goulden 404

436. Schmidt 205-206

437. Schmidt 205-206

438. Abels 207

439. Liberalism 261

440. McCoy 160-161

441. Phillips (Forties) 340

442. McCullough 681

443. Morris 449-450

444. O'Neill 101

445. Mooney 80

446. Clifford 234-235

447. Smith 505

448. Manchester 567.

449. Ferrell 283

450. Goulden 399-400

451. Goulden 398-400

452. Goulden 417

453. Goulden 414

454. Bess 379-380

455. Donovan 429

456. Donovan 430

457. Abels 242

458. Jenkins 138; Hamby, Man of the People, 457

459. Ross 234-235.

460. Smith 535

461. Liberalism 257

462. Donovan 428

463. Garson 309-310

464. Bess 383

465. Abels 264

466. Smith 20

467. Goulden 415

468. Baron 216

469. Smith 501

470. TIME Life 38

471. Smith 503

472. Abels 233-234

473. Abels 166

474. Smith 539

475. Phillips (Presidency) 245

476. Abels 181

477. The Kinsey report has been studied by numerous authors. See Manchester 584-589; Boorstin 239-241; Halberstam 272-281

478. Manchester 586.

479. Goulden 188-192

480. Christiansen 145

481. Christiansen 146

482. Manchester 588.

483. Chafe 13

484. Gilbert 15

485. In 1946, a survey by the Federal Women's Bureau of women workers in ten major war production areas revealed that most female workers hoped to stay on the job, even after the troops came home. Gilbert 15.

486. Gilbert 15.

487. Chafe 170

488. Patterson 32

489. Patterson 32

490. Patterson 10

491. Diggins 186

492. Baron 199

493. Jackson 241.

494. Patterson 63.

495. Patterson 11

496. Gilbert 22.

497. Diggins 99

498. TIME January 10, 1949

499. Gilbert 26.

500. See Halberstam, The Fifties, 157-8

501. Degler 45

502. Patterson 71

503. Rovere 72-73.

504. Gunther, Quint 67

505. Jones 40

506. Gunther, Quint 51

507. Golden 13

508. Newsweek, September 6, 1948

509. Gunther 907

510. Newsweek August 30, 1948

511. Castleman 41

512. The December 13, 1948 issue of Newsweek and the December 20, 1948 issue of TIME focus on the year in books.

513. Hart 106.

514. Hart 107

515. Manchester 590.

516. Smith 30

517. Smith 40

518. Smith 41

519. Miller 282

520. Smith 20

521. Manchester 572.

522. Ross 241

523. Smith 42

524. Smith 41-2

525. Phillips (Presidency) 245-246

526. Goldman 87

527. Donovan 433

528. Manchester 575.

529. Smith 46

530. Manchester 575.

531. Ferrell 281

532. Hamby, Man of the People, 463

533. Goldman 88

534. Abels 270

535. Marx 244-5

536. Cochran 240

537. See Manchester 569

538. Phillips (Forties) 343-344

539. Manchester 577

540. Abels 271

541. Harry Truman 47

542. Donaldson 209

543. Jenkins 141

544. Phillips (Presidency) 251

545. Donaldson 204

546. Barone 221-2

547. Barone 221

548. Goldman 89

549. Manchester 571

550. Manchester 577; Roper 118-119

551. Roper 119

552. Lash 133

553. Liberalism 268; TIME January 3, 1949

554. Phillips (Forties) 343-344

555. TIME Life 39

556. Walton 231; Garson 311

557. Chafe 114

558. Goldman 89

559. Barone 219

560. Barone 219

561. Hamby, Man of the People, 465

562. Schmidt 144-5

563. Schmidt 144-5

564. Yarnell 37

565. Barone 221-222

566. Smith 545

567. See Goulden 422

568. Goldman 85

569. Manchester 552

570. Bess 378-379

571. TIME Life 40

572. Bernstein 87

573. Siegel 71

574. Diggins 86-87

575. Harry Truman 449

576. Goulden 426

577. McCoy 141

578. Roper 113-114

579. Jones 1

580. Jones

INDEX

Acheson, Dean, 29,32,38,267
AFofL, 108
Alsop, Stewart and Joe, 37,72,84,86,108,206,227,250
Anderson, Clinton B., Secretary of Agriculture, 35
Andrews, Bert, 123
Arab League, 66,175
Arab Liberation Army, 61,168,173
Arvey, Jacob, 77,99
atomic bomb, 41,43,53
Austin, UN Ambassador Warren, 63,64,69
automobiles, 230,233-234,269
Baby Boom,, 5,132,145,221,227
Barkley, Alden, 97,98,101,102,181,269
Baruch, Bernard, 97,185
baseball, 211,236
Begin, Manachem, 60
Ben Gurion, David, 64,67,68,171,174
Benes, Eduard, President of Czechoslovakia, 36
Bentley, Elizabeth T., 118
Berle, Milton, 132,136,244
Berlin, 45,47-51,53-57,76,88,108,110,147,149,150,173,207,213
Berlin Airlift, 32,45,52,147-165,214,231,242,261,268,273
Bernadotte, Count Folke, 169-172,174,192,204,207,217
Bevin, Ernest, 32,39,47,147,174
Bradley, General Omar, 31,39
Brownell, Herb, Dewey Campaign Manager, 91,112,202,245,247, 248, 249
Burger, Warren, 25
Byrnes, Secretary of State James F., 46,47
Chambers, Whittaker, 118,119,121,123,180
Chek, Chiang Kai, 267-268
Chicago, 5,10,12,17,36,37,74,76,77,79,99,111,113
Churchill, Winston, 21,27,31,40,41,239
CIO, 108,191
Civil Rights, 13,14,16-18,35,71,75,95,99,100,102,103,107,108, 110-112,115,196,203,217,220,258,260
Clark, Attorney General Thomas Campbell, 17
Clay, Lucius, 45-50,52-55,149,156,159,162-164
Clayton, William L., 31

Clifford, Clark, 13,18,33,62,65-67,198,213
Cold War, 29,40,44,
Communism, domestic, 115-118
Como, Perry, 140
Connor, Bull, 100
containment, 27,30,31
Coon, Lt. Col. Forrest, 153
Crosby, Bing, 227,241
Crossley, Archibald, 186
Cunningham, Lt. Gen. Sir Alan Gordon, 69
Czechoslovakia, 36-37,108,271
Defense Department, 42,43,57
Dewey, Thomas, 11,13,22-25,60,71,81,84-88,90-91,103,107,112,121,
        174,179,181,186,200,201-210,212,243,262
Dixiecrats, 17,18,104,107,209,258,260,262
Dixon, Frank M., Governor of Alabama, 107
Douglas, William O., 95
Dulles, John Foster, 35,120-123,125
Eisenhower, Dwight, 16,42,62,71-73,77,83,95,96,181,239,255
electronics industry, 225
Ellis, Handy, 100
Epstein, Eliahu, 66
Famin, Charles A., 221
FBI, 17,118,128,161,
Ferdinand Magellan Railroad Car, 76,77,180,193,194,216,251
Flynn, Ed, 12,20,63,99,100,217
Ford, Gerald, 209,261
Forrestal, James, 35,40,42,53,62,149
Fulbright, J. William, 10
G.I. Bill of Rights, 226,228
Gallup, George, 11,16,71,83,84,87,104,110,186,213,218,244,247,
        249, 256
Ganeval, General Jean, 161,162
Gatow Air Base, 55,148,156,157,160,162
Godfrey, Arthur, 139
Gorgeous George, 135
Gottwald, Klement, 36
Great Depression, 3,5,6,117,221
Gunther, John, 179,196
Haganah, 60,65,68,167
Hague, Frank, 12,96,99,100,246,263

Halleck, Charles, 182,273
Halvorsen, Lt. Karl S., 162
Harding, Warren, 19
Harriman, Averel, 36
Hershey, Major General Lewis B., 44
Hiss, Alger, 2,115,119-121,125,204
Holocaust, 59,62
Hope, Bob, 131,240,241,249,268
House Un-American Activities Committee (HUAC),
        117,118,121,123,125, 127-129,177
Housing shortage, 5,7,8,108
Howdy Doody, 141-142
Hull, Cordell, 21
Humphrey, Hubert, 99,100
inflation, 6-8,232,261,269
Irgun, 60,167
Isacson, Leo, 20,108,260
Israel, 66,68,167-176,271,273
Jersey City, 12,60,74,246
Jerusalem, 59,61,65,168,169,171-173
Johnson, Louis, 185,186,251
Johnson, Lyndon, 120,209,210
Johnston, Olin, 18,72,251
Kai-shek, Chiang, 267-268
Kelly, Ed, 12
Kelly, Walt, 94
Kennan, George, 30
Kennedy, John F., 120,209
Khalidy, Awni, 67
Kinsey, Alfred, 221-224,273
Kinsey Report, 221,224,273
Knutson, Harry, 15
Koenig, Lt. Gen. Joseph P. L., 46
Korea, 41-42,271
Koseinkino, Oksana, 116
Ku Klux Klan, 16,17
Lafeber, Walter, 40
Laski, Harold J., 28
Lawrence, David, 99
League of Nations, 31,59
LeMay, Curtis, 50,53,54,148,154

Levittown, 8, 226
Lewis, John L., 189-191,232
Lie, Secretary General Trygve, 63
Louis, Joe, 83,89,135,196
Lovett, Robert, 56,57,63,65-67,269
Luce, Clair Booth, 78,90
Lukyanchenko, Lt. Gen. G., 49
Marshall Plan, The (European Recovery Program), 20,31,33,35-41,46,
        88,110,111,147,164,185,193,228,261
Marshall, George, 28-34,39,41,52,53,59,62-66,174,200,214,266
Marx, Groucho, 249
Mature, Victor, 242
McArthur, Douglas, 23,42,45,46,60,71,73,81,83,84
McCarthy, Joseph, 81,87,115
McGrath, J. Howard, 18,26,71,75,82,101,185,220
Mencken, H.L., 22,82,89,90,108,204,207,209,219
Mitchell, Hugh, 72
Morrison, Samuel Elliot, 57
movies, 240-242
Mumford, Lewis, 2
Mundt, Karl, Congressman, 117,121,195
Murphy, Ambassador Robert, 46,52
Murrow, Edward R., 71
Music, 240
Nebraska Primary, the, 83,87
New Hampshire Primary, the, 81
New York, 1,13,20,60,68,82,85,98,109,115,132,225,258
New York City, 60,82,116,217,246
Nixon, Richard, 2,86,94,117,119,121-125,127,144,209,212
Ohio Primary, the, 83,84
Oregon Primary, the, 85
Palestine, 28,59-62,64,66-68,71,168-170,173
Pegler, Westbrook, 21,22
Pendergast, Tom, 9,15,76,79,90
Pepper, Claude, 96
Philadelphia, 88,90,91,95,98,99,101,109
Progressive Party, 12,20,108,109,260
Race relations, 13,16-18,35,71,97,99,102,103,107,108,110, 113,195,
        208,209
Randolph, A. Philip, 110,111
Rankin, John, Congressman, 117

Rayburn, Sam, 59,97,100,105,170,181
Reston, James, 34,85,250,257
Rhein Main Airfield, 49,53,55,153,161,163
Ritchie, William, Democratic State Chairman of Nebraska, 77
Robertson, Lt. Gen. Sir Brian, 46,48
Roerich, Nicholas K., 21
Rogers, Roy, 241
Roosevelt, Elliot, 72
Roosevelt, Franklin, 9-12,16,18,19,24,71,72,77,95,98,102,
    187,190,218,238,255,256
Roosevelt, James, 72,95
Roosevelt, Jr., Franklin, 72
Roper, Elmo, 186,187,218,220,244,247,249,256,257
Ross, Charlie, 67,75
Rowe, James, 12-14,18,21,60,75,76,109,189,193,203,261
Royall, Secretary of the Army Kenneth, 56,159
Rusk, Dean, 67,120
Russell, Senator Richard, 35,101,111
Ruth, Babe, 237-238
Scott, Jr., Hugh, 112,204,246
Seattle, 76,77,144
Smith, Brigadier General Joseph, 55
Smith, Buffalo Bob, 142
Smith, Howard K., 110
Smith, Merriman, 243
Sokolovky, Marshall Vassily, 46,48,50,52,56
Spaatz, Air Force General Carl, 43
Stalin, Joseph, 27,30,36,37,39,41,45,47,78,90,108,117,147,204,
    207,214,253,261,268,271
Stassen, Harold, 23,25,71,73,81-87,125,187,192,205
State of the Union Address, 15,33,74,112,133,265
Stern Gang, The, 60,167,172
Stone, Columnist I. F., 62,115,117,203
Suburbia, 8,226,233,262
Sullivan, Ed, 138,219
Sullivan, Gael, 75
Taft, Robert A., 11,14,16,23-25,34,35,38,72,79,83-86,88,90,91,93,
    112, 138,215,261
Taft, Wm H., 24,179
Taft-Hartley Act, 15,24,181,182,191,203,220,232,269
Taylor, Glen, 20,88,104,109,207

Television, 104,131-146,248,263
Templehof Airfield, 53,57,149,154-156,160-162,269
Thomas, Parnell, Chairman of HUAC, 117,128
Thurmond, Strom, 18,107,113,186,209,213,218,236,253,254,256,
    258,260
Tito, Josef, of Yugoslavia, 147,271
Truman, Bess, 15,197,199,216
Truman, Harry S., 2,9-20,22,24,26,27,29,31,33,34,39,40,43,44,47,
    52, 56,59,60,62,66-68,71,72,74,75,78,79,86,88-90,93,95,
    97,99,100,107, 112,147,149,159,174,178,181,211,244,271
Truman, Margaret, 15,199
Truman Doctrine, 29-31,40,147,261
Turner, Ray, Governor of Oklahoma, 185
Turner, General Wm H., 152,155,156,159
Turnip Session, 103,107,111-113,118
Twain, Mark, 19
United Nations, 25,42,59-61,63,64,68,113,120,169,170-174,207
Van Fleet, Lt. Gen. Jim, 30,31
Vandenberg, Arthur, 10,23,29,34,35,37,38,40,71,88,91,112,182,
    114,202, 250,261,263,267
Wallace, Henry, 9,11,12,16,17,19-22,34,47,60,64,,71,77,90,100,
108,109,111,115,120,185,206,246,248,256,260
Warren, Earl, 23,73,91,93,103,185,258
Wedemeyer, Lt. Gen. Albert, 53
Weizmann, Chaim, 63
Wiesbaden AFB, 53
Willerford, Major Edward, 55
Willkie, Wendel, 23,83,91
Wilson, Woodrow, 31,60,201
Wisconsin Primary, 81,82
Woodard, Isaac, 17
World Series, 211
Wright, Fielding, Governor of Mississippi, 107

∼